中華現代學術名著叢書

現代吴語的研究

趙元任 著

圖書在版編目(CIP)數據

現代吴語的研究/趙元任著. —北京:商務印書館,2011(2024.6 重印)
(中華現代學術名著叢書)
ISBN 978 - 7 - 100 - 08620 - 2

Ⅰ.①現… Ⅱ.①趙… Ⅲ.①吴語—方言研究 Ⅳ.①H173

中國版本圖書館 CIP 數據核字(2011)第 192879 號

本書據清華學校研究院 1928 年版排印

中華現代學術名著叢書
現代吴語的研究
趙元任 著

商 務 印 書 館 出 版
(北京王府井大街36號 郵政編碼100710)
商 務 印 書 館 發 行
三河市春園印刷有限公司印刷
ISBN 978 - 7 - 100 - 08620 - 2

2011 年 12 月第 1 版 開本 880×1240 1/32
2024 年 6 月第 3 次印刷 印張 8⅜ 插頁 3
定價:58.00 元

趙元任

(1892—1982)

1927年秋，開始調查吴語方言

清華學校研究院

叢書第四種

現代吳語的研究

趙元任著

北京

清華學校研究院印行

中華民國十七年六月

Tsing Hua College Research Institute

Monograph No. 4.

Studies in the Modern Wu-Dialects

By Yuen Ren Chao

Peking

Tsing Hua College Research Institute

June 1928.

清華學校研究院1928年版《現代吳語的研究》封面

作者手迹(關於吴語方言調查的日記摘要)

出版説明

百年前，張之洞嘗勸學曰："世運之明晦，人才之盛衰，其表在政，其裏在學。"是時，國勢頹危，列强環伺，傳統頻遭質疑，西學新知亟亟而入。一時間，中西學并立，文史哲分家，經濟、政治、社會等新學科勃興，令國人亂花迷眼。然而，淆亂之中，自有元氣淋灕之象。中華現代學術之轉型正是完成於這一混沌時期，於切磋琢磨、交鋒碰撞中不斷前行，涌現了一大批學術名家與經典之作。而學術與思想之新變，亦帶動了社會各領域的全面轉型，爲中華復興奠定了堅實基礎。

時至今日，中華現代學術已走過百余年，其間百家林立、論辯蜂起，沉浮消長瞬息萬變，情勢之復雜自不待言。温故而知新，述往事而思來者。"中華現代學術名著叢書"之編纂，其意正在於此，冀辨章學術，考鏡源流，收納各學科學派名家名作，以展現中華傳統文化之新變，探求中華現代學術之根基。

"中華現代學術名著叢書"收録上自晚清下至二十世紀八十年代末中國大陸及港澳臺地區、海外華人學者的原創學術名著（包括外文著作），以人文社會科學爲主體兼及其他，涵蓋文學、歷史、哲學、政治、經濟、法律和社會學等衆多學科。

出版“中華現代學術名著叢書”，爲本館一大夙願。自一八九七年始創起，本館以“昌明教育，開啓民智”爲己任，有幸首刊了中華現代學術史上諸多開山之著、扛鼎之作；於中華現代學術之建立與變遷而言，既爲參與者，也是見證者。作爲對前人出版成績與文化理念的承續，本館傾力謀劃，經學界通人擘畫，并得國家出版基金支持，終以此叢書呈現於讀者面前。唯望無論多少年，皆能傲立於書架，并希冀其能與“漢譯世界學術名著叢書”共相輝映。如此宏願，難免汲深綆短之憂，誠盼專家學者和廣大讀者共襄助之。

商務印書館編輯部

二〇一〇年十二月

凡　　例

一、"中華現代學術名著叢書"收録晚清以迄二十世紀八十年代末，爲中華學人所著，成就斐然、澤被學林之學術著作。入選著作以名著爲主，酌量選録名篇合集。

二、入選著作内容、編次一仍其舊，唯各書卷首冠以作者照片、手迹等。卷末附作者學術年表和題解文章，誠邀專家學者撰寫而成，意在介紹作者學術成就，著作成書背景、學術價值及版本流變等情况。

三、入選著作率以原刊或作者修訂、校閲本爲底本，參校他本，正其訛誤。前人引書，時有省略更改，倘不失原意，則不以原書文字改動引文；如確需校改，則出脚注説明版本依據，以"編者注"或"校者注"形式説明。

四、作者自有其文字風格，各時代均有其語言習慣，故不按現行用法、寫法及表現手法改動原文；原書專名（人名、地名、術語）及譯名與今不統一者，亦不作改動。如確係作者筆誤、排印舛誤、數據計算與外文拼寫錯誤等，則予徑改。

五、原書爲直（横）排繁體者，除個别特殊情况，均改作横排簡體。其中原書無標點或僅有簡單斷句者，一律改爲新式標點,專名號從略。

六、除特殊情况外,原書篇后注移作脚注,雙行夾注改爲單行夾注。文獻著録則從其原貌,稍加統一。

七、原書因年代久遠而字迹模糊或紙頁殘缺者,據所缺字數用“□”表示;字數難以確定者,則用“(下缺)”表示。

目　　録

第一部　吴音

第二部　吴語

CONTENTS

序

研究中國語音最詳細又最多的，大概要首推瑞典的中國音韻家高本漢(Bernhard Karlgren)。他的成績都發表在1915—1926陸續出來的 *Études sur la phonologie chinoise*①。不過一個全國的方言調查不是個把人一年工夫或一個人年把工夫可以做得完的。高本漢的所得的材料可以够使他考定隋、唐時代的古音的大概，但是假如要做中國的方言志，那還得要許多人許多年有系統的調查跟研究才做得好吶。這種事業的重要，無論是本身的重要，或是在國學上地位的重要，或是應用於教育上的重要，也已經有過好些人談過的了，可是空談了許多時候怎末也没有結果吶？這大半是因爲有幾種必需的條件還不能實現。第一，要有永久性的組織跟經費能一致的辦這種事情，這是無消説的。第二，要有有相當訓練的工作者。但這是一種很專門的訓練，不是幾個月速成科可以練出來的。假如隨便到各處走走聽聽記記，那所得的東西的價值一定等於零，或小於零，因爲多錯誤的記載還不如没有記載。第三，要國内太平，不然最值得調查的區域往往不能去調查。可是要慢慢的等，等到哪一天才可以有大隊的語言學人馬，

① Archives d'Études Orientales, Vol. 15, Stockholm, 1915—1926.

大規模的來測量全中國的方言地理吶？所以還是先比較小規模的在一個比較安静的區域裡做一點比較簡略的研究，至少也可以做一個後來研究的格式。

這次調查能在這末短的時期内得這末許多材料，一大半是賴各地學商等界的熱心幫助；一方面幫找可以發音的人，一方面關於本地語言的特别有趣的而表格中没有問到的地方，也多有所指教，這是作者非常感激的。除已經專函致謝外，現在再對各地招待者跟發音者特别鳴謝。

INTRODUCTION OF ENGLISH

The present monograph is a preliminary report on the data obtained from a trip to the region of the Wu-dialects. So far as the discussions are concerned with questions of Chinese phonology, it is presumed that any reader who is seriously interested in it will have the necessary knowledge to read this in the Chinese. For these and for Chinese readers whose usage of modern linguistic terms may differ from mine, a glossary of terms is provided at the end of this introduction for reference. This introduction is written primarily for those who do not know Chinese, but who may be interested in the contents of this work as a field of general phonetics.

The Wu-dialects are a group of dialects extending over the South-eastern part of the province of Jiangsu(Kiangsu) and the North-eastern greater half of the province of Jehjiang (Chekiang); the south-western part of Jehjiang may belong to this group too, but it has not been studied.

The scope of study was to cover all the main features of each dialect studied, including the phonological classification of initials, finals and tones, the exact values of these classes, intonations of short phrases, vocabulary of the most common words and of peculiar words, and the grammatical particles.

The equipment used consisted of forms, or type-lists for each phase of the study which was printed before hand in the form of tables and pamphlets. The only other thing used was a sliding pitch-pipe for approximate matching of the intonations. All the consonant and vowel values were judged by ear.

The real content of this monograph are all given in the six tables as follows:

Table Ⅰ "第一表": Initials.

Table Ⅱ "第二表": Finals in the first three ancient tones.

Table Ⅲ "第三表": Finals in *ruhsheng*, or the 4th ancient tone.

Table Ⅳ "第四表": Tone graphs and formulæ.

Table Ⅴ "第五表": Vocabulary of common words.

Table Ⅵ "第六表": Grammatical particles.

All the rest is only talk, which it is presumed will help the reader read the tables.

In Tables Ⅰ—Ⅱ, the first two rows, and in Table Ⅲ, the first three rows give a sort of abstract phonological classification. In the notation of these rows, which is always given between single inverted commas, every character has always the same spelling no matter how it is pronounced. For instance, the character 班 belongs to the initial 'b' and the final 'an', and is therefore spelt 'ban', altho in actual pronunciation, it may be [pæ], or [be], or any sound whatever. This enables one to say that such and such a sound has such and such a pronunciation in such and such a place, which would be meaningless unless the 'sound' is taken not as a sound, but as a class. This idea is somewhat like that of *phoneme*, as used by Daniel Jones①, but still more radical than the phoneme, as the bringing in of different times and places makes it more inclusive and more complicated.

In the third row are given the names of the ancient initials and finals. These are cut up and scattered over different parts of each table, when it is found convenient to do so in order to conform to the main tendency of the modern Wu-dialects as to the coalescence or sub-division of sound-classes.

The fourth row, which is sometimes subdivided into two parts, states the conditions under which the ancient initial or final is pronunced in the way indicated by the present column. For instance, when ancient velar initials are followed by front vowels ('g_2, k_2, gh_2, gn_1', Table Ⅰ-2), as indicated by the condition '今齊攝', they will be found to become palatal sounds in most of the dialects studied. In Table Ⅱ, the factor which influences the final most is the *place* of articulation of the initials. This is

① For a definition of a phoneme, see Daniel Jones, *The Pronunciation of Russian*, Cambridge, 1923, pp. 49—50.

stated in terms of 'b 系, d 系, g 系, h 系, j 系, tz 系', which stands for the labial, dental (plosive, nasal and lateral) velar, glottal, alveolar or palatal, and dental (affricative and fricative) series, respectively. The character 文 in small print stands for the literary pronunciation and 白 for the colloquial pronunciation. The former is usually nearer to Mandarin and the latter usually nearer to the ancient pronunciation. Such cases of double reading are more numerous in the Wu-dialects than in most other dialects.

The fifth row gives characters of each class as illustrations; these are taken form the longer list of about 2700 characters used in the typelists.

The sixth row gives the pronunciation of the initials or the finals as they were pronounced in the North of China in the Swei or early Tarng dynasty, or about 600 A. D. The values given follow the reconstruction of Bernhard Karlgren①, except that it is here translated into the International Phonetic Alphabet (to be referred to as "IPA" from now on).

The seventh row gives the pronunciation of Gwoyeu, or Mandarin, which is taken to be approximately the same as the pronunciation of Peking.

---

① The most accessible form is in his *Analytic Dictionary of Chinese and Sino-Japanese*, Paris, 1923, and his "Dictionary of Dialects" Stockholm 1926, being the fourth volume of his *Études sur la Phonologie Chinoise*.

The body of the tables is given in a very "narrow " form of the IPA, two lists of which are given with examples in English, etc. in "甲表"(just before Table Ⅰ), and "乙表" (just before Table Ⅱ).

Additional signs to the IPA are as follows: For a medium *a*, a capital A is used, as Jespersen does in his *Lehrbuch der Phonetik*①. On the analogy of A, I, etc. , a medium [e] is indicated by a capital E. For the ancient palatal plosives, which came from archaic *t* and *d*, and later became palatal or alveolar affricates, it was thought advisable to use *t* and *d* with a horizontal hook to the left, after the fashion of the leftward-hooked *c* and *z*, thus leaving *c* and inverted *f* available for the back variety of palatal plosives. For apical vowels, the four signs proposed by Karlgren② are used instead of usng *i*-dieresis of *z* with a vertical stroke under it, etc.

A very important convention adopted in these tables concerns the use of superscripts and subscripts. A *super*script is always used in an *additive* sense, that is, a parasitic sound which lacks clearness, or intensity, or length, or any combination of these is written small as a superscript. It is also used for a sound which is sometimes present and sometimes absent in an initial or a final. A *sub*script is also used in an *adjectival* or *modifying*

① 2nd edition, section, 9. 92, p. 162.

② *Phonologie*, vol. 1, pp. 295—297.

sense, that is, it indicates that the sound denoted by the preceding letter has something of the manner or place of articulation of the sound denoted by the subscript. In case a sign which is itself a modifier, such as a nasal sign or a "higher" sign is found at the upper right-hand corner, it means that the sound of the preceding letter begins without the modification but finishes with that modification. Thus a diphthong of very narrow range may sometimes be indicated by a superscript modifier when it is thought not advisable to use two different letters.

Table Ⅳ gives the tones for single characters. The headings indicate the ancient classes and the influence of the manner of articulation on the modern subdivision. No actual values for the ancient tones were given, as nobody knows as yet what they were.

In the main body of the table, each space gives the name of the tone class, the time-pitch graph, and its notation in the numerical tonic sol-fa system. The original data were recorded in absolute pitch (with the aid of the pitch-pipe mentioned above) on the staff-notation, the relative time being also indicated. For the purpose of comparison, all the data were reduced to the same nameless key by regarding all the middle points of all sets as being *me* (*mi* flat) or *ri* in the scale. Inasmuch as the absolute *size* of the intervals in each tone also varies with individual temperament, momentary mood, etc. , this aspect of it should also have been reduced to a uniform scale, but sa no practical means has been divised for making such reduction, this has to be left alone. As a matter of fact, this does not seem to have given rise to much discrepancy in the comparisons, the worse case being that for No. 7 Jiang-in (江陰), where the tones were very much exaggerated and probably not consistently pronounced in one key of voice. ①

The first column to the right of the graphs gives the total number of tone classes in each dialect. The next column gives the absolute pitch of *do*, and the last column indicates the nature of the voice recorded, 成 stands for adult man, 童 for boy, and 女 for woman.

Part Ⅱ of this monograph gives a part of the data collected concerning vocabulary and grammar, or grammatical particles, the substance of which is given in Tables Ⅴ and Ⅵ. In Table Ⅴ, the top row gives the meaning in Mandarin, and the equivalents in the different dialects are given in a column. This vocabulary includes only the most common words and a small number of words peculiar to the Wu-dialects more or less in common. Then a series of words peculiar to only one or a very few dialects

---

① The shapes of curves for *inpyng*, *inshaanq* and *inchiuh* agree with, and that for *inruh* differs from those given by Dr. Liou Fuh ("Fu Liu") in his *Études Expérimentales sur les Tons du Chinoise*, Planches Ⅱ, figs. 17—20. Unfortunately, he did not take any record of the other three tones of Jiang-in, with which I could check my results.

are appended to the main vocabulary.

Table Ⅵ gives the grammatical particles. As the sentence structure of Chinese is nearly the same in all the dialects of China, the grammatical peculiarities of a dialect can practically all be given in the particles. In the first row of the table is given a brief statement of the functions, the second row gives approximate equivalents in the literary idiom, the third row gives the Mandarin equivalents, and the fourth row gives the reference numbers to an article written by the author in *Tsing Hua Journal* on grammatical particles. ①

Since the exact pronunciation of all the phonological classes are given in the first four tables, it will not be necessary to give the vocabulary in phonetic notation. A quite safe and dependable way is to give the exact sound (including tone) in terms of characters *as pronounced in the locality*, and whenever there is the slightest doubt as to whether the character used is the proper one (*i. e.*, the one used in that sense in several dialects over several hundred years), a small character "音" is placed after the nonce-character to indicate that it is used only for the sound. In many cases, an approximate pronunciation is given in terms of a dialect romanization, which is an extension of the National Romanization. The rough values of the letters used in this manner

① *Tsing Hua Journal*, Ⅲ, 2, pp. 865—917, Peking 1926.

are given in the two tables "甲表" and "乙表". For purposes of dialect writing, the tones are also indicated by variations of spelling on similar lines to the National Romanization.

The rules for tonal spelling are:

For *pyngsheng*(平聲):No special sign.

For *shaangsheng*(上聲): If the final has only one vowel, double it, as 李 l*ii*, 馬 m*aa*, Medial or "auslaut" *i* and *u* are changed into *e* and *o* respectively, as 廣 g*o*ang, 海 ha*e*. But the diphthongs *ei*, *ie*, *ou*, *uo*, have their *e* and *o* doubled instead of having their *i* and *u* changed, as 美 m*ee*i, 火 hu*oo*.

For *chiuhsheng* (去聲): "Auslauts "-*i*, -*u*, -*n*, -*ng*, -*l* change into -*y*, -*w*, -*nn*, -*ng*, -*ll* respectively. For other cases (including the cases of *i*, *u* as chief vowels) add a final *h*.

For *ruhsheng* (入聲):Add a final *q*.

The upper (陰) and lower (陽) series of tones are automatically indicated by the nature of the initial, surds always having the upper tones and sonants always the lower, words beginning with a vowel not spelt with an initial *y* or *w* are considered to belong to the upper series. For the small number of "liquid" sonants (nasals and laterals) which have the upper tones, an apostrophe is put after the initial, as ling 零, *yangpyng* (lower), l'ing 拎, *inpyng* (upper). In the National Romanization an *h* in used instead of the apostrophe.

The rules for tonal spelling in the National Romanization

are the same with two important modifications:

(1) Since Mandarin has surd initials in the *yangpyng* ('second tone') series, these need a special notation. When there is a medial *i* or *u*, it is changed into *y* or *w* respectively, as *y*ang 楊, *y*uan 元, h*w*ang 黄, when there is no medial, put an *r* after the vowels as cha*r* 茶, she*r*n 神.

(2) When a syllable begins with *i* or *u* in *shaangsheng* ("3rd tone") or *chiuhsheng* ("4th tone"), a *y* or *w* is always added to, or substituted for *i* or *u*(there being in Mandarin no distinction of upper and lower series in these two tones), as j*e*ang 講, but *y*eang 養, m*i*aw 廟, but *y*aw 要. This is only for graphical elegance and has no phonetic significance.

In words of more than one syllable, sometimes a syllable loses its etymological tone and has a short and neutral intonation, somewhat like the *ruhsheng*, but weaker, this is indicated by putting a dot before the syllable. In Table Ⅵ, no dots are used, as the particle seems to have a clear *ruhsheng* quality (tendency towards ending with a glottal stop), it is spelt with final *q*.

On the left hand side of each of the sound tables are given the names of the places whose dialects were studied. When a dialect is not urban, an arrow pointing from a circle indicates the direction of the country place from the city to which it belongs. The places are:

In Jiangsu Province

1. Yishing 宜興
2. Lihyang 溧陽
3. Jintarn Shigang 金壇 西岡
4. Danyang 丹陽
5. Danyang Yeongfengshiang 丹陽 永豐鄉
6. Jinqjiang 靖江
7. Jiang-in 江陰
8. Charngjou 常州
9. Wushi 無錫
10. Sujou (“Soochow”) 蘇州
11. Charngshwu 常熟
12. Kuenshan 崑山
13. Baoshan Shuangtsaoduen 寶山 霜草墩
14. Baoshan Luodiann 寶山 羅店
15. Joupuu 周浦
16. Shanqhae (“Shanghai”) 上海
17. Songjiang 松江
18. Wujiang Lilii 吴江 黎里
19. Wujiang Shenqtzer 吴江 盛澤

In Jehjiang Province

20. Jiashing 嘉興
21. Wushing Shuanglin 吴興 雙林
22. Harngjou 杭州
23. Shawshing 紹興
24. Juji Wangjiajiing 諸暨 王家井
25. Cherngshiann Chorngrenjenn 嵊縣 崇仁鎮
26. Cherngshiann Taypyngshyh 嵊縣 太平市
27. Yuyaw 餘姚
28. Ningbo（"Ningpo"）甯波
29. Hwangyan 黄巖
30. Wenjou（"Wenchow"）温州
31. Chyujou 衢州
32. Jinhwa 金華
33. Yeongkang 永康

A map of the region studied is given in the Chinese Introduction.

The general features of the Wu-dialects studied here may be summarized in the following points.

The ancient sonants 並，定，羣，牀，etc.（or aspirated sonants，according to Karlgren）remain as sonants or apparent sonants. The real nature of these initials，as was first noticed by Dr. Liou Fuh（"Fu Liu"），and later verified experimentally by the present writer, is that they begin with a quite voiceless sound and only finish with a voiced glide, usually quite aspirated, in the form of a voiced *h*. In the case of fricatives and affricatives (順,騎), the second half may be voiced; in plosives (旁), there is usually no voice at all until the explosion takes place. The only fully voiced sounds therefore are the nasals (忙) and laterals (來), and voiced *h* (毫) and its labial and palatal correspondents (王,沿). However, in intervocalic positions, all the quasi-voiced initials become true voiced sounds.

The plosives [p,t,k] have hard values as in French, and not the soft values of Peking (voiceless *b*, *d*, *g*). But in Joupuu (周浦), Songjiang (松江) and Yeongkang (永康), the sounds corresponding to [p, t] are [b, d] respectively, while [k] is still [k], the smallness of the air chamber between the glottis and the velar closure making it more difficult to form a voiced plosive here.

Ancient diphthong tend to become single vowels, *ai*, *ei*, *au*, *ou* tending towards *ä*, *é*, *ò*, *e*. The "raising" of vowels in some finals has gone further than in Mandarin. Thus Ancient back *a* become *o* in central Mandarin, but *u* or *ou* in the Wu-dialects. Ancient front *a* becomes medium or back *a* in Mandarin, but *o* in the Wu-dialects.

Initials of the 'j' series, which were palatals in ancient Chinese, have become dentals or retroflexes in a majority of the Wu-dialects agreeing with Mandarin.

There are no final consonants except *-n* and *-ng*. Where both *-n* and *-ng* occur in the same dialect, they are (except for some words in Shawshing (紹興)) either used at random or assimilated to the following sound. In either case, the speaker does not know that he is not using the same sound. Ancient finals of the types of *an* and *am* become purely oral vowels in the majority of places studied, and nasalized vowels in the rest. Ancient finals of the types of *ung* and *ang* mostly retain a nasal ending *ng*, or an imperfectly formed *ng*. Ancient finals of the types of *en*, *em*, *eng* usually retain either *-n* or *-ng* or both at random without the speaker knowing the difference. The last group is most susceptible to the assimilating influence of a following word. Thus 金 ji*n*, 金裱 ji*m*beau, 金剛 ji*ng*gang, 金針 ji*n*jen.

The endings *-p*, *-t*, *-k* in ancient finals are dropt, but a trace of a glottal stop is usually heard when a *ruhsheng* character is pronounced singly. In connected speech, however, when a syllable in the *ruhsheng* is followed by another syllable, its *ruhsheng* character is only shown by its brevity, there being no glottal stop.

The most frequent total numbers of tones are seven and eight.

Besides these general features, some points of special interest may be noted:

Danyang (丹陽) treats characters belonging to the ancient sonant *pyngsheng* series in two ways. The colloquial pronunciation for these gives a sort of quasi voiced initial, but the literary pronunciation makes it a complete aspirated voiceless sound after the fashion of Mandarin. This is an interesting case of a borderland dialect. Jingjing (靖江) is the only Wu-dialect belonging to the North of Yangtzyyjiang. Its sound system is quite Wu-like, but its personal pronouns have the Mandarin forms.

Charngjou (常州) has two kinds of tone-systems within the walls of the same city. This is a class distinction, the speech of the gentry following one system, that of the popular majority following the other. It is also interesting to note that the democratizing influence of modern schools, where children of different families mingle together, has resulted in a partial mixture of the two systems.

In Shanqhae (上海), the dialect is undergoing a more rapid change than in any of the other dialects. The sound system obtained here is noticeably different from that given by Karlgren in his Dialect Dictionary, and still further removed from that given in the *Shanghai Lessons* of F. L. Hawks Pott, the chief differences consisting in the obliteration of certain fine distinctions of tone and vocality. On the other hand, these differences given by Karlgren and Pott are still found to exist in Joupuu and

Songjiang, on opposite sides of Shanqhae. Another significant thing to note is that individuals differ more widely in Shanqhae than in any other dialect. Songjiang has true voiced [b] and [d] corresponding to the Joupuu and unaspirated [p] and [t] of the other dialects. But unaspirated [k] is still [k].

Harngjou (杭州), being the capital of the Southern Sonq Dynasty, retain a good deal of Mandarin influence. Whereas all the other Wu-dialects have a literary and a colloquial pronunciation for a large number of words, Harngjou uses only the literary form whether in speech or in writing. There is therefore no striking difference in pronunciation between reading a literary passage in the Harngjou dialect and reading it in the Shawshing dialect, while the colloquial speech of Harngjou sounds very different from the surrounding dialects.

Yuyaw (餘姚) has the French *gn* sound as *auslaut*, which is rather rare among Chinese dialects.

Hwangyan (黃巖) has a sort of dyssyllalic *Shaangsheng* that is, syllables of that tone class have a glottal stop in the middle of the vowel or between the vowel and a final nasal, thus giving the impression of two syllables. In connected phrases, the glottal stop is usually not present.

Yeongkang (永康) has true voiced [b] and [d] for sounds usually pronounced with unaspirated [p] and [t] in other Wu-dialects. In finals ending with a nasal, they become [m] and [n] respectively. But in all cases, the [k] of other dialects is still [k].

Yishing (宜興) has two finely distinguished varieties of *u*; Ningbo (甯波) (with some people) has two finely distinguished varieties of *i*; Harngjou (杭州) (with some people) has a front and a back variety of palatal affricates, Joupuu (周浦) can distinguish between two *o*'s, two *a*'s, an *é*, an *ö*, an inverted *e*, all of the same *ruhsheng* tone; Hwangyan (黄巖) can distinguish between two varieties of *iou*, the ending in one being only slightly more advanced and lower than the other. These examples constitute a phonetic lesson for the phonologist, namely, that he can never tell that a shade is too fine to make any difference until he finds out that it does not, or, in terms of phonemes, any (to the local car) noticeable difference between phones, however small, may serve as a basis of distinction between phonemes.

譯名表

affricative 破裂摩擦的

alveolar 牙齦的，舌尖後音

apical vowels 舌尖元音

aspirated 吐氣，次清

"auslaut"韻尾

character 漢字

consonant 輔音

dental 舌尖前音

diphthong 複合元音，兩合元音

final 韻母

fricative 摩擦的

front 前

glottal 喉的

high (vowel) 高(元音)

i-class (finals which begin with *i*-sound)齊齒

initial 聲母

interval 音程

intonation (廣義)腔調

iu-class (finals which begin with *iu*-sound) 撮口

kaikoou (finals that do not begin with *i*-, or *u*-, or *iu*-) 開口

labial 唇的

labiodental 唇齒的

lateral 邊音

liquid 次濁

low (vowel) 低(元音)

manner of articulation 發音方法

medial 介母

mixed (vowel) 混(元音)

nasal 鼻音

palatal 顎化的，舌面的

particles 語助詞

phonetics 語音學

phonology 音韻學
pitch 音高
place of articulation 發音部位
plosive 破裂的
rounded 圓唇
tone 聲調，四聲
triphthong 複合元音，三合元音
u-class（finals which begin with *u*-sound）合口
unaspirated 不吐氣，全清
unrounded 不圓唇
value 音值
velar 舌根的
voiced, sonant 帶音，濁
voiceless, surd 不帶音，清
vowel 元音

調查説明

名義:這次調查是清華學校研究院派出的工作,去的就是作者跟助教楊君時逢兩個人。從雙十節動身起到雲南起義節回到學校,一共去了兩個半月的工夫。除去在路上的時候,實在工作的時候大概有一個半月。

區域:廣義的吴語包括江蘇的東南部跟浙江的東北大半部。這吴語觀念的定義或這觀念的能否成立是要等詳細研究過後才能夠知道,現在暫定的"工作的假設"就是暫以有幫滂並,端透定,見溪羣三級分法爲吴語的特徵。第一圖所示有號碼的地方的方言,大都是在這個定義之内的。

第一圖中4,7—17,19—20,22—23,27—28是在本地找人發音的,其餘的地方因時間的限制没有來得及到本地去,是在附近的地方找人發音的,例如諸暨的音是在紹興做的,金華的音是在杭州做的。圖中又有南京,鎮江,揚州,跟句容橋頭的語言是順便調查的,因爲這些都不是照上述定義的吴語之内的了,所以結果不在本册裡發表。

内容:這次的調查是什末都問,共計用調查表格六種如下:

(一) 1. 發音人資格

2. 聲母音值

3. 韻母音值

4. 韻母與下字關係(鼻尾同化)

5. 單字聲調

6. 喻母等陰陽賞問題

7. 全濁上去問題(待代亥害之類)

8. 不成詞兩字聲調(兩字並重)

9. 成詞兩字聲調(有輕重者)

10. "北風跟太陽"故事。

(二) 成詞三字聲調 512 詞(或短句)(沒有很用)。

(三) 平上去單字表(約 2300 字)

(四) 入聲單字表(約 400 字)

以上兩表是方音的基本材料。

(五) a. 八百詞詞彙。

b. 語助詞。

(六) 讀文吟詩樂調(沒有很用)

本書所發表的材料只佔所得的材料的一部分。其餘的等整理出來了再發表。

與高本漢(Bernhard Karlgren)所作方音研究的比較:

彼	此
只記方音,未記詞類。	記方音,又記詞類跟語助詞。
只記聲母,韻母,未記聲調值。	聲韻調三種音值都記,並略記短語語調。
用3125 個例字,字字都記(大長處)。	大約用 2700 個例字,未字字都記(大短處)。

範圍大:33 處方音佔十一省,又加安南,高麗,日本三國。	範圍小:33 處方音限於江蘇南部及浙江(後者較略)。
33 處方音有 24 種是直接當地調查的,9 種是大半根據前人工作的發刊物作的。	33 處方音有 18 種是當地調查的,15 處是找已出鄉的人發音的。
書中用 Lundell 的瑞典方言字母(略加擴充)跟一種寬式音標註音。	書中用國際音標(略加擴充)跟註音羅馬字標音,用一種"吳語音韻羅馬字"標類。
書中有聲母變化規則歸納表而無韻母變化規則歸納表。	書中有變化規則歸納表,聲母韻母都有(第一至第三表)。
所調查單字音已全體在書的第四册(方音字典)中發表出來。	單字音只散見於音表的例字中,每處的全部字音還没有整理出來。
所用材料甚廣(彷彿測量的底線長),討論之後有許多關於古音的要緊發明。	所用材料範圍甚小(彷彿測量的底線甚短),對於吴語的事實雖多所發現,而對於空間與時間上遠處的推測没有什末發明。
調查時間較多。	調查時間甚少。

方法:到一處地方先物色可以發音的人,大都是找各處學界中人幫忙的,但是也有别界中人。假如可能的時候總是先找好幾個人發音,先審查他們過去的語言環境,再在第三第四方式表選些字給他們念。大概語音不雜者,他的讀音是内部一致的,受過别種語音的影響的,見了字容易會躊躇,或是即不躊躇,也會讀出

内部不一致的讀音。這末樣先約略試了一刻或半點鐘，就在這幾個人當中挑選一個或兩個人再從頭詳細問到底。問的時間大致從最匆促者只花兩個鐘頭到比較的最詳者花三四天。因爲時間多少的不同所得材料的份量也不同，最詳的什末都問，最簡的就只取聲調的音值，跟第三第四方式表（單字表）的一部分代表字。至於没有到的地方，只能就找得到的當中選人，有時候也没有選的餘地，但是從内部的徵狀上也可以看得出發音者是不是太受過别處的影響。

記單字聲調音值的方法是用一個漸變的音高管（sliding pitchpipe），讓發音者將一類的字一個一個的讀，同時用音高管一頭兒吹一頭兒移動著摹仿他的聲調，摹仿對了，就看音高管上是從什末音到什末音，再到什末音，用五線譜記下來；至於時間的比例只可以約略估一估，也用樂譜的音符記它。試擬的調類共有陰陽的平上去入八類，假如有陰去分爲兩類或陰入一部變入陽入等等現象，在試音值時就可以發現。等到聽熟了哪一調類是怎末一個腔調之後，就可以判斷某字讀（該處之）上聲，某字歸（該處之）某聲了。

聲母、韻母的音值是用最嚴式的國際音標註的。但不必每字都註，例如巴，邦，比，半等字的聲母是[p]只須在聲母行頭註一次，以後遇見不合例的特别註出，其餘的就打一個√（“check”）號，就是“合例”的意思。韻母也是一樣的辦法。有時候表格中暫擬爲同一類的在某處並不是一類，就須在行頭註出條件，比方某處布，都，孤，蘇等字的韻，看聲母發音部位不同而異其讀法，就得把條件註出。如果調查時臨時看不出原則出來，那就逐字用音標記下來，等帶回來才慢慢的做歸納。

聲調、聲母或韻母，三素當中有一素遇到難分辨的時候，就用異同法來解決。例如某處的全濁母（定義見第一章）的上去（如待代，是事，動洞，範飯之類），好像分好像不分，就找些這類的字叫發音者自己辨它的異同。假如他説能辨而調查者不相信時，就有兩種試法。一個是叫一個别的本地人（也相信能辨者），把代，待兩個字隨便换着讀（可由調查者背着第一個人指給第二個人讀）叫那個人辨得出是哪一個，再試動洞，範飯等字。假如每次能夠辨得出就是有兩類，假如平均十回只對五回，那就是只有一類。還有一個法子是把許多聲母韻母都同的字（如俟，士，柿，市，是，示，侍，逝）寫成小字塊兒，叫發音者歸成兩類，調查者把他的兩類抄了下來，把字塊弄亂了再叫他分，看前後分的一致不一致。同樣，遇到聲母或韻母有問題的時候也可以用這兩種方法。但是最要緊的是比字的時候，聲韻調三素之中除掉有問題的那一素，其餘的兩素都要（在該地方音中）完全相同，方能用異同的方法。因爲同音不同音是一個極淺顯的觀念，誰都能辨的（這回遇到過一個教育程度極低的賣餛飩的，他連同音不同音的觀念都没有，不過這是少見的）。假如問代怒，是否同聲調，或甚至代害是否同聲調，那就須得假定答者有一種作抽象分析的本事，這是很難有結果的，或是結果會很靠不住的。

兩字三字相連的聲調，這次做的不全，本書裡没有列入，做這種記載的簡而快的法子是用留聲機（dictaphone）把全套的幾百個句子都收了下來，可以帶回來再慢慢的聽了寫出來，但是這種機器不甚輕便，且又須用電，在没有電的地方不好用。這次曾經跟上海利商洋行商量好了可以找人在他們公司裡去收音的，後來從浙江回來了已經没有時候了，所以這三字表除四五處外，其餘的全没有做。

詞彙的調查格式是依國語羅馬字排列，以國語爲綱，每詞下又註已知的吴語（大半是蘇州的詞）。到每處就問什末叫什末，什末怎末説，問完了之後再看機會探詢跟觀察特别的詞類。詞類的記法注重音類而不注重音值，因爲音值已經在單音裡記過了。但是要不把音類（尤其是調類）弄錯了，聽的時候仍舊要極仔細的聽，不過記載的時候可以用簡略一點的符號就是了。但是遇到有的詞一時聽不出是屬於該地的哪一個聲韻調類，那就得暫用國際音標給它記下來。

語助詞是用蘇州話的句子作例，這是快完的時候的工作，也是最難做的。做到這時候那地方的聲韻調跟常用詞大致已經知道了，所以先把那些蘇州話改成該處的話，然後試用東西南北的煞，阿呐，咾，拉等音，看哪個合乎那種口氣，而且還要加許多同類的例來試試，以防誤認另一種口氣表示法爲所要問的口氣表示法。大概教育程度高一點的人差不多都能領略所要問的恰恰是怎末一個味兒，而且也能知道假如本地没有相當的語助詞就應該用一種什末説法或是什末語調來表示同樣的口氣。年紀太小的發音者往往因爲情感的經驗較少，有些口氣都是没有的，所以這時候問來問去總不得要領了。但不能因此就斷定那地方没有這種口氣。

方言調查方法當中最要緊的一層就是要叫發音者用本地自然的語音讀字跟説話。假如調查者是一個外國人倒也没有大關係,他能學多少就學多少就是了,假如是個别處的本國人,往往就引起一種對你説藍青官話的"complex",尤其是對於作者,他們總覺得這是一個調查國語教育的人來了,那非得要拿頂好的國語説給他聽不行。在這個情形之下,最好的自衛的方法就是充本地話,能充得幾分充幾分,充到後來,發音者覺得肯放心説自己的話了就好了。

發音人資格(只列正式長篇發音的人,初試的幾個跟遇機會偶耳請問或是側聽的一共許有二三百人,有的也没有問姓名的,這些都不在内):

姓名	年歲	職業	住過	家庭與小學語言環境
1.潘　照(榴楊)	'十八'	高中二	宜興城,近在常州一年。	本鄉
2.方龍章(博平)	'十六'	高中一	生在天津,家裡説溧陽城話,在家裡啓蒙,'七歲'進天津私塾,'十歲'回溧陽,進高小,近兩年在無錫,但年暑假回家。自稱無天津音。(是没有。)	
3.李　茂	——	高師一	一向住金壇西岡,初到鎮江。	本鄉
4.荆和籟	——	師三	丹陽城。	本鄉
5.康年(明德)	'二十三'	教員	丹陽永豐鄉童家橋,蘇州六年,近三年在丹陽。	本鄉
6.陳壽棣(萼華) 盛建康(南屏)	'十六' '十四'	高中一 初中三	靖江城,近在江陰{一/二}年。	本鄉
7.薛鴻遠(雲程) 王慰祖(誦陶)	'十八' '十九'	高中三	江陰城。	本鄉
8.吴亦璘(仲珂)	'三十五'	教員	常州城,在天津住過幾個月。	本鄉

9.（聲明名不發表）	‘三十四’	教員	無錫城，廿四至廿八歲住南延市。	本鄉
10. 盧玉如（式之）	——	高中師三	蘇州城中心。	本鄉
張啓明	——	高中三		
張静波	——	校長	蘇州城。	本鄉
11. 楊韻生（子韶）	——	高小六	常熟城。	本鄉
——	——	高小		
——	——	高小		
12. 秦家球（風俠）	‘十五’	初中二	崑山城。	本鄉
13. 顧慶枬	‘十七’	師三	寶山霜草墩，近在寶山城。	本鄉
14. 張雨庭	——	師四	寶山羅店，近在寶山城。	本鄉
15. 蔡雪香	‘二十’	高中二	南滙周浦，近在六里橋。	本鄉
16. 張阜生	‘十九’	高中（走讀）	上海城。	本鄉
張樹琨	‘十九’			
姚貽耕	‘十八’			
居　偉	‘十八’			
李世文	‘二十’	高中	上海城，但八九歲前往天津。	母蘇州人
17. 龔東英	——	中學	松江城。	本鄉
吴世英	——	中學	松江城。	
葛邦復	——	中學	松江西門外二里弱。	
葛邦敏	——	中學	松江西門外二里弱。	
朱紫雲	——	中學	松江西門外一里弱。	
查劍鋒	‘三十五’	學校職員	松江城。	
18. 汝佩玉	——	初中二	吴江黎里，近二年在蘇州。	本鄉
張民彝	——	初中三	吴江黎里，近三年在蘇州。	本鄉
19. 周志鴻	‘十六’	銀匠店	吴江盛澤。	母浙江烏鎮，近住盛澤十八年（自云無烏鎮口音）。

姚才觀	‘十六’	碗店	吴江盛澤。	父母泰州，近住盛澤約二十年，也不常互談泰州話，據本人云父母無泰州口音。
20.(聲明名不發表)	‘十五’	中學	嘉興城。	本鄉
21.黄敦德	‘十六’	初中一	吴興雙林，近在蘇州一年。	本鄉
22.陳逸然（希謙）	‘二十五’	教員	杭州城，在上海四年，南京三年，杭州一年，在外時放假均回家。	本鄉
23.張以鏞	‘十五’	初中二	紹興城。	本鄉
張錫恩	‘十五’	講習科學生	紹興城。	本鄉
孫貽謀	‘十五’	初中三	紹興城。	本鄉
24.俞鍾本（德安）	‘十八’	講習科學生	諸暨城南王家井，近在紹興三個月。	本鄉
阮俊成（文波）	‘十八’	中學	諸暨城南王家井，十三至十五住城内。	本鄉
25.裘震坤	——	中學	嵊縣崇仁鎮，近在紹興兩年半。	本鄉
26.劉承香	——	中學	嵊縣太平市，新到紹興。	本鄉
27.黄宗正	‘二十八’	教員	餘姚，十六至二十一在杭州。	本鄉
黄——	‘三十’	教員	餘姚。	本鄉
28.徐丕棣	‘三十一’	錢業	鎮海至十四歲，杭州二年，甯波八年，上海一年，以後在甯波。	（略有鎮海口音）

	姓名	年齡	職業	住處	籍貫
	倪仁壽	‘十八’	錢業	甯波。	父慈溪，母甯波，四歲時父過輩。
	水德生（啟湄）	‘十四’	錢業	甯波西鄉鳳奧市，近三年在城内。	鳳奧市
	李慶遠	‘十六’			
	張思僚	‘十九’			
	王純協	‘二十’	高中一	甯波城。	本鄉
	牛紀定	‘十八’			
	吴　華	‘十八’			
29.	毛進良（達性）	‘三十六’	功德林經理	黄嚴二十餘年，台州五年，上海十餘年。	本鄉
30.	周夫人	——	——	温州城，近在紹興	本鄉
	王梅菴	‘四十多’	教員	温州城，曾住北京，近在紹興。	本鄉
31.	何錫汝（禹疇）	‘十九’	高師二	衢州城，近在杭州一年半。	本鄉
	周和鈞（衡甫）	‘二十一’	高師二	衢州城，近在杭州一年半。	本鄉
32.	蔣汝源（君山）	‘二十’	高中一	金華城，近在杭州半年。	本鄉
33.	胡衛華（劍夷）	‘三十多’	教員	永康城，近在紹興。	本鄉

以上第 4，10 前二，17 前五，18，20，22，28 後三，30 前一都是女人，其餘的是男人。

本報告内容：本報告只發表這次成績的一部分，就是吴語聲母、韻母、聲調的**大致**分合法跟它們的音值；最常用詞跟一些特別詞；跟語助詞。還剩有每處的單字音全表（是問過的字都加入在内）；兩字相連的聲調；每處的詞彙（是問過的都加入）；跟“北風跟太陽”的故事，等有工夫再整理出來。

音標：

這次因爲所論的材料極複雜，所以須用極繁細的符號才能把有些比較的關係表示出來。但有時候標音的時候又注重音韻學的音類而不在語音學的音值，那就不能不用一種攏統一點的符號。爲各種用法都便利起見，現在擬定四種標音法如下：

1. 吴語音韻羅馬字——根據國語羅馬字拼法原則，擴充而標吴語的音類。這是一套純粹標類性的符號。比方古山刪咸銜韻的字，談寒韻的舌尖聲母的字，凡元合口韻唇音聲母的字，在這次所做過的方言之内，處處都是把他們歸併作一個韻讀。但是讀出來究竟是什末聲音（音值），那就一個地方一個樣子了，有的讀 a，有的讀 é，有的開一點有的關一點，有的帶半鼻音，有的全無鼻音。假如每次要説"宜興的山刪咸銜，談寒舌尖聲母，凡元合口唇音聲母讀如 a"，"蘇州的山刪咸銜云云云云讀如 é"……那豈不又麻煩又不清楚？所以最好把音類分合的趨勢相近的些字，不管它音值變的利害不利害都併起來給它一個抽象的總名叫'an'，以單引號爲記。凡是羅馬字加'　'號的都代表音韻的虚位。（看下第二表 3）因爲'an'不是音值符號，乃是音類符號，所以咱們可以説'an'韻在某處讀 an，在某處讀 ä，在某處讀 é 等等。同樣，假如用'ou'作爲古侯韻跟尤韻輕唇音聲母或莊初鋤山聲母的總名，咱們就可以説，"金華'ou'讀 éu"，"常州'ou'讀 ei"，等等。還有一樣便利就是遇到寫詞的時候（尤其是有音無字的詞），可以用這個寫。比方説蘇州話管没出息或不中用叫[ts'edʏ]，常州叫[ts'æ̃dei]，别處又叫什末，總一句話就可以説吴語叫'tsanndhou'（'ann'是'an'去聲,'dh'是定母)。這種音類的觀念有一點像 Jones 的 phoneme[①]的觀念,不過比 phoneme 還更廣就是了。

2. 注音羅馬字——爲行文上跟印刷上便利起見不便用精密音標的時候,就用國語羅馬字拼音的方法,約略表示語音,例如音韻上稱爲'ai'的韻,在宜興,溧陽,常州讀 ai(不用'　'號者是注音羅馬字),在蘇州,無錫讀 é。名爲'ch'母者在無錫音 ch,在上海音 ts,這種拼法最便於寫長篇的方言文用的。注音羅馬字的用法見第一章甲表,第二章乙表跟第五章的凡例。

3. 國際音標——爲標實在的音值最精密的方法當然只有用一種語音學的(非音韻學的)符號,因爲國際音標比較的最通行,所以就採用它,在平常行文中用到它的時候加[　]號來辨别它。比方説音韻羅馬字的'an'韻,用注音羅馬字寫可以辨 an, ä, é 幾種音。用國際音標就可以詳細註出[an],[æ̃],[æ],[ɛ],[ᴇ],[e]等等音。在長篇用國際音標時以不加表示上下前後等形容號爲原則,以求乾净整齊,但在做比較表的時候往往兩處語音的不同就是在那末一點,所以在本册的表當中都是用最詳的嚴式標音的。依平常習慣,用國際音標寫表時也可以把[　]號省掉。國際音標的全表見第一章甲表跟第二章乙表。

4. 漢字直音——一個地方的音類的音值大部分記下來之後,遇到有什末字怎末讀或遇到無正字的詞的時候,就可以用本地同音的字註直音,例如衢州勸(音串),假如串字的音已經用别種音

① Phoneme 的定義見 D. Jones, *The Pronunciation of Russian*, Cambridge, 1923, 第 49—50 頁。

標記準了，就可以知道勸字的的確確是什末音了。或是上海有句話叫 siah-ih（-h 表示去聲）第一個字不曉得是什末字，第二字大概是個意字，所以就可以寫作"瀉音意"一個小"音"字就是表示前頭那個字的音是對的，字不一定對。用這種方法的第一個條件是用本地音註本地字，依了這個條件結果就跟國際音標一樣可靠。假如拿別處的字音來註這處的音，那就全無價值，一定弄得亂不可言了。

第一部　吴音

第一章　吴語聲母

凡　　例

下列第一表(共五頁)是吴語聲母的音類跟音值的全表。第一橫行是吴語音韻羅馬字的聲母,共計有

‘b’系:	b	p	bh	m	f	v	
‘d’系:	d	t	dh	n		l’	
‘g’系:	g	k	gh	ng			
‘h’系:			h	hh			□
‘j’ 系:	j	ch	(dj)		sh	zh	
‘tz’系:	tz	ts	(dz)		s	z	

二十六類。‘j’系裡所以不一定加‘dj’,是因爲古音的牀禪跟今音的‘dj’,‘zh’都是一筆糊塗賬,能分辨的如常熟,常州,甯波等地,它們辨類的法子,又是一處一個樣子,所以只併爲一個‘zh’類。同樣,從邪母也一律用‘z’代表,不另加‘dz’。這一筆糊塗賬並不是不值得算,是因爲一時不容易算出來,等算出來了關於古今方

言的異同上可以有一種有趣的比較。上述'b'系,'d'系等等名稱是爲便於以後韻表當中註明分合條件之用,因爲同是一韻往往跟着'系'的性質而變的。

表第二行是第一行的細目,大概一個總目在一處方言未必全是一種讀法,所以再細分到不必再分爲止(除掉'dj,zh'跟'dz,z'的問題,以及有條件太複雜的時候)。所以粗略說起來,第一排的分法彷彿是吴語聲母的最大公因數,第二排的分法是吴語聲母的最小公倍數——不過是這末個意思罷了,至於在事實上遇到太不便的地方,也不能完全照這末分。

表第三行就是《切韻》、《廣韻》所代表的古聲紐。《廣韻》裡本來無所謂三十六字母,只有反切上字分合若干類,但是古公工等與居舉九等區别在吴語裡(除掉韻母不同的影響之外)並不發生影響,所以仍用見溪羣疑等名目。不過有兩樣還須分别的:一樣是幫滂並明非敷奉微的分法,雖然與《廣韻》的唇音上字八類的分法不合,但是跟吴語的系統相近,所以現在用前者而不用後者。還有照穿牀審的之昌乘式類跟它們的莊初鋤山類在吴語往往有不同的變法,因爲後者往往並入'tz'系的音,所以另外分出作'tz_1'系。在字母旁註上小字,例如第一表 4 頁's_1'下寫審山。

表第四行注的是分合條件。大概一個聲母變化的條件可以照下列的幾條説完它:

(1) 古一二三四等(照《切韻指掌圖》分法)。

現在這個表裡頭除'j'系跟'tz_1'系之外没有用到這一套話。但是表第三行已經有了之昌乘式,莊初鋤山的字了,所以二三等的註不過是加註的性質,並没有限制的效力了。

(2) 古開合。

這是跟着韻類定的。

(3) 今開齊合撮。

今音的分等,是看韻母是 i-頭叫齊齒,u-頭叫合口,iu-頭(國際音標[y])叫撮口。用今等註條件,是因爲古等跟今等往往不合,比方狂字在古音是三等合口,應作撮口。這字在大多數地方是用 gh(注音羅馬字)但在温州用 dj(i)。要是以古等論,這個規則就難説了。但是查韻表(第二表 8 頁)‘$uang_{3,4}$’行下這類字在多數地方是 uang 一類的音,而在温州讀撮口的[y 加倒寫草體 a],所以宜其爲 dj(i)了。這是用今等有時便利的地方。

(4) 古平仄。

這個在國語跟丹陽有一點關係。還有次濁上聲文言(清濁説見後聲母的討論)在靖江,江陰也有一點關係。

(5) 文言白話音。

在中國好些方言當中有些字讀書或“joai 文”時是一種念法,説話時又是一種念法。現在簡單用小“文,白”字樣註它。什末音有文白兩讀是一個地方一個樣子。比方丹陽‘bh’,‘dh’,‘gh’等母的平聲有文白兩讀,是别處没有聽見過的;金華有好些韻有文白兩讀,也是别處所没有的。還有交,間之類有‘giau’,‘jien’,跟‘gau’,‘gan’,文白兩讀,何以表當中没有註明呐?這是因爲在韻表裡(第二表 2,3 頁)‘au_3’,‘$an_{2,3}$’開口韻下已經註了“白”音,在(第二表 10 頁)‘iau_1,’‘$ien_{5,6}$’齊齒韻下已經註了“文”音;現在聲母表既然説逢‘今開合’怎末讀逢‘今齊撮’怎末讀,那就包括在裡頭了。

(6) 韻類。

有時聲母看什末韻怎末變,這種條件大概總不很簡單,在表格式裡不容易寫出,在這個情形之下,只得在一格之內寫幾種音。這是達不到"最小公倍數"分類法的標準的地方。

表第五行是每類下的例字。因爲這次調查的時候没有能够把處處的兩千七百多字全問一道,所以這些例字的代表價值也略有上下。大概問的最詳的是宜,丹,陰,常,錫,蘇,寶霜,寶羅,上,杭,紹,波,黄幾處,其餘的問的較略一點,本行的些例字差不多全是從實在問過的字裡選出來的。

表第六行列《切韻》時代的古音作參考。它的些音值是根據高本漢(Bernhard Karlgren)的工作①譯成國際音標寫出來的。(附《切韻》後發生的'輕唇音'四類。)

表第七行列國音作參考。它的音值是照民國十七年的修正《國音字典》定的(以京音系統爲原則),不過所用的音標因爲要跟吴語的音值作嚴密的比較,所以跟《國音字典》裡的所用的音標或略有出入。

表本身所用的聲母音標都是最嚴式的國際音標。它們的音值如下甲表。

① 最方便的查處是在他的《分析字典》(*Analytic Dictionary of Chinese and Sino-Japanese*, Paris, 1923),跟他的《方言字典》,就是他的(前述的) *Phonologie* 的第四本,Stockholm, 1926。

甲表:輔音音標表

方法 \ 部位			雙唇	唇齒	舌尖前	舌尖中	舌尖後	混合舌葉	舌面前	舌面中	舌根	喉
破裂	不帶音	軟	b̥			d̥					g̊	
		硬	p			t			ȶ	c	k	ʔ
		吐氣	pʻ			tʻ			ȶʻ	cʻ	kʻ	
	帶音	純	b			d						
		吐氣	bʻ			dʻ			ȡʻ	ɟʻ	gʻ	
鼻音			m	m_v		n			ȵ	ɲ⊣, ŋ⊢	ŋ	
破裂摩擦	不帶音	軟			dz̥		dʐ̥	dʒ̥	dʑ̥			
		硬			ts		tʂ	tʃ	tɕ			
		吐氣			tsʻ		tʂʻ	tʃʻ	tɕʻ			
	帶音	吐氣			dzʻ		dʐ	dʒʻ	dʑʻ			
摩擦	不帶音		φ,χ(u)	f,fʻ	s		ʂ	ʃ	ɕ	ç	χ	h
	帶音		β,w	v	z		ʐ	ʒ	ʑ	j	ɣ,w	ɦ
邊音						l						

國際音標	注音羅馬字	吳語例字		國語例字	外國語例字	符號叫名
[b]	b或bb	松江	巴[bo]	——	E. bow	——
[b˙]	b或bb	永康	巴[b˙ʌ]	——	E. tubbath	——
[b‘]	bh	上海	旁[b‘ɒ̃]	——	——	——
[ḅ]	b	丹陽	伴[ḅʊŋ]	伴[ḅan]	South G. Boden	"下圈b"
[β]	v	松江	附[βu]	——	一般 G. zwei	"beta"
[c]	g或j(i)	永康	雞[ciɛ]	——	Fr. qui	——
[c‘]	k或ch(i)	永康	啟[c‘iɛ]	——	G. Kiel	——
[ç]	h或sh(i)	黄巖	休[çiu]	——	G. märchen	——
[ɕ]	sh(i)	上海	興[ɕiəŋ]	興[ɕiŋ]	——	"平鈎c"
[d]	d或dd	松江	多[du]	——	E. do	——
[d˙]	d或dd	永康	多[doə]	——	E. midday	——
[d‘]	dh	上海	同[d‘ʊŋ]	——	——	——
[ḍ]	d	丹陽	動[ḍoŋ]	動[ḍʊŋ]	South G. das	"下圈d"
[ȡ‘]	dh$_{i}$	古澄母:池[ȡ‘i]			——	"平鈎d"吐氣
[dz‘]	dz	寧波	茶[dz‘o]	——	E. loads+[ɦ]	——

[dʑʻ]	dj(i)	上海	奇[dʑʻi]	——	E. judge + [ɦ]	——
[dʐʻ]	dj	常熟	城[dʐʻẽŋ]	——	——	——
[f]	f	上海	飛[fi]	方[faŋ]	E. fun	——
[fʻ]	fh	古敷母	紼[fʻi̯uət]		——	——
[ɟʻ]	gh或dj(i)	黄巖	瞿[ɟʻy]	——	E. dial. giarden + [ɦ]	"倒f"吐氣
[gʻ]	gh	上海	狂[gʻuɒ̃]	——	E. go + [ɦ]	"草體g"
[g̊]	g	丹陽	狂₆[g̊uaŋ]	逛[g̊uaŋ]	South G. gold	"上圈g"
[ɣ]	hh	古匣母	匣[ɣap]		一般G. lage	"gamma"
[h]	h	上海	好[hɔ]	(笑聲)	E. hall	——
[ɦ]	hh	上海	鞋[ɦa]	——	E. aha!	"彎頭h"
[j]	(i)或y	常熟	欲[jo]	銀[jin]	G. ja	——
[k]	g	上海	街[ka]	——	Fr. cas	——
[kʻ]	k	上海	鉛[kʻɛ]	開[kʻæ]	E. backhand	——
[χ]	h	溧陽	呼[χu]	好[χaʊ]	G. Aachen	"希臘chi"
[l]	l	上海	路[lu]	路[lu]	E. lose	——

國際音標	注音羅馬字	吳語例字	國語例字	外國語例字	符號叫名
[m]	m	上海 門[məŋ]	門[mən]	E. ma	——
[mᵥ]	mv	古微母:文[mᵥi̯uən]		E. triumvorate	——
[n]	n	上海 奶[na]	奶[næe]	E. no	——
[ŋ]	ng	上海 熬[ŋɔ]	——	E. singer	"ng"
[ɲ]	gn	上海 年[ɲɪ]	——	Fr. oignon	"gn"
[p]	b	上海 巴[po]	——	Fr. peau	——
[p']	p	上海 怕[p'o]	怕[p'ʌ]	E. haphazard	——
[φ]	f	松江 夫[φu]	——	——	"phi"
[s]	s	上海 三[sɛ]	三[san]	Fr. sa	——
[ʂ]	ʂ	常熟 商[ʂa˜]	商[ʂaŋ]	E. tree	"監鉤s"
[ʃ]	sh	金華 書[ʃɥ]	——	E. shoot	"積分s"
[t]	d	蘇州 多[tɜu]	——	Fr. ta	——
[t']	t	上海 梯[t'i]	梯[t'i]	E. hothouse	——
[ȶ]	di	古知母:知[ȶie̯]		——	"横鉤t"
[ȶ']	ti	古徹母:痴[ȶ'i]		——	——
[tɕ]	j(i)	上海 見[tɕɪ]	見[tɕien]	Fr.coll. tiens! tiens!	——

[tɕʻ]	ch(i)	上海	巧[tɕʻiɔ]	巧[tɕʻiau]	E achew!	——
[ts]	tz	上海	哉[tsɛ]	哉[tsæe]	——	——
[tsʻ]	ts	上海	菜[tsʻɛ]	菜[tsʻæe]	E. it's hot.	——
[tʂ]	j	無錫	真[tʂən]	真[tʂən]	——	——
[tʂʻ]	ch	常熟	川[tʂʻɤ]	出[tʂʻu]	E. true	——
[tʃ]	j	金華	準[tʃɥən]	——	——	——
[tʃʻ]	ch	金華	春[tʃʻɥən]	——	E. choose	——
[v]	v	蘇州	文[vən]	——	E. very	——
[z]	z	上海	事[zɿ]	——	Fr. zéro	——
[ʐ]	zh或r	無錫	善[ʐɔ]	人[ʐən]	E. draw	"竪鈎z"
[ʑ]	zh(i)	寧波	袖[ʑiʉ]	——	Fr. j'irai	"橫鈎z"
[ʔ]	不寫	上海	鴨[ʔa]	——	G. Ecke	"耳朵"
[O]	陰調不寫 陽調hh,y,w	丹陽	安[ʊŋ]	——	Fr. on	"元音起頭"

其他符號凡例：

上加或下加小圈表示不帶音(voiceless)。

⊢發音生阻處較前。

⊣發音生阻處較後。

上小字(superscript)表示微加一點某音，例如金華'hh'母是先有一點喉部破裂音["耳朵"]，然後再有帶音的 h[彎頭 h]，所以先寫一個上小字的耳朵，再寫一個大彎頭 h 作爲正音本部。

下小字(subscript)是形容性的註字，如 m_v 乃是用 v 音唇音齒性的部位所發的鼻音，並不是 m 之後又加一個 v 音(照第二講法就應該把 v 寫作上小字了)。

ˑ是長音符號，例如[bˑ]較[b]長些。

——表示某格當中没有調查清楚。

{　}表示某格當中所問字數太少或竟没有問，但從别的相關的音比較起來，想應作什末音(填在{　}號内)。

;　表示詳細條件寫不下或規則看不出來的時候，有些字是這種讀法;有些字是那種讀法。

,　表示有人這末讀，有人那末讀，或同一人有時這末讀，有時那末讀。

少　表示這類的字佔少數(假如有";"號)，或這末讀的人或次數佔少數(假如有","號)。

文,白表示文言音跟白話音。

(i)(u)等等表示這類的聲母後有這個元音，因爲它不是輔音，所以用括弧辨别它。

這些音標分是分得很細，但是只遇有分辨的必要時才分辨。不必分的時候還是從簡。最要緊的一種從簡的地方就是'bh，dh，

gh,zh,z,v'這幾個聲母音值的寫法。在這次所做過的方音裡，大多數把這個讀成'清音濁流'的音[①],例如'bh'讀如[下圈 b 加彎頭 h],或[p 加彎頭 h],又如'z'母讀如德文派的[sz],或[s 加彎頭 h]。但是這些在兩個元音當中(intervocalic position)的時候又都念成真的帶音的輔音了。所以簡單一律全寫[b',d',草體 g',横鈎跟竪鈎 z,z,v]的帶音字母字樣。

① 在作者所知道,最初留心到這一點的是劉半農先生,並且他還進而推測古音也許是這種音,所以他寫古羣爲[k 加彎頭 h]或[草體 g],古定爲[t 加彎頭 h]或[d],等等。看《國學季刊》一卷三號(1913)453 頁。

第一表：聲母表

（第一表 1）

聲母＼方言			今吳音聲母	'b'		'p'	'bh'			'm'		'f'				'v'						'd'		't'	'dh'		
				'b_1'	'b_2'	'p'	'bh_1'	'bh_2'	'bh_3'	'm_1'	'm_2'	'f_1'		'f_2'		'v_1'	'v_2'	'v_3'	'v_4'	'v_5'	'v_6'	'd_1'	'd_2'	't'	'dh_1'	'dh_2'	'dh_3'
			古母	幫		滂	並			明	微白	非	敷	非	敷	奉		微文				端		透	定		
			分合條件	口韵尾	鼻韵尾	全	平 文	平 白	仄	全	白	今合		今開齊		今合	今開齊	今合 平去入	今合 上	今開齊 平去入	今開齊 上	口韵尾	鼻韵尾	全	平 文	平 白	仄
縣名	區域	派別	例字／簡稱	巴	兵	怕	旁文	旁白	伴	門	問白	夫	副	方	費	附	墳	無文	武文	問文	尾文	多	丁	梯	同文	同白	動
古音		切韵時／切韵後	古	p		p'	b'			m	m／mv	p／f	p'／f'	p／f	p'／f'	b'／v		m／mv				t		t'	d'		
今國音			國	ḅ		p'			ḅ	m	(u)(=文)	f						(u)				ḍ		t'			ḍ
1. 宜興	城内		宜	p		p'	b'			m		f				v						t		t'	d'		
2. 溧陽	城内		溧	p		p'	b'			m		f				v						t		t'	d'		
3. 金壇	西岡		壇西	p		p'	b'			m		f				v						t		t'	d'		
4. 丹陽	城内		丹	p		p'		ḅ		m		f						v				t		t'		ḍ	
5. 丹陽	永豐鄉		丹永	p		p'	b'			m	m;v	f				v		ɦm;v				t		t'	d'		
6. 靖江	城内		靖	p		p'	b'			m		f				v		v	f	v	f	t		t'	d'		
7. 江陰	城内		陰	p		p'	b'			m		f				v		v	f	v	f	t		t'	d'		
8. 武進	城内	"紳談"／"街談"	常紳／常街	p		p'	b'			m		f				v						t		t'	d'		
9. 無錫	城内		錫	p		p'	b'			m		f				v						t		t'	d'		
10. 吳縣	城内	舊派／新派	蘇舊／蘇新	p		p'	b'			m		f				v						t		t'	d'		
11. 常熟	城内		熟	p		p'	b'			m		f				v						t		t'	d'		
12. 崑山	城内		崑	p		p'	b'			m		f				v						t		t'	d'		

地點				p	p'	b'	m	f	v	t	t'	d'
13. 寶山	⊖霜草墩		寶霜	p	p'	b'	m	f	v	t	t'	d'
14. 寶山	⊖羅店		寶羅	p	p'	b'	m	f	β,v / v / β,v / v	t	t'	d'
15. 南滙	⊖周浦		浦	b	p'	b'	m	f / f,h_y	v / β,v / v / β,v	d	t'	d'
16. 上海	城内	舊派 混合派 新派	舊 上混 新	p	p'	b'	m	f	β / ɦɑu,v / β / ɦɑu,v v	t	t'	d'
17. 松江	城内		松	b	p'	b'	m	φ / f,φ	β / β,v(ŋ) / β / β,v(ŋ)	d	t'	d'
18. 吳江	⊕黎里		吳黎	p	p'	b'	m	f	v	t	t'	d'
19. 吳江	⊕盛澤		吳盛	p	p'	b'	m	f	v	t	t'	d'
20. 嘉興	城内		嘉興	p	p'	b'	m	f	v	t	t'	d'
21. 吳興	⊖雙林鎮		湖	p	p'	b'	m	f	v	t	t'	d'
22. 杭縣	城内	'shi'派 'si'派	杭 shi si	p	p'	b'	m / v,m_y	f	v	t	t'	d'
23. 紹興	城内	普通 凡字眼	紹 □ 凡	p	p'	b'	m	f	v	t	t'	d'
24. 諸暨	⊕王家井		諸王	p	p'	b'	m	φ / f	β / v / β / v	t	t'	d'
25. 嵊縣	⊖崇仁鎮		嵊崇	p	p'	b'	m / —	f	—	t	t'	d'
26. 嵊縣	⊖太平市		嵊太	p	p'	b'	m / —	f	—	t	t'	d'
27. 餘姚	城内		姚	p	p'	b'	m	f	v	t	t'	d'
28. 鄞縣	城内		波	p	p'	b'	m	f	v	t	t'	d'
29. 黄巖	城内		黄	p	p'	b'	m / m,v	f	v	t	t'	d'
30. 永嘉	城内		溫	p	p'	b'	m	f	v	t	t'	d'
31. 衢縣	城内		衢	p	p'	b'	m	f	v	t	t'	d'
32. 金華	城内		華	p,m_y	p'	b'	m	f	v	t,n_y	t'	d'
33. 永康	城内		康	b· / m	p'	b'	m / v,ɦɑu	f	v	d· / n	t'	d'

（第一表2）

吴母	'n'	'l'	'g'		'k'		'gh'						'ng'		'gn'			
	'n'	'l'	'g1'	'g2'	'k1'	'k2'	'gh'1	'gh'2	'gh'3	'gh'4	'gh'5	'gh'6	'ng'1	'ng'2	'gn'1	'gn'2	'gn'3	'gn'4
古母	泥	來	見		溪		羣						疑			泥孃	日	
條件	今開合	全	今開合	今齊撮	今開合	今齊撮	今開合 平 文	今開合 平 白	今開合 仄	今齊撮 平 文	今齊撮 平 白	今齊撮 仄	今開	今u韻	今齊撮	今齊撮	多數	兒白 耳白 二白 等
例	奶	落	公	居	鉛	勸	狂文	狂白	共	求文	求白	件	熬	五白	牛遇	年女	讓白	
古	n	l	k		k'		g'						ŋ			n(j)	ɲʑ	
國	n	l	g̊	tɕ	k'	tɕ'	k'		g̊	tɕ'		tɕ	○	(u)	(i),n+	n	ʑ	(θr)(ɚr)
1.宜	n	l	k	tɕ	k'	tɕ'	g'			dʑ'			ŋ		ɲ,ɦ(i;y)+	ɲ		
2.溧	n;l	l	k	tɕ	k'	tɕ'	g'			dʑ'			ŋ		ɲ;(i;y)+	ɲ		
3.壇	l		k	tɕ	k'	tɕ'	g'			dʑ'			ŋ		ɲ;(i;y)+	ɲ		
4.丹	n	l	k	tɕ	k'	tɕ'	k'	g̊		tɕ'	dʑ		ŋ		ɲ;(i;y)+	ɲ	ɲ;n入	
5.丹文	n	l	k	tɕ	k'	tɕ'	g'			dʑ'			ŋ	ɦ(u,ɑ;ɑ)	ɲ,ɦ(i;y)+	ɲ	ɲ;ɦi	
6.靖	n	l	k	tɕ	k'	tɕ'	g'			dʑ'			ŋ	ŋ;(u)	ɲ;j+	ɲ		
7.陰	n	l	k	tɕ	k'	tɕ'	g'			dʑ'			ŋ	'ŋ;β	ɲ;j+	ɲ		
8.常	n	l	k	tɕ	k'	tɕ'	g'			dʑ'			ŋ		ɲ,ɦ(i;y)+	ɲ		
9.錫	n	l	k	tɕ	k'	tɕ'	g'			dʑ'			ŋ		ɲ,ç,ɦ(i;y)+	ɲ		
10.蘇	n	l	k	tɕ	k'	tɕ'	g'			dʑ'			ŋ		ɲ,ɦ(i;y)+	ɲ		
11.熟	n	l	k	tɕ	k'	tɕ'	g'			dʑ'			ŋ		ɲ;j+	ɲ		
12.崑	n	l	k	tɕ	k'	tɕ'	g'			dʑ'			ŋ	n	ɲ;j+	ɲ		

13.寶霜	n	l	k	tɕ	kʻ	tɕʻ	gʻ	dʑʻ	ŋ	n	ɲ,j˖	ɲ	
14.寶羅	n	l	k	tɕ	kʻ	tɕʻ	gʻ	dʑʻ	ŋ		ɲ,ɦ(i,y)˖	ɲ	
15.浦東	n	l	k	tɕ	kʻ	tɕʻ	gʻ	dʑʻ	ŋ		ɲ,ɦ(i,y)˖	ɲ	
16.上	n	l	k	tɕ	kʻ	tɕʻ	gʻ	dʑʻ	ŋ		ɲ,ɦ(i,y)˖	ɲ	
17.松	n	l	k	c,tɕ	kʻ	cʻ,tɕʻ	gʻ	ɟ,dʑʻ	ŋ		ɲ,ɦ(i,y)˖	ɲ	
18.吳黎	n	l.	k	tɕ	kʻ	tɕʻ	gʻ	dʑʻ	ŋ		ɲ,ɦ(i,y)˖	ɲ	
19.吳盛	n	l	k	tɕ	kʻ	tɕʻ	gʻ	dʑʻ	ɦ	ŋ	ɲ,ɦ(i,y)˖	ɲ	
20.嘉兴	n	l	k	tɕ	kʻ	tɕʻ	gʻ	dʑʻ	ɦ	ŋ	ɲ,ɦ(i,y)˖	ɲ	
21.湖	n	l	k	tɕ	kʻ	tɕʻ	gʻ	dʑʻ	ŋ		ɲ,ɦ(i,y)˖	ɲ		n
22.杭	n	l	k	tɕ	kʻ	tɕʻ	gʻ	dʑʻ	ŋ	ˣɦ(ɯ)	ɲ,j	ɲ	z (一χ)	l
23.紹	n	l	k	tɕ	kʻ	tɕʻ	gʻ	dʑʻ	ŋ		ɲ,ɦ(i,y)˖	ɲ	
24.諸	n;l˖	l;n˖	k	tɕ	kʻ	tɕʻ	gʻ	dʑʻ	ŋ		ɲ,ɦ(i,y)˖	ɲ	
25.嵊崇	n	l	k	tɕ	kʻ	tɕʻ	gʻ	dʑʻ	ŋ	—	ɲ, —	ɲ:n˖	
26.嵊太	n	l	k	tɕ	kʻ	tɕʻ	gʻ	dʑʻ	ŋ	—	ɲ, —	ɲ:n˖	
27.姚	n	l	k	tɕ	kʻ	tɕʻ	gʻ	dʑʻ	ŋ		ɲ, —	ɲ	ɲ;ŋ˖	
28.波	n	l	k	tɕ	kʻ	tɕʻ	gʻ	dʑʻ	ŋ		ɲ,ɦ(i,y)˖	ɲ	ɲ;ŋ˖	
29.黄	n	l	k,c,tɕ		kʻ,cʻ,tɕʻ		gʻ,ɟʻ,dʑʻ		ŋ		ŋ;ɲ,ɦ(i,y)˖	ɲ	ɲ;n˖	
30.溫	n	l	k	tɕ;ts	kʻ	tɕʻ;tsʻ	gʻ	dʑʻ;dzʻ	ŋ		ɲ;ŋ˖;n˖			ŋ
31.衢	n	l	k	tɕ;tʃ	kʻ	tɕʻ;tʃʻ	gʻ	dʑʻ;dʒʻ	ŋ		ɲ;(i;y)˖	ɲ	
32.華	n	l	k	tɕ; tʃ	kʻ	tɕʻ; tʃʻ	gʻ	dʑʻ; dʒʻ	ʔɦ	n	ɲ			n.
33.康	n	l	k;c		kʻ;cʻ		gʻ;ɟʻ		ŋ;ŋ˖;n˖				

(第一表 3)

吴母	'h'					'hh'	'hh(u)' 亦拼 'w'					'hh(i,iu)' 亦拼 'y' (u)				口		
	'h1'	'h2'	'h3'	'h4'	'h5'	'hh1'	'w1'	'w2'	'w3'	'w4'	'w5'	'y1'	'y2'	'y3'	'y4'	口1	口2	口3
古母	曉					匣	疑		匣		喻	匣		喻		影		
條件	今開	今合 u韵	今合 其餘	今齊	今撮	今開	今合 u韵	今合 其餘	今合 u韵	今合 其餘	今合	今齊	今撮	今齊	今撮	今合 u韵	今合 其餘	今開齊撮
例	好	虎	灰	希	虚	孩	吴(文)	危	胡	回	王	嫌	穴	沿	云	烏	汪	愛烟怨
古	χ					γ	ŋ		γ		(ɥ,j)	γ		(ɥ,j)		ʔ		
國	χ	χ(u)		ɕ		χ	(u)		χ(u)		(u)	ɕ		(i)		(u)		○(i,y)
1. 宜	{χ}	χ(u)		ɕ		{h}	ŋ,ɦ(u)	ŋ	{ɦ(u)}			ɦ(i,y)				{ʔ}		
2. 溧	χ	χ(u)		ɕ		χɦ	u					(i,y)				ʔ		
3. 壇	χ,h	χ(u)		ɕ		ʔ	u					(i,y)				—		
4. 丹	h	χ(u)		ɕ		χ,○	ŋ,v	v	χ(u),v		v	(i,y)				○,v	v	○
5. 丹(永)	h	χ(u)		ɕ	ʃ	χɦ	—		ɦ(u)			ɕ	—	ɦ(i,y)		ʔ○		
6. 靖	h	χ(u)		ɕ		hɦ	ŋ,ʔ	(u)	β,ʔ	(u)	(u)	j				ʔ		
7. 陰	{χ}	χ(u)		ɕ		χɦ hɦ	β	ɦ(u)				j				ʔ		
8. 常	χ,h	χ(u)		ɕ		ɦ	ɦ(u)					ɦ(i,y)				ʔ		
9. 錫	χ	χ(u)		ɕ		ɦ	ɦ(u)					ɕɦ(i,y)				ʔ		
10. 蘇	h		χ(u)	ɕ		ɦ	ŋ,ɦ	ɦ(u)				ɦ(i,y)				ʔ		
11. 熟	h	χ(u)		ɕ		(h)ɦ	ŋ,ɦ(u)	w				j				ʔ		
12. 崑	{h}		χ(u)	ɕ		ɦ	ŋ,ɦ	ɦ(u)				j				ʔ○		

13 寶霜	{h}	χ(u)		ɕ		ɦ	ŋ,ɦ(u)ᵧ	ɦ(u)				j		ʔ○		
14 寶羅	{h}	f		ɕ		ɦ	ŋ,β	β				ɦ(i,y)		ʔ○		
15 浦東	h	f,χ(u)ᵧ		ɕ		ɦ	ŋ,v, etc.		v	ɦ(u),v		ɦ(i,y)		ʔ	ʔ,v	ʔ
16 上	h	f	χ(u),fᵧ	ɕ		ɦ	ŋ,β	ɦ(u)	β	ɦ(u)		ɦ(i,y)		ʔ		
17 松	h	φ	f,φ,χ(u)	ɕ		ɦ	ŋ,β	β,v	β	ɦ(u),v		{ɦ(i,y)}		—		
18 吳黎	h,χᵧ		χ(u)	ɕ		ɦ	ŋ,ɦ(u)ᵧ	ŋ	ɦ(u)			ɦ(i,y),(i)(y)		ʔ○		
19 吳盛	h,χᵧ		χ(u)	ɕ		ɦ	ŋ,ɦ(u)	ɦ(u),ʔ	ŋ,ɦ(u)	ɦ(u),ʔ		ɦ(i,y),ʔ(i,y)		ʔ○		
20 嘉	h,χ		χ(u)	ɕ		ɦ;ʔ入	ɦ(u)			ɦ(u),ʔ(u)入	ɦ(u)	ɦ(i,y),ʔ(i,y)入		—		
21 湖雙	h,χ		χ(u)	ɕ		ʔɦ	ŋ,ʔɦ(u)		ʔɦ(u)			ʔɦ(i,y)		ʔ○		
22 杭	h		χ(u)	ɕ		ʰɦ	ˣɦ(u)					j ʔ ‡ ʔ j		ʔ○		
23 紹	h	χ(u)		ɕ		ɦ	ɦ(u)					ɦ(i,y)		ʔ		
24 諸王	h	φ	f	ɕ		ɦ	β	v	β	v		ɦ(i,y)		ʔ	v(u)	ʔ
25 嵊崇	h	—	f	ɕ		ɦ	—	{v}	—	{v}	ɦu	{ɦ(i,y)}		—		
26 嵊太	h	—	χ(u)	ɕ		ɦ	—	{ɦ(u)}	—	{ɦ(u)}	ɦu	{ɦ(i,y)}		—		
27 姚	{h}	f	χ(u)	ɕ		ɦ	v	ɦ(u)	v	ɦ(u)		ɦ(i,y)		ʔ		
28 波	{h}	f	χ(u)	ɕ		ɦ	v	ɦ(u)	v	ɦ(u)		ɦ(i,y)		ʔ		
29 黃	{h}	χ(u)		ɕ		ɦ;ʔ上	ŋ,ɦ(u)	ɦ(u)		ɦ(u),ɦ(y)ᵧ		ɦ(i,y),(i,y)		ʔ		
30 溫	χ	f,ɕ(y)		ɕ,s	ɕ	ɦ,ɦ(y)ᵧ	ŋ,vᵧ,ɲ		ɦ(u)	v	y	ɦ(i),z	ɦ(i,y)	ʔ○		
31 衢	χ	χ(u)		ɕ,ʃ	{ʃ}	ʔɦ,χ	(u)		(u),χ(u)文		(u)	(i),ɕ文	—; (i,y)	—		
32 華	χ	χ(u)		ɕ		ʔɦ	{u}					{(i,y)}		{ʔ}		
33 康	χ,ɕ					ɦ,ɦ(i)ᵧ	ŋ	ɦ,ɦ(u),ɦ(y)				ɦ,ɦ(i,y)		—		

（第一表4）

吳母	'j'				'tz'					'ch'				'ts'					'sh'		's'			
	'j1'		'j2'		'tz1'		'tz2'	'tz3'	'tz4'	'ch1'		'ch2'		'ts1'		'ts2'	'ts3'	'ts4'	'sh1'	'sh2'	's1'	's2'	's3'	's4'
古母	知	照(之)	知	照(之)	知	照(側)	精			徹	穿(昌)	徹	穿(昌)	徹	穿(初)	清			審(式)		審(山)	心		
條件	古三開		古三合		古二等		今開合	今齊	今撮	古三開		古三合		古二等		今開合	今齊	今撮	古三開	古三合	古二等	今開合	今齊	今撮
例	張	周	猪	專	劄	責	再	酒	(見上)	超	昌	寵	吹	撐	初	寸	千	取	少	書	山	三	相	宣
古	ȶ	tɕ	ȶ	tɕ	ȶ	tʂ	ts			ȶʻ	tɕʻ	ȶʻ	tɕʻ	ȶʻ	tʂʻ	tsʻ			ɕ		ʂ	s		
國	tʂ				tʂ;ts(少)		ts	tɕ		tʂʻ				tʂʻ;tsʻ(少)		tsʻ	tɕʻ		ʂ		ʂ;s(少)	s		ɕ
1. 宜	ts		ts;tɕ		ts			tɕ		tsʻ		tsʻ;tɕʻ		tsʻ			tɕʻ		s	s;ɕ	s			ɕ
2. 溧	ts;tɕ(少)				ts		ts;tɕ	tɕ		tsʻ;tɕʻ(少)				tsʻ		tsʻ;tɕʻ	tɕʻ		s;ɕ(少)		s	s;ɕ		ɕ
3. 壇(金)	ts;tɕ(少)				ts			tɕ		tsʻ;tɕʻ(少)				tsʻ			tɕʻ		s;ɕ(少)		s	s;ɕ		ɕ
4. 丹	ts;tɕ(少)				ts			tɕ		tsʻ;tɕʻ(少)				tsʻ			tɕʻ		s;ɕ(少)		s			ɕ
5. 丹(永)	ts		ts(少);tʃ		ts		ts;tʃ(少)	tɕ	tʃ(聖,顯)	tsʻ		tsʻ;tʃʻ		tsʻ		tsʻ;tʃʻ(少)	tɕʻ	tʃʻ	s	ʃ	s	s;ʃ(少)	ɕ	ʃ
6. 靖	ts		tɕ		ts					tsʻ		tɕʻ		tsʻ					s	ɕ	s			
7. 陰	ts		ts(少);tɕ		ts					tsʻ		tsʻ(少);tɕʻ		tsʻ					s	s;ɕ(少)	s			
8. 常	ts									tsʻ									s					
9. 錫	tʂ;tɕ(少)				ts					tʂʻ;tɕʻ(少)				tsʻ					ʂ;ɕ(少)		s	s;ʂ(少)		s
10. 蘇(舊)	ts									tsʻ									s					
10. 蘇(新)	tʂ;ts(少)				ts					tʂʻ;tsʻ(少)				tsʻ					ʂ;s(少)		s			
11. 熱	tʂ;ts(少)				ts					tʂʻ;tsʻ(少)				tsʻ					ʂ;s(少)		s			
12. 崑	ts									tsʻ									s					

13. 寶霜	ts				tsʻ				s			
14. 寶羅	ts				tsʻ				s			
15. 浦東	ts				tsʻ				s			
16. 上	ts				tsʻ				s			
17. 松	ts				tsʻ				s			
18. 吴黎	ts				tsʻ				s			
19. 吴盛	ts				tsʻ				s			
20. 嘉興	ts	ts, tɕ$_{y}$	ts	tɕ	tsʻ	tsʻ; tɕʻ$_{y}$	tsʻ	tɕʻ	s	s; ɕ$_{y}$	s	ɕ
21. 湖雙	ts; tɕ$_{y}$		ts	tɕ	tsʻ; tɕʻ$_{y}$		tsʻ	tɕʻ	s; ɕ$_{y}$		s	s; ɕ
22. 杭	ts			tɕɹ ts; tɕɹ	tsʻ			tɕɹʻ tsʻ; tɕɹʻ	s			ɕɹ s; ɕɹ
23. 紹	ts	ts, tɕ$_{y}$	ts	tɕ ts	tsʻ	tsʻ; tɕʻ	tsʻ	tɕʻ tsʻ	s	s; ɕ$_{y}$	s	ɕ
24. 諸王	ts	ts; tɕ$_{y}$	ts	tɕ	tsʻ	tsʻ; tɕʻ$_{y}$	tsʻ	tɕʻ	s	s; ɕ$_{y}$	s	ɕ
25. 嵊崇	ts				tsʻ				s			s; ɕ
26. 嵊太	ts$_{y}$, tɕ	ts, tɕ$_{y}$	ts		tsʻ$_{y}$, tɕʻ	tsʻ; tɕʻ$_{y}$	tsʻ		ɕ	s		s; ɕ
27. 姚	ts			tɕ	tsʻ			tɕʻ	s			ɕ
28. 波	ts; tɕ		ts	tɕ	tsʻ; tɕʻ		tsʻ	tɕʻ	s; ɕ		s	ɕ
29. 黄	ts$_{y}$; tɕ		ts	ts$_{y}$; tɕ	tsʻ$_{y}$; tɕʻ		tsʻ	tsʻ$_{y}$; tɕʻ	s$_{y}$; ɕ		s	s$_{y}$; ɕ
30. 温	ts; tɕ		ts	ts; tɕ	tsʻ; tɕʻ		tsʻ	tsʻ; tɕʻ	s; ɕ		s	s; ɕ
31. 衢	ts$_{y}$; tʃ		ts	tɕ; tʃ	tsʻ$_{y}$; tʃʻ		tsʻ	tɕʻ; tʃʻ	s$_{y}$; ʃ		s	ɕ; ʃ
32. 華	ts; tɕ; tʃ		ts		tsʻ; tɕʻ; tʃʻ		tsʻ		s; ɕ; ʃ		s	
33. 康	ts; tɕ		ts		tsʻ; tɕʻ		tsʻ		s; ɕ		s	

（第一表 5）

<table>
<tr><td>吳母</td><td colspan="16">'zh'(dj)</td><td colspan="10">'z'(dz)</td></tr>
<tr><td></td><td colspan="6">'zh₁'</td><td>'zh₃'</td><td>'zh₃'</td><td colspan="6">'zh₂'</td><td>'zh₃'</td><td>'zh₄'</td><td colspan="4">'z₁'</td><td colspan="3">'z₂'</td><td colspan="2">'z₃'</td><td>'z₄'</td></tr>
<tr><td>古母</td><td colspan="2">澄</td><td colspan="2">牀乘</td><td colspan="2">禪</td><td colspan="2">日文</td><td colspan="2">澄</td><td colspan="2">牀乘</td><td colspan="2">禪</td><td colspan="2">日文</td><td colspan="2">澄</td><td colspan="2">牀鋤</td><td colspan="2">從</td><td>邪</td><td colspan="2">從</td><td>邪</td></tr>
<tr><td>條件</td><td colspan="8">古三開</td><td colspan="2">古二三合</td><td colspan="6">古三合</td><td colspan="2">古二開</td><td colspan="2">古二等</td><td colspan="3">今開合</td><td colspan="3">今齊撮</td></tr>
<tr><td>例</td><td>陳</td><td>直</td><td>乘繩</td><td>食</td><td>成</td><td>上</td><td>平去入 仍</td><td>上 忍</td><td>傳</td><td>儔</td><td>船</td><td>順</td><td>垂</td><td>樹</td><td>平去入 如</td><td>上 乳</td><td>茶</td><td>宅</td><td>查</td><td>助事</td><td>殘</td><td>字</td><td>遂</td><td>牆</td><td>匠</td><td>詳</td></tr>
<tr><td>古</td><td colspan="2">ȡ'</td><td colspan="2">dʑ'</td><td colspan="2">ʑ</td><td colspan="2">ȵʑ</td><td colspan="2">ȡ'</td><td colspan="2">dʑ'</td><td colspan="2">ʑ</td><td colspan="2">ȵʑ</td><td colspan="2">ȡ'</td><td colspan="2">dʐ'</td><td colspan="2">dz'</td><td>z</td><td colspan="2">dz'</td><td>z</td></tr>
<tr><td>國</td><td>tʂ'平</td><td>tʂ仄</td><td>tʂ'平 ʂ平</td><td>ʂ仄</td><td>tʂ'平</td><td>ʂ仄</td><td colspan="2">ʐ</td><td>tʂ'平</td><td>tʂ仄</td><td>tʂ'平</td><td>ʂ仄</td><td>tʂ'平</td><td>ʂ仄</td><td colspan="2">ʐ</td><td>tʂ'平</td><td>tʂ仄（但入文:ts）</td><td>tʂ'平</td><td>tʂ仄 ʂ仄</td><td>ts'平</td><td>ts仄</td><td>s（但隨:ts）</td><td>tɕ'平</td><td>tɕ</td><td>ɕ</td></tr>
<tr><td>1. 宜</td><td colspan="8">dz';z</td><td colspan="8">dz';z, dʑ';ʑ</td><td colspan="7">dz';z</td><td colspan="3">dʑ';ʑ</td></tr>
<tr><td>2. 溧</td><td colspan="16">dz';z; dʑ';ʑ</td><td colspan="4">dz';z</td><td colspan="3">dz';z;dʑ';ʑ</td><td colspan="3">ʑ</td></tr>
<tr><td>3. 壇</td><td colspan="16">dz';z;dʑʏ';ʑʏ</td><td colspan="4">dz';z</td><td colspan="3">dz';z;dʑ';ʑ</td><td colspan="3">ʑ</td></tr>
<tr><td>4. 丹</td><td colspan="6">ts';dz;s;tɕ';dʑ;ɕ</td><td colspan="2">(i)</td><td colspan="6">ts';dz;s;tɕ';dʑ;ɕ</td><td colspan="2">l</td><td colspan="7">ts';dz;s</td><td colspan="3">tɕ';dʑ;ɕ</td></tr>
<tr><td>5. 丹文</td><td colspan="6">dz';z</td><td colspan="2">ɦi</td><td colspan="6">dzʏ';dʒ;ʒ</td><td colspan="2">ʒ</td><td colspan="7">dz';sɦ</td><td colspan="3">dʑʏ';ʑ;dʒʏ';ʒʏ</td></tr>
<tr><td>6. 靖</td><td colspan="7">dz';z</td><td>{s}</td><td colspan="6">dʑ';ʑ.</td><td>ʑ</td><td>ɕ</td><td colspan="10">dz';z</td></tr>
<tr><td>7. 陰</td><td colspan="7">dz';z</td><td>s</td><td colspan="6">zʏ;dʑ';ʑ</td><td>ʑ</td><td>ɕ</td><td colspan="10">dz';z</td></tr>
<tr><td>8. 常</td><td colspan="20">dz';z</td><td colspan="6">dzʏ';z</td></tr>
<tr><td>9. 錫</td><td colspan="16">z;ʑʏ</td><td colspan="10">dz';zʏ</td></tr>
<tr><td rowspan="2">10. 蘇舊新</td><td colspan="16">z;zʏ</td><td colspan="10">z</td></tr>
<tr><td colspan="26">z</td></tr>
<tr><td>11. 熟</td><td colspan="16">dz';z;dzʏ';zʏ</td><td colspan="10">dz';z</td></tr>
<tr><td>12. 崑</td><td colspan="16">dz'(?);z</td><td colspan="10">dzʏ'(?);z</td></tr>
</table>

<table>
<tr><td>13.寶</td><td colspan="5">z</td></tr>
<tr><td>14.寶</td><td colspan="5">z</td></tr>
<tr><td>15.浦</td><td colspan="5">z</td></tr>
<tr><td>16.上</td><td colspan="5">z</td></tr>
<tr><td>17.松</td><td colspan="5">z</td></tr>
<tr><td>18.吳</td><td colspan="5">dzʻ;z</td></tr>
<tr><td>19.吳</td><td colspan="5">dzʻ;z</td></tr>
<tr><td>20.嘉</td><td>dzʻ;z</td><td colspan="2">dzʻ;z,dzʻ;z</td><td>dzʻ;z</td><td>dʑʻ;ʑ</td></tr>
<tr><td>21.湖</td><td colspan="3">dzʻ;z,dʑʻ;ʑ</td><td>dzʻ;z</td><td>z;dʑʻ;ʑ</td></tr>
<tr><td rowspan="2">22.杭</td><td colspan="4" rowspan="2">dzʻ;z</td><td>dʑʻ;ʑ</td></tr>
<tr><td>dzʻ;z,dʑʻ;ʑ</td></tr>
<tr><td rowspan="2">23.紹</td><td rowspan="2">dzʻ;z</td><td rowspan="2">dzʻ;z,dʑʻ</td><td rowspan="2">ʑ</td><td rowspan="2">dzʻ;z</td><td>dʑʻ;ʑ</td></tr>
<tr><td>dzʻ;z</td></tr>
<tr><td>24.諸</td><td>dzʻ;z</td><td colspan="2">dzʻ;z,dʑʻ;ʑ</td><td>dzʻ;z</td><td>dʑʻ;ʑ</td></tr>
<tr><td>25.嵊</td><td colspan="4">dzʻ;z</td><td>dzʻ;z,dʑʻ;ʑ</td></tr>
<tr><td>26.嵊</td><td colspan="3">dzʻ;z,dʑʻ;ʑ</td><td>dzʻ;z</td><td>dzʻ;z,dʑʻ;ʑ</td></tr>
<tr><td>27.姚</td><td colspan="4">dzʻ;z</td><td>dʑʻ;ɦi</td></tr>
<tr><td>28.波</td><td colspan="3">dzʻ;z,dʑʻ;ʑ</td><td>dzʻ;z</td><td>dʑʻ;ʑ</td></tr>
<tr><td>29.黃</td><td colspan="3">dzʻ;z,dʑʻ;ʑ</td><td>dzʻ;z</td><td>dzʻ;z,dʑʻ;ʑ</td></tr>
<tr><td>30.溫</td><td colspan="3">dzʻ;z,dʑʻ;ʑ,ɦi</td><td>dzʻ;z</td><td>dzʻ;z,dʑʻ;ʑ,ɦi</td></tr>
<tr><td>31.衢</td><td colspan="3">dzʻ;z,dʒʻ;ʒ</td><td>dzʻ;z</td><td>dʑʻ;ʑ,dʒʻ;ʒ</td></tr>
<tr><td>32.華</td><td colspan="3">dzʻ;s,dʑʻ;ɕ,dʒʻ;ʃ</td><td colspan="2">dzʻ;s</td></tr>
<tr><td>33.康</td><td colspan="3">dzʻ;z,dʑʻ;ʑ</td><td colspan="2">dzʻ;z</td></tr>
</table>

聲母的討論

1. 發音方法

古音聲紐關於發音方法可以分爲下列的類數：

清	全清：	幫	非,敷	端		見	曉	影	知	照	審	精	心
	次清：	滂		透		溪			徹	穿		清	
濁	全濁：	並	奉	定		羣	匣		澄	牀	禪	從	邪
	次濁：	明	微	泥	來	疑		喻	孃		日		

凡是古音的不帶音不吐氣的破裂，破裂摩擦，摩擦都叫全清。吐氣的破裂跟破裂摩擦音叫次清；帶音破裂，破裂摩擦，摩擦都叫全濁。帶音的鼻音，邊音，元音（喻），鼻音兼摩擦（日）叫次濁。這樣分法與平常的分法略有出入，但在討論吴語的時候最爲便利，所以以下就當這末講了。

帶音跟吐氣問題。——吴語全清次清的聲紐除松，浦東，康的'b'，'d'用真[b，d]跟影母一部分有地方讀 v 外，都是不帶音的，這是與古音相合與今國音也相合的。全清不吐氣，次清吐氣，也是與古音相合，不過敷母今音讀成不吐氣的摩擦音所以歸全清了。

吴語的幫端見破裂音讀法是法文派的硬音，比北京的讀法較緊而脆。所以在國音下的註音用 b，d，g 下加圈（軟派清音），而在表的正文中大都用[p，t，k]標音。（松，浦東，康當然除外。）

吴語的濁類聲紐的發音最特别。在大多數地方這些字都用一個帶音的氣流就是[彎頭 h]音。假如是個破裂音,那音的本身並不帶音,换言之當它閉而未破的時候,聲帶並不顫動,等開的時候接着就是一個帶音的 h,就是[彎頭 h],因此聽起來覺得像很"濁"似的。因爲這個緣故,劉半農先生主張用[b̥ 加彎頭 h],[d̥ 加彎頭 h]等等標吴語並定等母的音值,或簡直就寫[p 加彎頭 h],[t 加彎頭 h]等等更好。若是摩擦音呐,乃就起頭不帶音到後半再帶音,或又加一點帶音氣流,例如表中所列的些[z]音細説起來都是[sz]或是[s 加彎頭 h]。不過遇到匣母喻母跟疑母不念鼻音的時候,就簡直全用[彎頭 h]。還有丹,温的'v'是用軟的真[v],不用[fv]。要是破裂摩擦音呐,那就在關閉的時候不帶音,到摩擦的時候恐怕起初也不帶音,到後半才帶音,而且總是帶一點[彎頭 h],例如表中所列的[dz']，細説起來是[下圈 d 加 z 加彎頭 h],或是[tsz 加彎頭 h]。

還有剩下來的次濁類的些字,因爲這些字的發音阻礙很少,所以仍是全部帶音,不過發音時所出的氣比發音所需者多,所以仍有[彎頭 h]在裡頭,不過没有先後的次序,是同時帶吐氣的聲音。例如上海龍字跟北京攏字聲母韻母聲調(論調值)都相近,但是上海的音聽起來像"濁"一點,就是因爲上海的'l'不是純[l],乃是[l 右下角加小彎頭 h]。因爲這些特點都是吴語跟别省語不同而内部大體一致的地方,所以在符號只須用較"寬"一點的寫法,除掉此處説明以外,就不在表當中處處註明了。

以上都是講這些字獨立重念時候的音。遇到輕讀而前頭有字(在 intervocalic position)的時候呐,那就都又念作普通不吐氣純帶音的[b,z,dz,l]等等聲音了。

有好些次濁母的字在好些地方(江蘇多,浙江少)不用吐氣的讀法而讀如北方的 m,n,l 等母的讀法。這些字在上聲文言尤多,例如了用不吐氣的 l 音或甚至帶[耳朵]的音。喻母字遇到這種讀法時就念成影母的念法了。

破裂摩擦問題。——非敷奉母在《切韻》時代還是破裂音,後來變成摩擦音,現在吳語也都作摩擦音。見溪羣母在齊齒撮口韻前變成顎化音,而且變成[t 加横鈎 c],[t 加横鈎 c‘],[d 加横鈎 z‘]的破裂摩擦音了。匣母本是所謂叫"淺喉音",就是舌根的摩擦,在吳語大部分讀成"深喉音",就是真喉音的[彎頭 h],雖然仍是一種摩擦音,但是因爲這種喉部的摩擦凡是次濁母都有的,因而匣母,喻母跟疑母的一部合併了。

知照精兩系的變法在吳語最不一致。知徹澄母在古音是純粹破裂音,照穿牀跟精清從是破裂摩擦音,審心邪是摩擦音。在清音方面,吳語跟今國語一樣,就是知徹變破裂摩擦音,照穿精清與古音同是破裂摩擦音,審心同是摩擦音。可是那些濁音就一處一個樣子了。有的一律念成摩擦音,例如上海,有的有破裂摩擦跟摩擦兩種,但是各處的分法不一致,既與古音的分法不同,又與國音不同,所以表當中只得暫把幾種混起來用";"號表示有些字這末念有些字那末念(例如[dz‘;z])。但是有一種與今國音一致的,就是澄母也仿知徹例不用破裂音,而變成破裂摩擦音(除非更進而一律變成純粹摩擦音如上海)。

日母在古音是鼻音加摩擦音,吳語文言中取它的摩擦成分,拿它當牀禪看待,白話取它的鼻音成分,拿它當泥孃看待。但牀禪母在吴音本有破裂摩擦跟純摩擦的兩種發音方法。所以日母也是的，例如江陰人 *z*eng，仍 *dz*eng。

鼻音問題。——明泥孃母古音是鼻音，吴語也全用鼻音，這是大多數方言一樣的，没有像厦門明母有[b]音的讀法。

疑母開口差不多全是 ng 音起頭，合口'u'韻的字(國音作 wu 的)，好些地方文言作 wu，白話作 ng，例如吴字文言讀 wu，白話云"吴先生"讀 ng。但這類字白話也不盡讀 ng，文言也有不讀 wu 而讀 ngu 的，非但處處不一致，而且同一處自己也不一致。疑母齊撮没有文白的關係，但是用 gn 還是用 y-聲母的音，各處也不一致。但古山咸那類韻如顔眼等字文言(齊齒)用 y-聲母，白話(開口)用 ng 聲母，没有地方既齊齒而仍用 gn 讀顔如嚴的。

微母大致白話讀 m(明母讀法)，文言讀 v(奉母讀法)。但文言上聲不變去聲，跟奉母變法不同，所以歸它入次濁(看第四表)。

日母大致白話讀 gn(泥母齊齒跟孃母讀法)，文言讀摩擦或破裂摩擦音(澄牀禪母讀法)。但文言上聲不變去聲，跟澄牀禪母不同，所以歸它在次濁(看下第四表)。日母支脂之韻元音大多數地方讀成元音或[彎頭 h]。

2. 發音部位

'b'系——幫滂並用雙唇，非敷奉(除幾處有字用雙唇摩擦音[phi，be，ta]外)用唇齒，這是跟國音一樣的。微母白話用雙唇鼻音，近廣東音跟古音；文言用唇齒摩擦音，近國音。

'd'系——端透定大都用舌尖破裂音，來母用邊音，這都是很簡單的。不過泥母只有現在開合讀舌尖的 n,現在齊撮的就讀成舌面的 gn 音了,就是舊式國音的ㄏ母。

'g'系——古舌根音見溪羣疑今開合口讀 g,k,gh,ng 舌根音,今齊撮就變成 j(i),ch(i),dj(i),gn 舌面音(疑母有時失去鼻音變 y-音),這是跟國語一樣的原則。但原則雖一樣,而應用的條件不同,因爲國語的韻頭未必盡跟吴語一致,比方江,庚,麻,山,咸,肴那些韻的'g'系字的文言讀法都變成齊齒,跟國音一樣,在白話就是開口,跟古音一樣了。

在齊撮韻讀 j(i),ch(i),dj(i),gn 音的時候,是不前不後的顎化音,比北京的基,欺,希的部位較後,但是比英文 key,geer 等字的 k,g 音要前得多。有幾處讀得特別後,變成純破裂音的,表中特別註出[c,c']等字樣。

'gn'母包括古泥母的齊撮,孃母,跟日母的文言音。但日母的脂,支,之韻在浙江常常讀成 n,ng 音,並不另加韻母。

'h'系——古曉匣是舌根摩擦音('淺喉音'),影喻是(深)喉音。現在吴語把這類字的開口大都讀成深喉音。曉母讀合口時,大都有一點舌根摩擦,讀齊撮時就移到舌面上來,跟國音一樣,但是它的部位比德文 ich 的 ch 音略前,比北京希字的音又略後。

疑母不讀鼻音時,跟喻母匣母可以相提並論,開口是喉音[彎頭 h],合口大致是一種 w 音,但是往往聽不見舌根或兩唇的摩擦,仍是喉音重,這是跟法文的 w 大不同的地方。齊撮音也是一種 y-母,但是這種音也是舌面不大有摩擦而用喉部摩擦的居多,有時簡直就是簡單的元音 i 起頭。

影母大都是用喉部破裂音,跟古音一樣,但在有的地方讀得很輕。

以上講的'h'系的發音部位跟'g'系的變法大致很相近,不過有時候不同,所以分作兩系。

'j,tz'系——這兩系的部位問題像它們的方法問題一樣複雜。現在討論的是發音部位,可以只講知照精三母,因爲'j,tz'系其餘的聲母都是它們同部位異方法的音。最簡單的就是上海派,一律讀成 tz。在餘姚遇到齊撮不能作 tzi 音而讀成 ji,與見母齊撮併,這又是一派。在蘇州(舊派)把知照的三等字讀如國語的舌尖後音,以辨知茲,招糟,這又是一派。但這一派的分法跟國語略有出入而跟天津的分法較近一點,就是表中'tz_1 系'的字,在國語往往讀 j 系音而在吴語(指能辨 j,tz 者言)歸 tz,例如初,山,士,在國語是 *ch*u,*sh*an,*sh*yh,天津作 *ts*u,*s*an,*s*yh,蘇州(舊派)*ts*ou,*s*é,*z*yh。還有一派,例如甯波,他的'j'系也跟蘇州似的另分出來,但不讀舌尖後音的 j(如國音)而讀舌面的 ji,因此跟見母的齊撮混。還有些再細分的地方,跟各派複合相配的地方看表就可以知道,總計四派的辨音可以比較如下例:

大略讀法	giau	jiau	jau	tziau	tzau
古音	驕	招		焦	糟
國語		驕焦	招		糟
上海派		驕		焦	招糟
蘇州舊派		驕	招	焦	糟
餘姚派		驕焦			招糟
甯波派		驕招焦			糟

第二章　吴語韻母

凡　例

下列第二表(共十三頁)是平上去韻母表,第三表(共八頁)是入聲韻母表。這兩表的標題跟第一表差不多的排法。頭一排是韻總目,第二排是細目(入聲第二排下又一排註平上去相配的韻目,這是照古音相配的説的,跟今音不盡合。以後計算標題排數的時候入聲的這一行算“又第二排”)。這一排也是大致成一種最小公倍數的韻目,但第一排比最大公因數的標準較細一點,因爲韻母的變化比聲母參差得利害得多,要是照著最大公因數的標準來定韻類(就是要有豎隔線一直到底的地方才始分類)那就一共没有多少類的韻母了。

第三行是《廣韻》韻目,舉平以概上去,入聲另列。一韻有幾類的就在右下角用小字註明是哪一類,例如麻韻的三類就拿它們的反切下字代表加,邪,瓜三個字註在麻字右下角。

第四行是分合條件。韻母的分合條件差不多全是跟着現在聲母發音部位而定的,所以最多見的就是註某系某系聲母的字樣。若是同一系裡不一樣變法就只好註出某母某母。有時候跟着古母變的就寫出古母見溪羣疑的字樣出來。還有時候有些單字有特別的讀法，就寫“一個字”。還有文言白話讀音不同的地方也照聲母表的註法寫文白字樣。

第五行是例字。

第六行韻音的古音也是照高本漢考定的古音，譯成國際音標，不過上小字的“^{w}”仍照他的寫法，究竟是加性的 w，還是形容性的 w(照本書例後者應作下小字“$_{w}$”)現在誰也不能定。

第七行列國音的韻音作參考。音值也是照民國十七年的《國音字典》寫的。

表本身所用的國際音標總表如下乙表。

乙表:元音音標表

高低 \ 唇圓度 / 前後 / 生阻處		舌尖元音					舌面元音														
		前		混或後			前					混					後				
		不圓	圓	不圓	畧圓	圓	特開	中性	畧圓	圓	最圓	特開	中性	畧圓	圓	最圓	特開	中性	畧圓	圓	最圓
高	最高	ɿ	ʮ	ʅ	ʯ	ʮ	i				y		ɨ			ʉ		ɯ			u
	次高						I			Y						ᵾ					U
中	高中						e			ø			ɘ		ɵ			ɤ		o	
	半中			$ə_r$			E						ə						or		
	低中						ε		œ				ɜ	ɵ				ʌ	ɔ		
低	次低			$ɐ_r$			æ						ɐ						ɒ		
	最低						a					A						ɑ			

國際音標	注音羅馬字	吳語例字		國語例字	外國語例字	符號叫名
a	a或á	無錫 法[fa]	江陰 生꜀[saᵑ]	蘭[lan]	Fr. patte	"刻板a"
A	a或á	宜興 鞋[ɦA]	永康 方[fAŋ]	他[t'A]	——	"大寫a"
ɑ	a或à	江陰 家꜀[kɑ]	常州 奥[ɑɤ]	方[fɑŋ]	Fr. pas	"草體a"
ɒ	ò或à	蘇州 家꜀[kɒ]	上海 方[fɒ̃]	——	S. Eng. not	"倒寫草體a"
ɐ	a或e	金華 麥[mɐʔ]		——	S. Eng. up	"倒寫刻板a"
æ	ä	常州 蘭[læ̃]	嵊縣 蘭[læ]	來[læe]	E. hat	"ae合字"
ɐr	al或el	——		二[ɐr]	Am. art	"倒寫刻板a捲舌"
e	é(齊撮省作e)	無錫 梅[me]	杭州 謀[meɪ]	——	G. geben	——
E	é(齊撮省作e)	常熟 梅[mE]	靖江 恆[ɦEŋ]	梅[meɪ]	E. get	"刻板大寫e"
ɛ	é或ä	寧波 三[sɛ]	松江 硯꜀[ŋɛ̃]	先[ɕiɛn]	Fr. mêler	"草體大寫e"

ɘ	e	江陰 噎[iɘ]		—	—	"反寫e"
ə	e或ö	上海 黑[hə]	金華 倫[lən]	嫩[nə˞n]	E. fallen	"倒寫e"
ɜ	e或ö	溫州 好[hɜ]	蘇州 奴[nɜu˞]	—	S. Eng. her	"亞拉伯三"
ər	el	靖江 兒[ɦər]		兒[ər]	Mid. W. Am. her	"倒寫e捲舌"
i	i	崑山 未[vi]	杭州 烟[Ĭ]	衣[i]	Fr. si	—
ɪ	i	無錫 連[lɪ]	崑山 星[sɪn]	星[ɕɪŋ]	E. sin	"大寫i".
ɨ	i	雙林 鬼[kuɯɨ]		—	Rus. быть [bɨl]	"橫杠i"
ɿ	y	上海 斯[sɿ]	永康 孫[sɿə˞]	斯[sɿ]	—	"前舌尖韻"
ʅ	y	—		詩[sʅ]	—	"後舌尖韻"

國際音標	注音羅馬字	吳語例字	國語例字	外國語例字	符號叫名
o	o	蘇州 沙[so]　常州 風[foŋ]	——	G. so	——
o˒	o或ó	黄巖 東[to˒ŋ]	——	——	"特别加圓唇o"
o˕	q	丹陽 木[mo˕]	摟[lo˕u]	Am. so[so˕u]	"中o"
ɔ	o或ò	蘇州 木[mɔ]　寧波 江[kɔ̃]	——	E. for	"倒c"
ɵ	ö	江陰 干[kɵ]	——	——	"横杠o"
ø	ö	上海 干[kø·]　蘇州 摟[lᵉʏ]	——	Fr. queue[kø·]	"斜杠o"
œ	ö	周浦 脱[t'œ]	——	Fr. heur	"oe合字"
ɞ	ö	寧波 小[ɕiɞ·]	——	——	"腰子式oe"
u	u	松江 蘇[su]	蘇[su]	Fr. sou	——
ʊ	u	常熟 綠[lʊ]　紹興 松[sʊŋ]	松[sʊŋ]	G. lung	"大寫u"

ɯ	ou或e	常熟 多[tɯ]	常州 多[tʌɯ]	——	——	“倒寫m”
ʉ	u	靖江 君[tɕyʉŋ]		——	S. E. Am. who [hʉ]	“橫杠u”
ᵿ	u	餘姚 谷[kᵿ]		——	——	“橫杠大寫u”
ʊ	u	蘇州 布[pʊ]		——	日本ウ[ʊ]	“縫狀脣u”
ɤ	ou或e或ɤ	常熟 看[k‘ɤ]	金壇 毛[mɑɤ]	河[χɤʌ]	——	“開口8字”
ʌ	ou或e或ö	松江 脫[t‘ʌ]	寶山 口[k‘ʌɪ]	河[χɤʌ]	Am. up	“倒寫v”
y	iu或ü	無錫 女[ɲy]	杭州 君[tɕym]	去[tɕ‘y]	Fr. une	——
Y	iu或ü	丹陽 宣[sʏ]	寧波 陳[dz‘ʏŋ]	——	G. hütte	“大寫y”
ɥ	u或ÿ	上海 書[sɥ]	杭州 車[ts‘ɥᵊi]	——	——	“平底y”
ɥ	u或ÿ	金華 吹ₒ[tʃ‘ɥɥ]		——	——	“兩頭彎y”

其餘符號凡例：

⊢ 發音生阻處較前。

⊣ 發音生阻處較後。

⊥ 發音生阻處較上。

⊤ 發音生阻處較下。

⌒或⌣ 短音符號。

▼ 長音符號。

） 圓唇度增加。

（ 圓唇度減少。

⊖ 唇不圓而作縫狀。

⊂̃ 半鼻音符號。

上小字(superscript)表示微加一點某音，例如 a^n 是 a 音後加一點舌尖鼻音，但不强也不長，也許舌尖碰不到。

下小字(subscript)是形容性的註字，如[i_j]乃是 i 音帶一點摩擦(因爲[j]是摩擦音)，[i_z]是讀[i]音時舌比[i]更前，且作一點摩擦，並不是先[i]後[z]。

假如上小字是正字的變形者，例如 $a^{\tilde{a}}$，$e^{e\vdash}$，$a^{\tilde{a}\dashv}$ 之類，可以省寫作 $a^{\sim}$，$e^{\vdash}$，$a^{\tilde{\dashv}}$。

吴語韻母音標特别從略的地方：

(1) 吴母[i，u，y]等韻頭(“介母”)往往是聲母的形容者，或不是形容者也很短，不像在國語那末比較的長，因此介母嚴格的應改寫作上小字或下小字，但因爲吴語都是這樣，所以都從簡寫成大字。例如虐瓜雪有些地方實在讀作[“gn”a]，[kuo]，[sye]或[“gn”^{i}a]，[$k_u$uo]，[$s_y{}^y$e]，但爲省事起見，一律用大字寫作

[“gn”ia],[kuo],[sye]。遇到似介母而實在是主音,似主音而實在是韻尾的例,就把尾韻寫作上小字,例如永康貼:[t‘iᵃ]。

(2) 長短音大致是平上去長,入聲短,所以沒有個個韻都註,有幾種特別短的非入聲字(如永康的陰去)在第三章聲調表裡可以看得出來。

(3) 入聲韻尾單字重讀時有時有一點[ʔ]音,但在句中差不多都沒有,所以入聲表當中都沒加[ʔ]音韻尾。

第二表：平上去韻母表　　　　　　　　（第二表 1）

韻母 \ 方言	今吳音韻母			'm'		'ng'		'y'		'o'						'a'		
				'm'1	'm'2	'ng'1	'ng'2	'y'1	'y'2	'o'1	'o'2	'o'3	'o'4	'o'5	'o'6	'a'1	'a'2	'e'3
	廣韻韻			虞	侯	模	魚	脂支之祭		麻邪		麻瓜	麻加			麻加	入声字長讀	皆佳
縣名	區域	派別	分合條件	微 白	明 白	疑 白	疑 一个字 白	'j'系	'tz'系	'j'系 文	'j'系 白	'ng'母 白	'b'系	'tz'系	'h'系 白	'g'系 白		'g, h'系 白
			例字簡稱	嘸白	畝白	五白	魚白	試	玆	捨文	捨白	瓦白	巴	沙	啞白	家白	拉	街白 鞋白
古音			古	i̯u	əu	uo	i̯wo	i i₂	ie iæi	i̯a		ʷa	a				—	ai a:i
今國音			國	u (=文)			y (=文)	ʅ	ɿ	ɤʌ		uA	A		iA (=文)		A	ie
1.宜興	城内		宜	m	—	ŋ	(ŋ)yⱼ (=文)	ɿ		A;O˔		O˔					A	
2.溧陽	城内		溧	m	—	ŋ	(ŋ)y₂ (=文)	ɿ		A,O˔		O˔					A	
3.金壇	西岡		壇西	m	—	ŋ	(ŋ)y (=文)	ɿ		—	ɔ˔						—	æe, a
4.丹陽	城内		丹	m,n	ʌɤ	ŋ	(ŋ)y₂ (=文)	ɿ		ie	a	ua˔	o白,a˔文		o		a	
5.丹陽	永豐鄉		丹永	(不用)	ʌɤ (=文)	u (=文)	yч (=文)	ɿ		ɒ								aɪ
6.靖江	城内		靖	(不用)	ʌ-ɤ (=文)	u	yч (=文)	ɿ		iæ˔	iA,O˔	O˔(à la Fr.)					a	
7.江陰	城内		陰	m	əɤ	ŋ	yч (=文)	ɿ		a		o				a		æ
8.武進	城内		常	m	—	ŋ	y (=文)	ɿ		a		o					a	
9.無錫	城内		錫	m		ŋ		чʅ	ɿ	a˔		ᵘu					a	
10.吳縣	城内	舊派 新派	蘇舊 蘇新	m		ŋ		чʅ;ʅ少 / ɿ	ɿ	ᵊY	o;ɒ少	o				ɒ		
11.常熟	城内		熟	m		ŋ	(ŋ)E	чʅ	ɿ	E,ɤ	u					a		
12.崑山	城内		崑	m,n 次濁上	n			ч˔	ɿ	E	O˔					a		

13.寶山	⊖霜草墩		寶霜	m	—	n		ɿ		e,ʌɪ	~ɤ				{ɑ}		
14.寶山	⊘羅店		寶羅	m	—	ŋ		ɿ		e,ʌɪ	~ɤ				{ɑ}		
15.南滙	⊖周浦		浦周	m	—	ŋ		ɿ		e	iɔ	o˔	iɔ	ɒ(但…)	ɑ		
16.上海	城内	舊派 混合派 新派	上舊派新	m		ŋ		ɿ		e;ø / E;ø	o˔(但唇母:ɔ; 靴:ø)				ɑ		
17.松江	城内		松	m		ŋ		ɿ		e˔	o˔(但唇母ɔ˔; 靴:ø)				ɑ		
18.吳江	⊕黎里		吳黎	m		ŋ		ɿ		ɵ	o				ɒ		
19.吳江	⊕盛澤		吳盛	m		ŋ		ɿ		E	ɔ˔				ɑ		
20.嘉興	城内		嘉興	m		ŋ		ɿ		ɤə	ɔ˔				ɑ		
21.吳興	⊖雙林鎮		湖雙	m	—	ŋ		ɿ		ø	ʊ				ɑ		
22.杭縣	城内		杭	(不用)	°u (=文)	u (=文)	yɥ (=文)	ɿ		ɥəɪi	=文	uɑ (=文)	ɑ	iɑ (=文)		ɑ	iE (=文)
23.紹興	城内		紹	m	—	ŋ		ɿ		e	o˕					ɐ	
24.諸暨	⊕王家井		諸王	—	—	ŋ		ɿ		e	—	—	o			ɑ	
25.嵊縣	⊖崇仁鎮		嵊崇	—				ɿ		—	{o}				{ɑ}		
26.嵊縣	⊘太平市		嵊太	—				ɿ		—	{o}				{ɑ}		
27.餘姚	城内		姚	m	—	ŋ		ɿ		e;ɔ		ɔ				ɑ	
28.鄞縣	城内		波	m	—	ŋ		ɿ;ɥʅi	ɿ	ø˔	o˔					a	
29.黄巖	城内		黄	m		ŋ		ɿ(但…:ʅ)	ɿ	A;o		o(但墨,金:A)				A	
30.永嘉	城内		温	n	m…	ŋ		祭… ʅi 支…	脂… 之 ɿ	ᶻi		o(但金:A)				—	ɑ
31.衢縣	城内		衢	—		ŋ		(韵母還原) yɥ	ɿ	ɛ	ɑ						ɛ
32.金華	城内		華	m	—	n	(ŋ)ỹ (=文)	ɿ		ie	uɤ…; ɥɑ	uɤ	ɑ	ɑ(文), uɤ…	uɤ	—	ɑ
33.永康	城内		康	—			(ŋ)ỹ 上…	i;ɿ	ɿ	iA		—	A	A;uA		—	iA

（第二表 2）

<table>
<tr><td rowspan="2">吳韻</td><td colspan="5">'a'</td><td colspan="4">'ai'</td><td colspan="6">'ei'</td><td colspan="3">'au'</td></tr>
<tr><td>'a'4</td><td>'a'5</td><td>'a'6</td><td>'a'7</td><td>'a'8</td><td>'ai'1</td><td>'ai'2</td><td colspan="2">'ai'3</td><td>'ei'1</td><td>'ei'2</td><td>'ei'3</td><td>'ei'4</td><td>'ei'5</td><td>'ei'6</td><td>'au'1</td><td>'au'2</td><td>'au'3</td></tr>
<tr><td>廣韻</td><td>皆
佳</td><td>泰
哈佳</td><td colspan="2">皆
佳</td><td>泰哈佳</td><td>哈</td><td>泰</td><td>哈
(泰)</td><td>哈</td><td>脂
支</td><td>灰
泰</td><td>脂灰
支泰</td><td>灰
泰</td><td>脂
支祭</td><td>灰
泰</td><td>豪</td><td colspan="2">肴</td></tr>
<tr><td rowspan="2">條件</td><td>'b, tz'
系</td><td>'d'
系</td><td>'b'
系</td><td>'tz'
系</td><td>'d'
系</td><td rowspan="2">'g'
系</td><td rowspan="2">'h'
系</td><td rowspan="2">'d'
系</td><td rowspan="2">'tz'
系</td><td colspan="2" rowspan="2">'b'
系</td><td rowspan="2">'n','l'
母</td><td rowspan="2">'d,t,
dh'
母</td><td colspan="2" rowspan="2">'tz'
系</td><td rowspan="2">全</td><td rowspan="2">'b,d,tz'
系</td><td rowspan="2">'g,h'
系</td></tr>
<tr><td colspan="2">白</td><td colspan="3">文</td></tr>
<tr><td>例</td><td>敗白豺白</td><td>泰白</td><td colspan="2">敗文豺文</td><td>泰文</td><td>該</td><td>海</td><td>胎</td><td>菜</td><td>悲</td><td>梅</td><td>類</td><td>推</td><td>歲</td><td>最</td><td>操</td><td>包鐃抄</td><td>交白</td></tr>
<tr><td>古</td><td>ai uai
ai ua·i</td><td>a·i
ai a·i</td><td colspan="3">見左邊</td><td>ai</td><td>a·i</td><td>ai
a·i</td><td>ai</td><td>ʷi
ʷie̯</td><td>uai
uɑ·i</td><td>見左</td><td>見左</td><td>ʷi
ʷie̯ iʷæi</td><td>uai
ua·i</td><td>au</td><td colspan="2">au</td></tr>
<tr><td>國</td><td colspan="9">æe</td><td colspan="3">ɛɪ</td><td colspan="3">uᴱɪ</td><td colspan="2">ɑʊ</td><td>iaʊ
(=文)</td></tr>
<tr><td>1.宜</td><td colspan="5">A</td><td colspan="10">ɐɪ (僅嘴：ɥɐɪ)</td><td colspan="3">ʌ˞ɤ</td></tr>
<tr><td>2.溧</td><td colspan="5">A</td><td colspan="8">æᴇ</td><td colspan="2">ɥæᴇ</td><td colspan="3">ʌ˞ɤ</td></tr>
<tr><td>3.壇西</td><td colspan="2">ɑ</td><td colspan="9">æe</td><td colspan="4">uei</td><td colspan="3">ɑɤ</td></tr>
<tr><td>4.丹</td><td colspan="2">ɑ˔;æ˔y</td><td colspan="3">æ;ɑ˔y</td><td colspan="4">æ</td><td colspan="2">ɛi</td><td colspan="2">ue</td><td colspan="2">ye</td><td colspan="3">ɔ˔</td></tr>
<tr><td>5.丹永</td><td colspan="9">aɪ</td><td colspan="4">ai;ei</td><td colspan="2">yɥᴱɪ</td><td colspan="3">ɐɤ</td></tr>
<tr><td>6.靖</td><td colspan="9">æ˔</td><td colspan="6">e˔</td><td colspan="3">ɒ˔</td></tr>
<tr><td>7.陰</td><td colspan="9">æ</td><td colspan="6">ᴇɪ</td><td colspan="3">ɒ</td></tr>
<tr><td>8.常</td><td colspan="5">ɑ</td><td colspan="8">æe</td><td colspan="2">ɥæe</td><td colspan="3">ɑɤ</td></tr>
<tr><td>9.錫</td><td colspan="5">ɑ</td><td colspan="10">e</td><td colspan="3">ʌ˔</td></tr>
<tr><td>10.蘇</td><td colspan="2">ɒ</td><td colspan="13">ᴇ（男ɪ）</td><td colspan="3">ɐ˔男人多
æ女人多</td></tr>
<tr><td>11.熱</td><td colspan="2">ɑ</td><td colspan="7">æ</td><td colspan="6">ᴇ</td><td colspan="3">ɔ</td></tr>
<tr><td>12.崑</td><td colspan="2">ɑ</td><td colspan="3">ɑ;ɛy</td><td colspan="4">ɛ</td><td colspan="6">ᴇ</td><td colspan="3">ɔ˔（à la Fr.）</td></tr>
</table>

13. 寶	{a}	a;e	e	ʌɪ		o
14. 寶	{a}	a;e	e	ʌɪ		o
15. 浦	[illegible]	e			ø或ø̃	ɔ
16. 上海	a	a;e	e (人多) / E	e	ø˔	ɔ˕
17. 松	a	e˔或E / E	e˔(但圭:ø)		ø,ø˔(有人)	ɔ˔
18. 吴	ɒ	E				A˞(少数)
19. 吴	a	E				Aa
20. 嘉	a	—	E²	e	ɥe	ɔ˕
21. 湖	a	—	e(但g-后:ɤ)	ᵊɣ(但affric.后ʅᵊɣ)		ɔ
22. 杭	E			eɪ / ʉəi(但|后:ɥəi)	ɥəi	ɒ / iɒ
23. 紹	a˂(但鉗:e)		e(但ɣ后:ɪe)	e		aɒ
24. 諸	a(但'b'后:ɒ)	—	ᶦe˔	e˔(à la Fr.)		aɒ
25. 嵊	{a}	—	E		{E}	ɑᵒ
26. 嵊	{a}	—	E		{E}	ᵃɒ
27. 姚	a		ᵊɐ	e(但至:i)		ɒ
28. 波	a,ɛ,e		e	E˔I		ɔ˔
29. 黄	A		ᵊe / e˔	iⱼ;e˔ / e	yɥ(但…) / e˔	ɒ
30. 温	a		e	æi	æi; yɥ / æi	з / ɔ
31. 衢	ɛ			əɪ(但…:i)		ɒ˔
32. 華	a˂	æɛ		eɪ;i / eɪ文;æɛ白 / eɪ;i / eɪ文;æɛ白	eɪ;{i} / eɪ文;æɛ白	ɒu
33. 康	iA		ɵɪ			AU

（第二表 3）

<table>
<tr><td rowspan="2">吴韻</td><td colspan="6">'ou'</td><td colspan="5">'an'</td><td colspan="9">'on'</td></tr>
<tr><td>'ou'1</td><td>'ou'2</td><td>'ou'3</td><td>'ou'4</td><td>'ou'5</td><td>'ou'6</td><td colspan="3">'an'1</td><td>'an'2</td><td>'an'3</td><td>'on'1</td><td>'on'2</td><td>'on'3</td><td>'on'4</td><td>'on'5</td><td>'on'6</td><td>'on'7</td><td>'on'8</td><td>'on'9</td></tr>
<tr><td>廣韻</td><td>侯尤</td><td>尤</td><td colspan="4">侯</td><td>凡 山合 删開 元原</td><td>談寒</td><td>山咸</td><td colspan="2">删銜</td><td colspan="3">桓</td><td colspan="2">寒</td><td colspan="2">覃</td><td colspan="2">覃談</td></tr>
<tr><td>條件</td><td>'b'系</td><td>'tz'系</td><td>'d'系</td><td>'tz'系</td><td>'h'系</td><td>'g'系</td><td>'b'系</td><td>'d,tz'系</td><td>'tz'系</td><td>'h'系</td><td>'g'系</td><td>'b'系</td><td>'d'系</td><td>'tz'系</td><td>'g'系</td><td>'h'系</td><td>'d'系</td><td>'tz'系</td><td>'g'系</td><td>'h'系</td></tr>
<tr><td>例</td><td>否</td><td>鄒</td><td>頭</td><td>走</td><td>歐</td><td>口</td><td>反</td><td>難三</td><td>斬</td><td>晏</td><td>閂</td><td>半</td><td>暖</td><td>酸</td><td>看</td><td>安</td><td>南</td><td>蠶</td><td>敢</td><td>庵</td></tr>
<tr><td>古</td><td>əu iəu</td><td>iəu</td><td colspan="4">əu</td><td>i^wɐm ^wan ^wan i^wɐn</td><td>ɑm₂ ɑn</td><td>an am</td><td colspan="2">an₂ am₂</td><td colspan="3">uan</td><td colspan="2">ɑn</td><td colspan="2">ɑm</td><td>ɑm</td><td>ɑm₂</td></tr>
<tr><td>國</td><td colspan="6">o-u</td><td colspan="3">an</td><td colspan="2">iɛn (=文)</td><td>an</td><td colspan="2">uan</td><td colspan="6">an</td></tr>
<tr><td>1.宜</td><td colspan="6">ɤɯ</td><td colspan="5">ʌ</td><td>eᴗ (='ien,文)</td><td colspan="8">e (f'],口母:eᴗ)</td></tr>
<tr><td>2.溧</td><td colspan="6">ei</td><td colspan="5">ʌ</td><td colspan="2">u</td><td>撮口</td><td colspan="3">u (Lundell也)</td><td>撮口</td><td colspan="2">u</td></tr>
<tr><td>3.壇</td><td colspan="6">e-i</td><td colspan="5">æ</td><td colspan="2">ɵ̃</td><td>撮口ɵ̃</td><td colspan="3">ɵ̃</td><td>撮口ɵ̃</td><td colspan="2">ɵ̃</td></tr>
<tr><td>4.丹</td><td colspan="6">ɛi</td><td colspan="5">æ</td><td>æ文, uŋ白</td><td colspan="3">ʊŋ</td><td>uŋ</td><td colspan="4">ʊŋ</td></tr>
<tr><td>5.丹</td><td colspan="6">ei</td><td colspan="5">ɑ</td><td colspan="2">u</td><td>撮口</td><td colspan="3">u (Lundell也)</td><td>撮口</td><td colspan="2">u</td></tr>
<tr><td>6.靖</td><td>ɒ;əɤ eifʏ</td><td>ᵊY; əɤ</td><td>ᵊY</td><td>ᵊY; əɤ</td><td colspan="2">ᵊY</td><td colspan="5">æ̃</td><td colspan="9">ɯ̃</td></tr>
<tr><td>7.陰</td><td colspan="6">ɛɪ</td><td colspan="5">æ</td><td colspan="9">ɵ</td></tr>
<tr><td>8.常</td><td colspan="6">e-i</td><td colspan="5">æ̃</td><td colspan="9">ɜ</td></tr>
<tr><td>9.錫</td><td colspan="6">ɛi</td><td colspan="5">æ̃ (~甚微)</td><td colspan="9">o</td></tr>
<tr><td>10.蘇</td><td colspan="6">ᵊY</td><td colspan="5">ɛ</td><td colspan="9">ɵ</td></tr>
<tr><td>11.熟</td><td colspan="6">ɛ</td><td colspan="5">æ</td><td colspan="5">ɤ (但…)</td><td colspan="4">ɜ</td></tr>
<tr><td>12.崑</td><td colspan="6">ɛ</td><td colspan="5">ɛ</td><td>ɵ, ɤ; ɛ</td><td colspan="8">ɵ, ɤ</td></tr>
</table>

13.寳霜	ʌI	e	^ɤ;I / ^ɤ (但睾:I) / I (但含,搭^ɤ韵)
14.寳羅	ʌI	e	^ɤ;I / ^ɤ (但睾:I) / I (但含,搭^ɤ韵)
15.浦東	ɤ^	ɛ	ẽ / ø̃ (~有時無) / ẽ
16.上海	ɤ	E	e / ø˧ / e / ø˧ / e ø˧ (ã)ã Fr., 舒緩些)
17.松	ɯ˧	E	e˧ / ø, ø˧ / ɵ˧
18.吳黎	ie˧ɵ	E	ɵ
19.吳盛	i˧əʉ˧	E	ɵ˧
20.嘉興	e	E^ɛ	ɤə˧ (但 s 母: uɤə˧)
21.湖雙	^əɣ (但 affric. 用 i^əɣ)	e (但蠶: I;ɛ̃ 母 om: I)	
22.杭	eI	ɛ̃ / Ĩ (=ɛ̃)	õ / ɛ̃
23.紹	ɤ / Iɤ (但...)	æ̃	ɵø̃˧ (但...) / ø̃˧ / e (但...)
24.諸王	e˧i (但...) / e˧i / Iɵ	ɛ / Iɛ	ɤ˧ (但...)
25.嵊崇	ø / Iø	æ̃	ø̃
26.嵊太	^ɛɤ	æ̃	ɑõ
27.姚	ɤ / Iɤ	ɛ̃ (但...) / Iɛ̃	ø̃˧ / e (但...)
28.波	œY, œø (但...)	ɛ	ũ / ø˧ / I / EI / ɛ,EI / ,I;ɛ / EI
29.黄	i·eɵ	ɛ˧	ø˧ / i^e / ɛ˧ / i^e (但...)
30.温	ɜ / ʌ˧u	ɑ	ɵ / ɵ;yø / ɵ
31.衢	əI / ɤ˧ɯ˧	ã	ə̃˧
32.華	eu˧ / ieu˧ / eu˧	ɛ̃e,ɑ˧ / ɑ˧	ɯɛ̃e,ɯə̃ / uɛ̃e,ɯə̃ / ɛ̃e,ə̃ / —
33.康	ə˧u˧	A	o / ɤ / —

（第二表 4）

吳韻	'en'														
	'en'$_1$	'en'$_2$	'en'$_3$		'en'$_4$		'en'$_5$		'en'$_6$	'en'$_7$	'en'$_8$	'en'$_9$	'en'$_{10}$	'en'$_{11}$	'en'$_{12}$
廣韻	魂 文	登	痕	登	痕	登	痕	魂		諄	侵	庚$_{耕}$	耕$_{爭}$	庚$_{耕}$耕$_{爭}$	登
條件	'b' 系	'd,tz' 系	'g' 系	'k' 母 一个字	'h' 系		't' 母 一个字	'd' 系	'tz' 系	l 母	'tz'$_1$ 系 一个字	'g' 系 文	'd,tz' 系	'b' 系 文	
例	本	能	根	肯	恨	恆	吞	嫩	寸	倫	森	更$_{文}$	爭$_{文}$	孟$_{文}$	朋$_{文}$
古	uən iuən	əŋ	ən	əŋ	ən	əŋ	ən	uən		iuĕn	iəm	ɐŋ	ɐŋ$_2$	ɐŋ ɐŋ$_2$	əŋ
國	ə·n	ə·ŋ	ə·n			ə·ŋ	uᵊn (但嫩：ə·n)				ə·n	ə·ŋ（但猛；打耍；耕地：ɛŋ）			
1.宜	əŋ														
2.溧	ən														oŋ
3.壇$_{西}$	əŋ														
4.丹	ɛ[n/ŋ]（任意）（但数$_{文}$，缒：開口）								yɛ[n/ŋ]	合口文 開口文白	ɛ[n/ŋ]				
5.丹$_{永}$	ə·ŋ									合口文 開口文白	ə·ŋ			oŋ	
6.靖	ɛŋ													o·ŋ	
7.陰	e·ŋ													o·ŋ	—
8.常	ə·ŋ													oŋ	ə·ŋ
9.錫	ən														—
10.蘇	ən														
11.熟	ɛ̃·ⁿ														—
12.崑	ə·n														—

<table>
<tr><td>13.寶</td><td colspan="9">ẽ˔ⁿ</td><td colspan="3">ẽ˔ⁿ; ã (=白)</td><td>—</td></tr>
<tr><td>14.寶</td><td colspan="9">ẽ˔ⁿ</td><td colspan="3">ẽ˔ⁿ; ã (=白)</td><td>—</td></tr>
<tr><td>15.浦</td><td colspan="12">əŋ</td><td>—</td></tr>
<tr><td>16.上</td><td colspan="12">əŋ</td><td>—</td></tr>
<tr><td>17.松</td><td colspan="11">ə̃ŋ</td><td colspan="2">—</td></tr>
<tr><td>18.吴</td><td colspan="11">əŋ</td><td colspan="2">—</td></tr>
<tr><td>19.吴</td><td colspan="13">ə˔[n ŋ]</td></tr>
<tr><td>20.嘉</td><td colspan="9">ɵ[n ŋ] (任意)</td><td colspan="4">—</td></tr>
<tr><td>21.湖</td><td colspan="13">ən</td></tr>
<tr><td>22.杭</td><td colspan="4">ə˔n</td><td>—</td><td>uən</td><td>ɥən</td><td>ɥən</td><td colspan="3">ə˔n</td><td colspan="2">o˔ŋ</td></tr>
<tr><td>23.绍</td><td>ẽ</td><td>əŋ</td><td>ᶦəŋ</td><td>ẽ, əŋ</td><td colspan="2">ø̃˔</td><td>Y[n ɲ ŋ]</td><td colspan="2">ø̃˔</td><td>ᶦəŋ</td><td>əŋ</td><td colspan="2">—</td></tr>
<tr><td>24.諸</td><td colspan="2">ẽĩ
(à ln 南…)</td><td>ĩ</td><td colspan="5">ẽĩ (但恩：ĩ; 杏：ɤ˔˧)</td><td colspan="3">—</td><td>Ã</td><td>ẽĩ</td></tr>
<tr><td>25.嵊</td><td colspan="11">eŋ</td><td>—</td><td>eŋ</td></tr>
<tr><td>26.嵊</td><td colspan="11">eŋ</td><td>—</td><td>eŋ</td></tr>
<tr><td>27.姚</td><td colspan="4">e˔ŋ</td><td colspan="4">Yɲ˔</td><td>—</td><td colspan="4">e˔ŋ</td></tr>
<tr><td>28.波</td><td colspan="8">ə˔ŋ</td><td>—</td><td colspan="4">ə˔ŋ; ã (=白)</td></tr>
<tr><td>29.黄</td><td colspan="4">ə˔ŋ</td><td colspan="4">uə˔ŋ</td><td>ɥə˔ŋ</td><td colspan="3">a˜</td><td>o˔ŋ</td></tr>
<tr><td>30.温</td><td colspan="4">ʌ˔ŋ (但豐：ɵ)</td><td colspan="4">ɵ</td><td>ʌ˔ŋ</td><td colspan="3">ɛ (=白)</td><td>oŋ</td></tr>
<tr><td>31.衢</td><td colspan="8">ə˔n</td><td>—</td><td colspan="2"></td><td colspan="2">oŋ</td></tr>
<tr><td>32.華</td><td colspan="8">ən</td><td>—</td><td colspan="2"></td><td>—</td><td>ən</td></tr>
<tr><td>33.康</td><td colspan="4">əŋ</td><td colspan="2">ɤ^ə˔</td><td>əŋ;
(但…
ŋə˔)</td><td>ə˔ŋ</td><td>—</td><td colspan="2">ai (=白)</td><td>—</td><td>eŋ</td></tr>
</table>

（第二表 5）

吳韻	'ang'						'áng'					'ong'							el
	'ang'1	'ang'2	'ang'3	'ang'4	'ang'5	'ang'6	'áng'1	'áng'2	'áng'3	'áng'4	'áng'5	'ong'1	'ong'2	'ong'3	'ong'4	'ong'5	'ong'6	'ong'7	el
廣韻	唐	陽方	江		陽良		庚貴		耕爭		登	耕宏	東紅冬	東融	鍾	鍾	東弓	鍾	脂支之
條件	全	'b'系	'b'系	'g,h'系	'tz'1系	照系（變tz系）	'g'系	'h'系	'tz'系	'b'系		h系	全	'b'系	'l'母	'tz'系	'g'母	'g'系	日母 / 文
例	剛	方	邦	江白	雙 爽	嘗白	硬白	杏白	爭白	孟白	朋白	轟	公 宋	馮	龍	從	弓	共	耳文
古	aŋ	iʷaŋ	ɔŋ		i̯aŋ		ɐŋ		ɐŋ₂		əŋ	ʷɐŋ₂	uŋ uoŋ	i̯uŋ	i̯ʷoŋ	i̯ʷoŋ	i̯uŋ	i̯ʷoŋ	i / i̯ə i₂
國	aŋ			iAŋ（一文）	uaŋ	aŋ	ə·ŋ,ɪŋ（一文）	ɪŋ（一文）	ə·ŋ（一文）			ʊŋ	ʊŋ（侵筋：uəŋ）	ə·ŋ	ʊŋ				əʳ平 ɐʳ仄
1. 宜	Aŋ				uAŋ	Aŋ						o›ŋ							ᵊl
2. 溧	a·ŋ					A	ən				oŋ								—
3. 壇	aŋ				aŋ;uaŋ	æ	əŋ					oŋ							—
4. 丹	a·ŋ					æ	æ;ɛ[n ŋ]			ɛ[n ŋ]		o›ŋ							eⁱʳ
5. 丹永	aŋ				yᵤaŋ	aŋ	ə·ŋ			oŋ（農字：ioŋ）									əʳ
6. 靖	Aŋ				yAŋ	iã	ɛŋ			o›ŋ									əᵣ
7. 陰	ɒᵑ					aᵑ				oŋ	aᵑ	o›ŋ（供（l漢）又可用ioŋ）							ᵊḷ
8. 常	aŋ				ɥaŋ	aŋ						oŋ（農字：ioŋ）							əᵣ
9. 錫	ɒ̃˜					ã˜						oŋ（農字：ioŋ）							əᵣ
10. 蘇	ɒ̃ᵑ						ã					o›ŋ							ɜɹ
11. 熟	ɒ˜						a˜					ʊŋ							ḷ
12. 崑	ɑ̃						ã					oŋ							ᵊl

13.寶霜	ɒ̃	ã	o^ŋ	ᵊɿ
14.寶羅	ɒ̃	ã	o›^ŋ	ᵊɿ
15.浦東	ɒ̃ / — / ɒ̃	ɑ̃ / — / ɑ̃	o›ŋ	ɿ
16.上	ɒ̃	ã˧	ʊŋ	ɵɿ
17.松	ɑ̃	ɛ̃	ʊŋ;(… ʊŋ) / ʊŋ ; ʊŋ	ᵊɿ
18.吳黎	ɑ̃	ã	o›ŋ	ɜɿ
19.吳盛	ɑ̃	ã	(o›ŋ)	ᵊɿ
20.嘉興	ɑ̃	ã (—)	(oŋ)(但口,hh母以后ũ)	—
21.湖雙	ɔ̃˩	ã˧	oŋ(但紅(ɒ):ŋ)	əɿ
22.杭	Aŋ / iAŋ (=文) / ɥAŋ / Aŋ	ə˧n (=文) / In (=文) / ə˧n (=文) / oŋ (=文)	oŋ(但畫:ioŋ)	ɿ
23.紹	ɒŋ	a˧ŋ	ʊŋ (但口,hh母:uoŋ) / ʊŋ	ɿ
24.諸王	ɒ̃ / ɒ̃,Ã	Ã / ẽɪ	o›ŋ	ɿ
25.嵊崇	ɒ̃ / —	Ã	u^ŋ	ɿ
26.嵊太	ɒŋ / —	Aŋ	ʊŋ	ɿ
27.姚	ɔ̃˩	ã˧	ʊŋ	ɿ
28.波	ɔ̃	ã	oŋ	ɿ
29.黄	ɒ̃^ŋ / ɒ̃^ŋ;ã	ã / o›ŋ	o›ŋ / i›o›ŋ	ʅ
30.温	ɒ / yɒ;ɒ / iɛ	ɛ / oŋ / uɛ	oŋ / iə / yɒ;oŋ / oŋ;yuŋ / yɒ	ʅ;ŋ (=文)
31.衢	ɒ̃	ã / (—)	oŋ	—
32.華	Aŋ / yɥAŋ / iAŋ	Aŋ / ən / —	oŋ	ᵊɿ
33.康	Aŋ / ɥAŋ / iAŋ	ai / — / eŋ (=文) / —	oŋ / ioŋ	ɜɿ

（第二表 6）

吳韻	'u'								'ù'											
	'u'1	'u'2	'u'3	'u'4	'u'5	'u'6	'u'7	'u'8	'ù'1	'ù'2	'ù'3	'ù'4	'ù'5		'ù'6		'ù'7	'ù'8	'ù'9	'ù'10
廣韻	虞尤	模							戈			歌	戈		歌		歌	戈	魚虞	泰上
條件	'f,v'母	'b,p,bh'母	'm'母	'hh'口母	'h'母	'g'系	'd'系	'tz'系	'b,p,bh'母	'm'母	'□,hh'母		'h'母	'g'系	'h'母	'g'系	'd'系	'tz'₂系	'tz'₁系	d系一个字白
例	夫無文	布	暮	烏	虎	姑	都	蘇	婆	摩	禍	阿	火	過	呵	個	多	左	初數	大白
古	i̯u i̯ə̯u	u							ua			a	ua		a		a ua		i̯ʷo i̯u	a:i
國	v	u							uoː		uo;ɤʌ	ɤʌ	uoː;ɤʌ		ɤʌ		uoː		u	ʌ(文)
1.宜	u								ʌɤ		ᵘu									
2.溧	u								ʌɯ˗											
3.壇	ᵊu		ɤɯ˗	ᵊu (但'hh'母:u)					ɤɯ˗										ɤɯ˗;ᵝu	ɤɯ˗
4.丹	v	u	ʌɤ	ᵊu (但'hh'母:v)			ᵊu		ʌɤ										ʌɤ;ᵊu	ʌɤ
5.丹永	v;u	u							ʌɤ											
6.靖	v	u	ʌ˖ɤ	u			u (但n母:ʌ˖ɤ)	u	u	ʌ˖ɤ									ʌɤ;ᵊu	ʌ˖ɤ
7.陰	v	u	ɜɤ	u			ɜɤ		u	ɜɤ										
8.常	v	u	ʌɯ	u				ɥ	ʌɯ										ʌɯ;ɥ	ʌɯ
9.錫	(v)	ʌɤ		ᵘu			ʌɤ													
10.蘇	vʉ	ʑ	ɜu˖; o(入聲)	ɜu˖					ʑ	o	ɜu˖									
11.熟	(v)	u (ng母:ɯ)					ɯ		u		ɯ									
12.崑	(v)	u	—	əu					u	əu										

13.宜興	v	u	ᵊu	u	ᵊu					
14.宜興	u	u	⁽ᵊ⁾u	u	⁽ᵊ⁾u					
15.浦東	(v)	u ch'-微讀f時用v韵)								
16.上	v;u	u ( )								
17.松	u									
18.吳	v	ẙ	ɜu	uᵣ	ɜu	ẙ	ɜu文 o白	uᵣ	ɜu	
19.吳	v	ẙ	ẙ/ɜu	ɜu	ẙ	ẙ/ɜu	ɜu			
20.嘉	(u)	u	ᵊu	u	ᵊu	u	ᵊu	u	ᵊu	
21.湖	v	ẙ	uᵣ	ᵊẙ	əẙ	ẙ	ɯ	ᵊẙ	əẙ	
22.杭	(v)	⁽ᵒ⁾u	u	⁽ᵒ⁾u	ᵒu	⁽ᵒ⁾u	u	⁽ᵒ⁾u (但𧼮:ɒ)	ᵒu	ɑ (=文)
23.紹	u	o	u	o	u	o				
24.諸	u	ɤ	u	ɯ (但𫗏:ɑ;餓:u)						
25.嵊	u	o (但𫗏:ɑ;我:uɑ)	—							
26.嵊	u	o (但𫗏:ɑ;我:uɑ)	—							
27.姚	v	ẙ	ᵒẙ	v	ẙ	ᵘẙ	ɥ	ᵒu (但我:ɔ)	ɥ	ᵒu
28.波	(v)	u	ə·u	u	ə·u (但我:o)	u	ə·u			
29.黃	v	u	ᵒu	u	o	u	o	ᵘu	o;ᵒu	ᵒu
30.溫	ʉ;u	ʉ	u (但薑:ʉ)	ʉ (但'n'母:u)	u (但'ng'母:ŋ)	o;u	u			
31.衢	ᵛu (但'b','p','bh','f','v',口,'bh'母:u)	—								
32.華	v	u	(o)	u	o文,oə白 (但'h'母:uɤə;我:ɑ)	oə				
33.廣	o (但'w'母:uo)	oᵊ	—	oᵊ						

（第二表 7）

吳韻	'uo'			'ua'				'uei'					
	'uo'₁	'uo'₂	'uo'₃	'ua'₁	'ua'₂	'ua'₃	'ua'₄	'uei'₁	'uei'₂	'uei'₃	'uei'₄	'uei'₅	'uei'₆
廣韻	麻瓜	麻瓜佳蛙	麻瓜佳蛙夬快	皆喈佳蛙夬快				灰泰外		微歸脂追支爲齊圭祭歲			
條件	'ng'母 [illegible]	'g'系	'h'系	'g'系 白	'h'系 白	'g'系 文	'h'系 文	'g'系	'h'系	'g'系 文	'h'系 文	'g'系 白	'b'系 白
例	瓦	瓜掛	花畫話	怪白	懷白	怪文	懷文	塊	會	鬼文	爲文	鬼白	喂白
古	ʷa	ʷa ʷaˑi	ʷa ʷaˑi ʷaˑi₂	ʷai ʷaˑi ʷaˑi				uɑi	uɑˑi	ʷe̯i ʷi ʷie̜		iʷei	i̯ʷæi
國	uA			uæé				uæe;uᴱɪ		uᴱɪ			
1.宜	=白	uo˦		uʌ				uɐɪ					
2.溧	ɔ˦			uʌ				uæᴇ					
3.童	—	uɔ˦		uɑ		uæ		uei					
4.丹	ɑ白, uɑ˧文			uɑ˧	(v)ɑ˧	uæ		u/(v)}æ白	u/(v)}e文	u/(v)}e			y_2
5.丹永	uɒ;ɒ$_y$			uaɪ				uᴇɪ					—
6.靖	o˨			uæ˨				ue˨					
7.陰	o (接'w'ʒ: uo)			uæ				uᴇɪ					
8.常	uɔ			uɑ				uæe					
9.錫	ᵛu			uɑ˧				uᴇ					y
10.蘇	o			uɒ		uɒ;uᴇ		uᴇ					y(少)
11.熟	u			uɑ				uᴇ					y
12.崑	o˨			uɑ				uᴇ					y

13.衢州	uʌɤ		ua;ue				uʌɪ				y
14.衢州	uʌɤ	uʌɤ,(v)ʌɤ	ua;uė入少,(v)e入少				uʌɪ	uʌɪ,(v)ʌɪ	uʌɪ	uʌɪ,(v)ʌɪ	y
15.浦江	uo˩		ua	ua,(f)a	—	(v)e	ue	(v)e	ue	(v)e	y
16.上	o˩		ua,(f)a入少				ue,(f)e入少				y
17.松	o˨(但話,畫:ɔ˧)		ua		—	(v)e	ue˩	(v)e˩	ue˩	(v)e˩	y
18.吴江	o		uɒ		uE						y_j
19.吴武	ɔ˩		ua		uE						y
20.嘉兴	ɔ˩		ua		uE^ε		ue				y
21.湖州	ʊ		ua		ue		uɯi				i_z
22.杭	ua		uE				uə˩i				
23.紹	uo˥(但[illegible]白:o˧)		ua˧				ue				y_j
24.諸暨	o		ua				ue˩	(v)e˩	ue˩	(v)e˩	yɥ
25.嵊崇	uo (但[illegible],(ʔ)o)		ua	—	—		(uE)	—	uE	—	(y)
26.嵊太	uo		ua	—	—		(uE)	—	uE	—	(y)
27.姚	ɔ	uɔ	ua				ue˩				(y)
28.波	yo˩	uo,o入少	ua		(ua)	ue	uEɪ				yɥ
29.黄	uA						uø˩		yɥ(但[illegible]白:uø˩)		
30.温	o		a	ua,(v)a	a	ua,(v)a	ai	(v)ai	yɥ		
31.衢	ua		uɛ				uəɪ				—
32.華	uo˧文,oɤ白		ua˧		uæɛ		uɪ文,uæɛ白		uɪ		ɥy
33.康	o˩A		yA				uəɪ				

（第二表 8）

吳韻	'uan'		'uon'		'uen'			'uang'				'uáng'
	'uan'$_1$	'uan'$_2$	'uon'$_1$	'uon'$_2$	'uen'$_1$	'uen'$_2$	'uen'$_3$	'uang'$_1$	'uang'$_2$	'uang'$_3$	'uang'$_4$	'uáng'
廣韻	删(關)山(鰥)		桓		魂		庚(横)	唐(光)		陽(方)		庚(横)
條件	'g'系	'h'系	'g'系	'h'系	'g'系	'h'系	'h'系(文)	'g'系	'h'系	'g'系	'h'系	'h'系(白)
例	慣	還	官	歡	困	昏	横(文)	光	荒	狂	王	横(白)
古	ʷan	ʷan$_2$	uɑn		uən		ʷɐŋ$_2$	uɑŋ		i̯ʷɑŋ		ʷɐŋ$_2$
國	uan				uᵊn		ə·ŋ	uɑŋ				ə·ŋ (=[illegible])
1. 宜	uʌ		ue·		uəŋ			uʌŋ				
2. 溧	uʌ		u·		uon			uɑ·ŋ				uən
3. 壇(西)	uæ		ᵘʊ		uəŋ			uɑŋ				uəŋ
4. 丹	u)(v)æ		ʊŋ		u)(v)ɛ[n ŋ			u)(v)ɑ·ŋ				vɛ[n ŋ
5. 丹(永)	uɑ		u·		ue·ŋ		ə·ŋ	uɑŋ				uə·ŋ
6. 靖	uã		uɯ (g,k,h,ŋ可[illegible])		uɛŋ			uɑŋ				
7. 陰	uæ		ue,-e (g,k,h 用e入[illegible])		uəŋ		uaᵑ	uɒᵑ				uaᵑ
8. 常	uæ̃		uɜ̃·		uə·ŋ			uɑŋ				
9. 錫	uæ̃ (~甚微)		uo·		uən			uɒ̃~				uã~
10. 蘇	uɛ		ue·		uən			uɒ̃ᵑ				uã
11. 熟	uæ		uɤ		uẽ·ŋ		uã~ (=白)	uɒ~				uã~
12. 崑	uɛ		ue·		ue·n		—	uɑ̃				uã

13.寶	uɐ		uɪ		uẽ·ⁿ		—	uɒ̃				uã
14.寶	uɐ	uɐ;(v)ɐ	uɪ	uɪ;(v)ʌɪ	uẽ·ⁿ	uẽ·ⁿ;(v)ɐ·n	—	uɒ̃				uʌ̃
15.浦	uẽ⁽ᵑ⁾	(v)ẽ⁽ᵑ⁾	uẽ·	(v)ẽ·	uəŋ	(v)əŋ;uəŋ	—	uɒ̃	(f)ɒ̃;uɒ̃	uɒ̃	(f)ɒ̃;uɒ̃ ([illegible])	(β)ɑ̃
16.上	uɛ		uɐ		uəŋ;(f)əŋ		—	uɒ̃;(f)ɒ̃				uæ̃·
			uɐ;uø·ɐ·		uəŋ			uɒ̃				
17.松	uɛ	(v)ɛ	ue·	(v)e·	uẽŋ	(v)ẽŋ	—	uɑʔ	uɑʔ;(β)ɑʔ	uɑʔ	uɑʔ;(β)ɑʔ	(v)ɛ̃
18.吴	uɛ		ɵ		uəŋ		—	uɑ̃				uæ̃
19.吴	uɛ		ɵ·	uɵ·;ɵ·	uə[ⁿ ŋ [illegible]]		—	ɑʔ (sic)				uæ̃
20.嘉	uɛᵋ		uɤə·		uəŋ		—	ɑʔ (sic)				—
21.湖	uɐ				uəŋ		—	ʒ·([illegible], w [illegible] uɒ·)				uæ̃·
22.杭	uõ				uən		ə·n	uʌ̃ŋ				ə·n (=[illegible])
23.紹	uæ̃ẽ, uæ̃		uẽ·ẽ·		uən, uəŋ, uẽ([illegible])		—	uɒŋ				uʌŋ
24.諸	uɛ	(v)ɛ	uɤ·	(v)ɤ·	uə̃ĩ	(v)ə̃ĩ	—	uɒ̃	uɒ̃;(v)ɒ̃	uɒ̃	uɒ̃;(v)ɒ̃	uʌ̃
25.嵊	uæ	—	uə̃	—	uəŋ	—		uɒ̃				—
26.嵊	uæ	—	uoə̃	—	uəŋ	—		uɒŋ				—
27.姚	uẽ		uẽ·		uʔŋ·([illegible] w [illegible] —)		uæ̃· (=[illegible])	uɔ̃·				uæ̃·
28.波	uɛ		ũ		uəŋ		—	uɔ̃				uæ̃
29.黄	uɛ·		uø·		uə·ŋ		uã (=[illegible])	uɒ̃ʔ		yɒ̃ʔ ([illegible]: uɒ̃ʔ)		uã
30.温	ɑ	(v)ɑ	yø;ɑ		ʌ·ŋ	yø;(v)ʌ·ŋ	uɛ	ɒ·		yɒ·		uɛ
31.衢	uã		(õ·)	uõ·	uə·n			uɒ̃				yã
32.華	uẽẽ, uoɐ				uən			uʌŋ				
33.康	o·ʌ				o·əŋ		uai (=[illegible])	uʌŋ				uai

（第二表 9）

吴韵	'i'						'io'	'ia'				'iai'			
	'i'₁	'i'₂	'i'₃	'i'₄	'i'₅	'i'₆	'io'	'ia'₁	'ia'₂	'ia'₃	'ia'₄	'iai'₁	'iai'₂	'iai'₃	'iai'₄
廣韻	脂齊開支移 祭開微開齊合	之齊開 脂去祭例	脂去微去支移 齊開之祭例	脂去 支移之	齊祭例	魚	戈群	麻加		麻邪				皆諧	佳
條件	'b' 系	'd' 系	'g,h' 系	日母 / 西	'tz' 系	'g' 系 一个字	一个字	'h' 系 (文)	'g' 系 (文)	'h' 系 (白)	'tz' 系 (白)	'h' 系 (文)	'tz' 系 (文)	'g' 系 (文)	'h' 系 (文)
例	鄙未	低例	記希	耳白二白	西	去白	靴	下文	家文	也白	謝白	也文	謝文	戒文	諧文
古	i ʷi iei ie̯ / jæi ʷe̯i i̯ʷei	i_2 iei / i i̯æi	i e̯i ie̯ / iei i_2 i̯æi	i / ie̯ i_2	iei i̯æi	i̯ʷo	i̯ua	a		i̯a				ai	a'i
國	i (位對各音 uᵉɪ; ɛɪ)			ər 平 / ɐr 仄	i	y (=文)	yɛ	iA		iɛ					
1.宜	i_z						io˞			iA		ɪ,io		iA	
2.溧	i_z					—	io˞			iɔ˞,iA,i_z				iA	
3.壇西	i_z (聲擦重)					æe	ua	—	iɑ (且:iæe)					iæe	
4.丹	i_z					y_z (=文)	yɑ	iɑ				ie			
5.丹西	i_j;ei_j;uɛɪ	i_j		eʳ (=文)	i_j	—	yɒ	iɒ						iaɪ	
6.靖	i			əʳ (=文)	i		yæ	iA				i;ĩ;iA		iæ	
7.陰	i			i;ə (=文)	i	ɛɪ	io	iä						iæ	
8.常	i						y	iɑ							
9.錫	i						iᵘu			iɑ					
10.蘇	i,i_j (人家)						io		iɒ			iɪ;i_y		iɒ	iɪ
11.熟	i					ɛ	—	iu	iɑ			iᵉ;i_y		iɑ	iæ
12.崑	i					ɛ	y	io	iɑ			嗟 姐 且 / y i ɪ		iɑ	

<table>
<tr><td>13.寶霜</td><td colspan="5">i</td><td>y</td><td>i^ʌɤ</td><td colspan="3">iɑ</td><td colspan="2">ie;ɪ</td><td colspan="2">iɑ</td></tr>
<tr><td>14.寶羅</td><td colspan="5">i</td><td>y</td><td>i^ʌɤ</td><td colspan="3">iɑ</td><td colspan="2">ie;ɪ</td><td colspan="2">iɑ</td></tr>
<tr><td>15.浦東</td><td colspan="5">(i)</td><td>yʊ</td><td colspan="4">iɑ</td><td colspan="2">ĩ</td><td>iɑ</td><td>iɛ</td></tr>
<tr><td>16.上</td><td colspan="5">i,i_j</td><td>iu</td><td colspan="4">iɑ</td><td colspan="2">iɛ;i_j,ɪ</td><td>iɑ</td><td>iɛ</td></tr>
<tr><td>17.松</td><td colspan="5">i</td><td>iu</td><td>(iɑ)</td><td colspan="3">iɑ</td><td colspan="2">—</td><td>iɑ</td><td>—</td></tr>
<tr><td>18.吳黎</td><td colspan="5">i_j</td><td colspan="2">io</td><td colspan="3">iɒ</td><td colspan="2">iɪ</td><td>iɒ</td><td>—</td></tr>
<tr><td>19.吳盛</td><td colspan="5">i</td><td colspan="2">iɔ˔</td><td colspan="3">iɑ</td><td colspan="2">iɪ</td><td>iɑ</td><td>iɪ</td></tr>
<tr><td>20.嘉興</td><td colspan="4">(i)</td><td>—</td><td>yə˔</td><td>—</td><td colspan="3">iɑ</td><td>ie</td><td>—</td><td colspan="2">—</td></tr>
<tr><td>21.湖雙</td><td colspan="2">i_z（z甚微）</td><td>n</td><td>i_z</td><td>—</td><td>iʊ</td><td>—</td><td colspan="3">iʌ</td><td>ie</td><td>—</td><td colspan="2">—</td></tr>
<tr><td>22.杭</td><td colspan="2">i</td><td>l
(=文)</td><td colspan="2">i</td><td>yɥ</td><td colspan="2">iɑ</td><td colspan="4">i</td><td colspan="2">iɛ</td></tr>
<tr><td>23.紹</td><td colspan="5">i,i_j</td><td>yɥ</td><td colspan="2">io˕</td><td colspan="2">iɐ˧</td><td>ie</td><td>ie;ĩ</td><td colspan="2">iɐ˧</td></tr>
<tr><td>24.諸王</td><td colspan="4">i_z</td><td>e˔</td><td>yɥ</td><td>(io)</td><td>io</td><td colspan="2">iɑ</td><td>ie</td><td>—</td><td colspan="2">ie</td></tr>
<tr><td>25.嵊崇</td><td colspan="5">i</td><td>y</td><td>(io)</td><td>io</td><td colspan="2">iɑ</td><td colspan="2">ĩɪ̃</td><td colspan="2">iɑ;ĩɪ̃</td></tr>
<tr><td>26.嵊太</td><td colspan="5">i</td><td>y</td><td>(io)</td><td>io</td><td colspan="2">iɑ</td><td colspan="2">ĩẽ˔</td><td colspan="2">iɑ;ĩɛ̃</td></tr>
<tr><td>27.姚</td><td>i</td><td>i_z</td><td>i_z;ŋ</td><td colspan="2">i_z</td><td>y</td><td colspan="2">iɔo</td><td colspan="2">iɑ</td><td colspan="2">iɛ̃,io</td><td colspan="2">iɑ</td></tr>
<tr><td>28.波</td><td>i</td><td>i_z</td><td>i_z,ŋ</td><td colspan="2">i_z</td><td>yɥ</td><td>yo˔</td><td>yo˔,iɐ</td><td colspan="2">iɐ</td><td colspan="2">iɛ,i</td><td colspan="2">iɛ</td></tr>
<tr><td>29.黄</td><td>i</td><td>i_j,i（gn'韻）</td><td>n</td><td>i_j</td><td>ᵉe</td><td>yɥ</td><td colspan="2">o˕
(=ɑ)</td><td colspan="4">iʌ（但嘘:ʌ；姐:i_j）</td><td colspan="2">A
(=ɑ)</td></tr>
<tr><td>30.温</td><td>ᶻi</td><td>ᶻi; i_z</td><td>ŋ</td><td>ᶻi</td><td>(k)i</td><td>y</td><td colspan="2">o</td><td colspan="4">ᶻi</td><td colspan="2">ɑ</td></tr>
<tr><td>31.衢</td><td>i</td><td>ʅ（但鼠書:i）</td><td>i</td><td>ʅ_i</td><td>(k)i</td><td>—</td><td colspan="4">iɑ</td><td colspan="4">iɛ</td></tr>
<tr><td>32.華</td><td colspan="2">i（但齊韻{字韻}:ie）</td><td>n</td><td>i_ɣ,ie</td><td>ɯ</td><td>—</td><td colspan="3">iɑ˧</td><td>iæ</td><td>ie</td><td>eɪ</td><td colspan="2">iæɛ</td></tr>
<tr><td>33.康</td><td colspan="2">i,iᵉ 齊韻,{字韻}</td><td>—</td><td>iᵉ</td><td>ə˕ʊ˕</td><td>—</td><td colspan="2">uʌ
(=ɑ)</td><td colspan="6">iʌ</td></tr>
</table>

（第二表10）

吳韻	‘iau’						‘iou’						‘ien’							
	‘iau’₁	‘iau’₂	‘iau’₃	‘iau’₄	‘iau’₅	‘iau’₆	‘iou’₁	‘iou’₂	‘iou’₃	‘iou’₄	‘iou’₅	‘iou’₆	‘ien’₁	‘ien’₂	‘ien’₃	‘ien’₄	‘ien’₅	‘ien’₆	‘ien’₇	‘ien’₈
廣韻	肴	蕭	宵	宵			尤幽			尤			先仙	先天仙延	添鹽	先天元言仙延添鹽嚴	山艱刪顏	咸銜	鹽	添
條件	‘g,h’系文	‘b,d’系	‘g,h,tz’系	日母 白	日母 文	‘ji’系其餘	‘g,h,tz’系		一个字	l母	日母	‘ji’系其餘	‘b’系	‘d’系	‘tz’系	‘g,h’系	‘g’系 文	‘h’系 文	‘gn’母一个字	‘gn’母一个字
例	交孝文	表	橋	繞白	繞文	超	九	就	謬	劉	柔	周	變	點	千	兼現	間文	陷文	驗	念
古	au	ieu	jæu	jæu			i̯əu iəu			i̯əu			先: ien 仙: jæn 元: jɐn 添: iem 鹽: jæm 嚴: jɐm				an am an₂ ăm₂		jæm	iem
國	iau			au			iºu平 iɔu仄				oᵘ		ien							
1.宜	iʌɤ				ʌɤ		iᵊɯ				ɤɯ		ə		ɪ					
2.溧	iʌɤ			—		ʌɤ	iʌɯ		=廟	ei, iʌɯ	—	ei	i (≠i₂)							
3.壇	iaɤ			aɤ, iaɤ	aɤ		iɯ			e·i			i_j							
4.丹	iɔ					ɔ	ʏ				ie	ɛi	ɪ							
5.丹永	iɐʌ					ɐɤ	iɯᵘ		eɪ				ɪ (微有~，右同)							
6.靖	iɒ						gn:ᵊʏ; 其餘:ʏ	ᵊʏ	iɒ	ᵊʏ	ʏ		ɪ̃							
7.陰	iɒ				ɒ		iɯ				EI		ɪ							
8.常	iaɤ				aɤ		iɯ		e·i				ɪ̃							
9.錫	iɤ				ʌ		iʌɤ		ɛi				ɪ							
10.蘇	iɐɤ 男人多 iæ 女人多				ɐ æ		ʏ (但?ʏ)	ᵊʏ					iɪ							
11.熟	iɔ					iɔ,ɔ	iɯ		iɔ	iɯ	iɯ 寅 ɯ 人		ie							iæ白
12.崑	iɔ				—	ɔ	ɪ (sic!) (但?白:E)				E		ɪ							ie白

13.寳霜	io	o			y	ʌɪ	y	ʌɪ			ɪ (但阳去: ie)			
14.寳罗	io	o			y	ʌɪ	y	ʌɪ			ɪ (但阳去: ie)			
15.浦东	iɔ	—	(ɔ)		iɤ	iɔ	iɤ	ɤ			ĩ	ĩ;ie	—	ie
16.上	iɔ	ɔ			iɤ	ɤ					ɪ	iE	ɪ	iE(旧)
17.松	iɔ	—	ɔ		iɯ	—	iɯ	ɯ			i	—	i	iE
18.吴黎	iA	—	A		ie-ɵ						iɪ	iE		
19.吴盛	iAɑ	—	Aɑ		i-ɵʊ						iɪ	iE		
20.嘉兴	iɔ	—	ɔ		iəu	e					ie	iE		
21.湖双	iɔ	—	ɔ		ᶿY (但affric前iᶿY)						ɪ			
22.杭	iɒ	ɔ			Y	eɪ	Y	eɪ			ĩ			
23.绍	iɑɒ	ɑɒ			iɤ	ɤ					ɪ	iẽ		
24.诸王	iɑɒ	ɑɒ			iɵ	ei					iɪ			
25.嵊崇	iɑᵒ	ɑᵒ			iø	—	Iø	—	ø		ĩɪ			
26.嵊太	iᵅɒ				Y	Y,ᶿY	—	ᶿY	—	ᶿY	iẽ			
27.姚	iɒ	ɒ			I-E-ɤ						ĩ	iẽ		
28.波	iə				Y,i-ɵ入声	iɵ	Y,i-ɵ入声				ɪ; ɪ; i(入声) e前i'的	ie		
29.黄	ɒ (=ɐ)	iɒ			i-u (但ts:i-ɵɤ)	iɒ	i-u				ie			
30.温	ɔ	iə	Yɐ		iʌu (但iʌu)	iʌu, iu	iə	iu	iʌu;iu		ɪ;iE(规则不明)	ɑ	ɪ	ie
31.衢	iɒ	ɒ			iɯ	ɤ-ɯ	iɯ				iẽ	(—)		
32.華	iɑʊ				iɯu	eu	iɯu				iẽ	iẽ, iɐ	iẽ	(—)
33.康	—	iAU	—	iAU	iəʊ (—)						iə;iᴱ;iᴬ(规则不明)	A	iᵉ	iᴬ

（第二表 11）

吳韻	'ien'			'in'											'iàng'	
	'ien'9	'ien'10	'ien'11	'in'1	'in'2	'in'3	'in'4	'in'5	'in'6	'in'7	'in'8	'in'9	'in'10	'in'11	'iàng'1	'iàng'2
廣韻	仙鹽			真臻 庚	侵 真人 青經 清征 蒸		侵 真人 欣 庚京 蒸 青經 清征	清傾	庚耕	侵 真人 青經 清征 蒸	侵真人		青經 清征 蒸		江	陽方
條件	日母 白	日母 文	'j'系其餘	'b'系	'd'系	'tz'系	'g,h'系	'g,h'系	'h'系 文	日母 白	日母 文	'j1'系其餘	日母 文	'j1'系其餘	'g,h'系 文	喻母一个字 白
例	染白	染文	扇	命品	丁	尋	金興	傾營	行文	認白	忍文	陳	仍文	程	講文	旺白
古	iæn iæm			侵:iəm 真人:iěn 真質:iʷěn 欣:iən 青:ieŋ 清征:iæŋ 清傾:iʷæŋ 庚耕:ɐŋ 京:iɐŋ 榮:iʷɐŋ 耕爭:ɐŋ2 蒸:iəŋ											ɔŋ	iʷaŋ
國	an			古-n,-m: in; 古-ŋ: iᵊŋ						ə·n,ə·ŋ (=文)	ə·n		ə·ŋ		iʌŋ	uɑŋ
1.宜	I	I,Yẽ		iŋ		iŋ;yiŋ	iŋ				əŋ				iʌŋ	
2.溧	—		i(≠iɪ)	i[n/ŋ]		i[n/ŋ];yi[n/ŋ]	i[n/ŋ](任意)				ən				ie	
3.壇	iⱼ			iŋ		iŋ;yiŋ	iŋ				əŋ				iaŋ;ie	
4.丹	I	—	I	iŋ		iŋ;yiŋ	iŋ				iɛ[n/ŋ]	ɛ[n/ŋ]	iɛ[n/ŋ]	ɛ[n/ŋ]	ie	iaŋ
5.丹	I˧	—	I˧	iŋ						iə·ŋ	ə·ŋ				iaŋ	yɥaŋ
6.靖	ɪ̃		yɪ̃	iŋ							iɛŋ				ĩ	yaŋ
7.陰	I	ɵ		iŋ							e·ŋ				iɒŋ;(但姓 iəŋ)	uɑŋ
8.常	ɪ̃	ɜ̃˦		iŋ		iŋ;yiŋ	iŋ				ə·ŋ				iaŋ	
9.錫	I	o˦		I[n/ŋɣ](任意)			iə˦[n/ŋɣ](任意)				ən				iɒ̃	
10.蘇	iɪ	ɵ˦		iɪn			iən				ən				iɒ̃ŋ,yɒ̃ŋ人少	iɒ̃ŋ,yɒ̃ŋ人多
11.熟	iᵉ	ɤ,e		Iŋ							ɛ̃˦				iɒ̃	
12.崑	I˧	—	ɵ˧,ɤ˧人少	ɪn			ie·n				ə·n				iɑ̃	iã

13.嘉	ɪ	—	ɪ	ɪn						ɛ̃˧^{n}				iɒ̃	
14.宝	ɪ	—	ɪ	ɪn						ɛ̃˧^{n}				iɒ̃	
15.浦	ĩ	—	ĩ	iɪn		iə˧ŋ				(əŋ)				iɑ̃	iɒ̃
16.上	ɪ	e / ø˧		iŋ		iəŋ				əŋ				iɒ̃;iɑ̃	iɒ̃
17.松	i	(e˩)	e˩	iəŋ		iɐ˧ŋ				(ɐ̃ŋ)				iɛ̃;iɑ̃ʸ	iɑ̃
18.吴	iɪ	ɵ		ɪŋ		iə˧ŋ				əŋ				iɑ̃	
19.吴	iɪ	—	ɵ˧	ɪ[n/ŋ (任意)		iɪ[n/ŋ				ə˧[n/ŋ				iɑ̃	
20.嘉	—		ɣə˧	ɪŋ						ə[n/ŋ				iã (但匣:iɑ̃)	iɑ̃
21.湖	—		e	ɪn	iən					ən				iõ	—
22.杭	ŏ			ɪn˞					ə˧n					iʌŋ	uʌŋ (=文)
23.绍	ẽ			ɪŋ						e˧n,ẽ(南人)		əŋ		iɒŋ,(但匣:iɑ˧ŋ)	—
24.诸	iɪ	ɣ˧˧		ĩ						(eĩ) ẽĩ (ẽĩ)			ẽĩ	iõ	—
25.嵊	—		ɤ̃,ĩĩ	i^{ŋ}						eŋ				õ	—
26.嵊	—		iaɤ̃,ĩẽ	iŋ						ieŋ				ɒŋ	—
27.姚	—		ɤ̃	e˧ŋ	iŋ					e˧ŋ				yɔ̃˞ (但匣:iɑ̃)	—
28.波	[illegible]			ɪŋ						Yŋ,ɪŋ		ɪŋ		yɔ̃ (但匣:进)	uɔ̃
29.黄	iᵉ			iɪŋ				a (=白)	iᴵŋ					ɒ̃ŋ(=白) (但匣:[illegible])	uɒ̃ŋ
30.温	ɪ;(iɛ)			e˧ŋ	e˧ŋ(但疑母及影ʌ˧ŋ)	iʌ˧ŋ	Yuŋ	ɛ	iʌ˧ŋ (但合:ʌ˧ŋ)	ʌ˧ŋ		e˧ŋ		ɒ˞ (=白)	
31.衢	—	ə̃		i^{ŋ}						—	ə˧n	—	ə˧n	iɒ̃	—
32.華	—		ɥyEe文, ɥyə̃白	ɪn		iɪn	—		iɪn					iʌŋ	—
33.康	—		iᴱ,øᴬ	ie˧ŋ			—	ai (=白)	(ie˧ŋ) (但合:[illegible])	əŋ		ie˧ŋ		ʌŋ (=白)	—

（第二表 12）

吳韻	'iang'					'iong'						'iu'					
	'iang'1	'iang'2	'iang'3	'iang'4	'iang'5	'iong'1	'iong'2	'iong'3	'iong'4	'iong'5	'iong'6	'iu'1	'iu'2	'iu'3	'iu'4	'iu'5	'iu'6
廣韻	陽良					青螢	庚榮	東融			東融鍾	魚虞					
條件	'l'母 'gh'系 'tz'系	日母 白	日母 文	知徹澄母	照之系 文	'g'母	'h'系	'k,gh,y,'母	日母 白	日母 文	'j'1系 其餘	'l'母 白	'tz'系 白	'l'母 文	'tz'系 文	'g,h'系	'j'1系
例	兩香相	讓白	讓文	長	嘗文	迥	兄	窮熊	絨白	戎文	中重	濾白	徐白	慮文	須文	居雨	朱如
古	iaŋ					iʷeŋ	iʷeŋ	iuŋ			iuŋ iʷoŋ	iʷo iu					
國	iʌŋ	ɑŋ				iʊŋ			ʊŋ			y					u
1.宜	iʌŋ	ʌŋ				iɔ:ŋ				ɔ:ŋ		yч					
2.溧	ie	—		A		ioŋ (但丞:yɪ'n)				oŋ		yz					
3.壇白	ie	æ				ioŋ (但丞:yiŋ)				—	oŋ	y					ᵊu
4.丹	ie			æ		iɔ:ŋ (但丞:iyŋ)					ɔ:ŋ	yz					ᵊu
5.丹永	iaŋ			ɑŋ		—	ioŋ (但丞:[illegible])	oŋ	ioŋ		oŋ	l母:yч,tz系:yч,yчEI				yч	
6.靖	ĩ	iã				iɔ:ŋ (但丞:yɤŋ)						i		yч			
7.陰	iaⁿ	aⁿ				iɔ:ŋ				ɔ:ŋ		i;y(ч)		y(ч)			
8.常	iaŋ	ɑŋ				ioŋ (但丞:yiŋ)				oŋ		y					ч
9.錫	iã~	ã~				ioŋ (但丞:yɪn)				oŋ		i				y	ч
10.蘇	iã	ã				iɔ:ŋ				ɔ:ŋ		i				y(ч)	ч
11.熟	ia~	a~				iʊŋ				ʊŋ	ʊŋ文,iчʊŋ白	y (驟白:i)					ч
12.崑	iã	ã			ɑ̃;ã	ioŋ				oŋ		y (驟白,徐:i)					ч

13.賓霜	ia˜		ɒ˜	a˜	ɒ˜	iɔ·ŋ				oᵑ		y,i		y			ɿ
14.賓羅	iɑ˜		ɒ˜	a˜	ɒ˜	iɔ·ŋ				ɔ·ᵑ		y,i		y			ɿ
15.浦東	iɑ˜		—	ɑ˜	=ɐ;ɑ˜	iɔ·ŋ				ɔ·ŋ		y (但騷條:i)					
16.上	iã		ã			iʊŋ				ʊŋ		y (但騷條:i)					ɥ
17.松	iɛ̃		ɛ̃			iʊŋ				ʊŋ		y (但條:i)					
18.吴	iã		ã			iɔ·ŋ				ɔ·ŋ		yɥ (但條:iɿ)					ɥ
19.吴	iã		ã			(iɔ·ŋ)				(ɔ·ŋ)		i		y			ɥ
20.嘉	iã (—)		—	ã		(ioŋ)				(oŋ)		y,(i)				y	ɥ
21.湖	iã˧		—	ã˧	ɔ̃˩	ioŋ				oŋ		i					ɿ
22.杭	iʌŋ	ʌŋ				ioŋ (sic)				oŋ		yɥ					ɥ(舌尖高)
23.紹	ia˧ŋ		a˧ŋ			iɔʊŋ				ʊŋ		yɥ (但騷口條:i)					
24.諸	iã˧		Ã			iɔ·ŋ				ɔ·ŋ		i,yɥ		yɥ			
25.嵊	iÃ	—		Ã		—		iuᵑ	—	(uᵑ)		i				y	ɿ
26.嵊	iʌŋ	—		iʌŋ		—		iuŋ	—			i				y	ɿ
27.姚	ia˜		ã˧?ɔ̃˩	ã˧	ɔ̃˩	iɔʊŋ				ʊŋ		y (但騷:u;條:i)					ɥ
28.波	iã				ɔ̃	yoŋ				oŋ		i	ɥɿ	i	ɥɿ	yɥ	ɥɿ
29.黄	ia˜				ia˜;ɔ̃ᵑ	iᶦŋ	iɔ·ŋ		—	ɔ·ŋ		yɥ					
30.温	iɛ					ʏʊŋ			oŋ		ʏʊŋ	yɥ (但條:ʻi)				yɥ ([illegible])	i
31.衢	iã	—		ã		—	(ʃ)oŋ; yiᵑ	(dʒ)oŋ,ioŋ	ioŋ	oŋ		yɥ (但'ɿ'母:i;'gn'母:y)					
32.華	iʌŋ					—	(ɥyən)	ioŋ				(但騷:u;條:i) ɥy (但'gn'母:ỹ)					
33.康	iʌŋ	—		iʌŋ		—	ye˧ŋ	ioŋ	—		oŋ	Y					

（第二表13）

吴韵	'iu'		'iuei'		'iuon'						'iuin'					
	'iu'7	'iu'8	'iuei'1	'iuei'2	'iuon'1	'iuon'2	'iuon'3	'iuon'4	'iuon'5	'iuon'6	'iuin'1	'iuin'2	'iuin'3	'iuin'4	'iuin'5	'iuin'6
广韵	脂合支合祭合				元合仙合先合		仙合				谆文真合		谆			
条件	日母 白	'j'1 其余系 白	日母 文	'j'1 其余系 文	'g'系	'h'系	日母 白	日母 文	'j'1系 其余	'tz'3系	'g'系	'h'系	'tz'系	日母 白	日母 文	'j'1系 其余
例	蕊白	吹白水白	蕊文	吹文水文	捐	玄	软白	软文	川	全	君	允	巡	闰白	润文	春
古	ʷi ʷie̯ i̯ʷæi				i̯ʷɐn i̯ʷæn i̯ʷen		i̯ʷæn				i̯uěn i̯uən i̯ʷěn			i̯uěn		
国	uᵋɪ				yan		uan			yan	yn			uᵊn		
1.宜	yj		ɐɪ		yẽ,ue		yẽ				yiŋ					
2.溧	yz		ɥæɛ		yu						yɪ·n,-ŋ(任意)					
3.壇山	—	ᵊu	ɥei		yʊ̃						yiŋ			—	uəŋ	
4.丹	—	yz	ye		y			—	uŋ	y	ⁱyŋ			uɛ[n/ŋ]	yɛ[n/ŋ]	
5.丹城	yɥɛɪ				iou,ɪ						yɥəŋ					
6.靖	yɥ	[illegible]	e	ye	yʊ̃					ĩ	yuŋ		—	yɛŋ		
7.阴	y(ɥ)		ɛɪ		ye			—	ɵ	ɪ	ioŋ			ioŋ,eŋ(任意)		
8.常	y	ɥ	ɥæe		iɔ̃		ɔ̃			iɔ̃	yiŋ			ɥəŋ		
9.锡	y	ɥɿ	e		iɔ			—	ɔ	ɪ	yɪn		ɪ[n/ŋ]	iə[n/ŋ]	en	
10.苏	y(ɥ)	ɥɿ	ɛ		iɵ		ɵ	—	ɵ	iɪ	yən		iɪn	ⁱyən	ən	
11.熟	y	ɥɿ	ᴇ		iɤ		ɛ̃~	—	ɤ,e	iᴱ	iuŋ		ɪⁿ	iuŋ	ẽ~	
12.昆	y	ɥ	ɛ		yɵ		ɵ,ɤ	—	ɵ,ɤ	ɪ	yən		ɪn	ən		

13.寶霜	y	ɿ	ʌɪ		iʌɤ	ɪ	—	ɪ		ɪn				ẽ,ⁿ	
14.寶羅	y	ɿ	ʌɪ		iʌɤ̃	ɪ	—	ɪ		ɪn				ẽ,ⁿ	
15.浦周	—	ɿ	(~)ø		yɤ̃		—	ẽ	ɪ̃	yɤ̃,iɔŋ		iɪŋ	iə·ŋ	əŋ	
16.上舊派新	y	ɿ	ø·		yø·		ø·		ɪ	iuŋ / yŋ		iŋ	iəŋ	əŋ	
17.松	—	ɿ	ø,ø·		yø		(e·)	e·	i	yɐ~	iuŋ	iəŋ	iɐŋ	ɐ·ŋ	
18.吳黎	—	ʮ;ɿ	E		iɵ		—	ɵ	iɪ	yEŋ,iɔŋ 少		ɪŋ	—	əŋ	
19.吳盛	—	ɿ	EʒUE 人少,多少		iɵ·		(ɵ·)	ɵ·	iɪ	yə[n/ŋ](彼此: iɪ[n/ŋ])		ɪ[n/ŋ]	ə·[n/ŋ]		
20.嘉興	—	ɿ	ʮ·e		yɤə·	—		ɤə·	ie	yə[n/ŋ]		ɪŋ	—		ə[n/ŋ]
21.湖雙	—	ɿ	ᵊy (但affric.用iᵊy)		ɪ		—	e	ɪ	iən				ən	
22.杭	ʮ	ʮə·i			yõ	õ			ɪ̃	yɪn		ɪn	ʮən		
23.紹	yʮ	ɿ	e		yẽə̃		—	ẽ	ɪ̃	y·n, y·ŋ, y~ (人異)				e·n,ẽ(人異)	
24.諸王	—	ɿ	e·		iɤ·		—	ɤ·	iɪ	iɔŋ		ɪ̃	—		ẽɪ
25.嵊崇	—	(ɿ)	—	ɛ	yɤ̃	—		ɤ̃	ĩɪ	ỹ		—			eŋ
26.嵊太	—	(ɿ)	—	E	ioɤ̃	—		oɤ̃	ĩẽ	ỹŋ		—			eŋ
27.姚	iuŋ	ɿ	e		yɤ̃·(或yən)		—	ẽ	ɪ	yɲ·		iŋ	yɲ·	e·ŋ	
28.波	yʮ	ʮ₁	ɛ·ɪ		yʮ, yø· 人少					yŋ					
29.黃	yʮ				yø·		(—)	ø·		ye·ŋ		uəŋ	yeŋ	uəŋ	
30.溫	y	i_z	ɿ	i_z	yø					yuŋ					
31.衢	yʮ		əɪ		ə̃	—		ə̃		yiⁿ		iⁿ	—		ən
32.華	—	ʮy	eɪ		ʮyɤẽẽ_ɤ, ʮyɤə̃_e				iẽẽ_ɤ, ie_e	ʮyən		ɪn	—		ʮyən
33.康	—	y	—	əɪ,yə	(y)øᵊ	—		øᵊ		ye·ŋ		ʮə·ŋ	—		yə·ŋ

第三表：入聲韻母表　　　　（第三表 1）

方言／韻母			'oq'												aq				
今吳音韻母			'oq'1	'oq'2	'oq'3	'oq'4	'oq'5	'oq'6	'oq'7	'oq'8	'oq'9	'oq'10	'oq'11	'oq'12	'aq'1	'aq'2	'aq'3	'aq'4	'aq'5
與上去相配韻			'ong1-2'	'ong3,4,5'			'ong1-2'	—	'ong3'	'ang1-5'					'in11'	—	'ang1,2'		
廣韻韻			沃	燭	屋六		屋谷沃	屋六	屋谷沃	鐸	覺	鐸落	覺		昔	麥	陌麥		
分合條件			'h'系 一等	'l''tz'母系		'f,v'母	'd,g,tz'系	'm'母 一等	'b'系	'b'系	'b'系	'd,g,tz'系	'g,h'系	'tz'1系	'j1'系 讀如去音	'b'系		'g,h'系	'tz'系
縣名	區域	簡稱／例字	沃	綠俗	陸縮	伏	谷酷	目	僕木	博	剝	落各作	覺學	朔	尺石	麥	白	格	策
古音		古	uok	iʷok	iuk		iuk uok	iuk	uk uok	ak	ɔk	ak	ɔk		iæk	ʷɐk2	ɐk		ɐk2
今國音		國	uo	u (但綠…y，六…iou)						uo, o, ao	uo, au, u	uo, ɤ, ʌ, au	iau, yɛ	uo	ʅ	æe		ɤʌ(=文)	æe; ɤʌ(=文)
1. 宜興	城內	宜	o˔												ɑ				
2. 溧陽	城內	溧	ɔ												ə(=文)				
3. 金壇	西岡	壇	ɔ												ə(=文)				
4. 丹陽	城內	丹	o˧												ɛ(=文)				
5. 丹陽	永豐鄉	丹永	o˧												ə˦	(o˧)		ə	
6. 靖江	城內	靖	uɔ	ɔ										iɔ	ə(=文)	ɔ		ə(=文)	
7. 江陰	城內	陰	ɔ												ɑ				
8. 武進	城內	常	uɔ	ɔ											ə˦	ɔ		ɑ˧	
9. 無錫	城內	錫	uɔ	ɔ											ɑ˧				
10. 吳縣	城內	蘇	ɔ												ɑ˧				
11. 常熟	城內	熟	uʊ	ʊ				ɔ							ɑ				
12. 崑山	城內	崑	o˧												ɑ (但麥：ə)				

地点				1	2	3	4	5	6	7	8	9	10	11	12	13	14	15	16	17
13.寶山	霜草墩		寶霜	uɔ	o								ɔ			a				
14.寶山	羅店		寶羅	uɔ	o								ɔ			ɑ				
15.南滙	周浦		浦東	uɒ	o（但蝠,醋:ɒ）				ɒ							ɑ				
16.上海	城内	旧派 混合派	上旧混	o									ɔ			A				
		新派	上新	o																
17.松江	城内		松	—	o				ɒ（但尉,蹚,搪,莫:o）				ɒ			A				
18.吴江	黎里		吴黎	o												A				
19.吴江	盛澤		吴盛	ɔ												ɑ				
20.嘉興	城内		嘉兴	o												A				
21.吴興	雙林鎮		湖双	—	u;ᵒu	ᵒu	[illegible]	ᵒu,ʊ	ʊ			[illegible]	ʊ			ɑ				
22.杭縣	城内		杭	ɔ（但d,j,tɕ,系習）										（=文）（但鬼:ɔ）	ɔ	ə				
23.紹興	城内		紹	uo	o			uo	o（但蟛:ɑ）							ə（=文）	A	ɑ（但安A）	A	
24.諸暨	王家井		諸王	o												ɐ（=白）	A			
25.嵊縣	崇仁鎮		嵊崇	—		o		(ʊ,o)	—	(o)	o		(o,ɔ)	—		ɑ				
26.嵊縣	太平市		嵊太	—		o		(o)	—	(o)	o		ɔ	—		ɑ				
27.餘姚	城内		姚	uɔ	ɵ								ɔ			a				
28.鄞縣	城内		波	ɔ（但耋:ɔ,æ）												æ				
29.黄巖	城内		黄	uɔ	ɔ（但耋:ø）											iɪ（=文）	ɑ			
30.永嘉	城内		温	o	o;yo	u;iu	u				o				yo	ʳi	ɑ			
31.衢縣	城内		衢	uə	ə			uə	ə								iæ,ə		A	ə
32.金華	城内		華	o					o				o			iɐ	(ɐ)			
33.永康	城内		康	o	o;u				o		ʌʊ				—	ə-i	ai			

（第三表2）

吳韻	'aq'										'eq'								
	'aq'6	'aq'7	'aq'8	'aq'9	'aq'10	'aq'11		'aq'12	'aq'13	'aq'14	'eq'1	'eq'2	'eq'3	'eq'4	'eq'5	'eq'6	'eq'7	'eq'8	'eq'9
	'an1'		'an2'	'an3'	'an'1			'an'1 'on'8	'on'6	'on'7	'an1	'on1	'on2	'on3	'on4	'on5	'on8	'on7	'en1
廣韻	黠洽	乏 黠洽月越	黠札鎋瞎洽狎		曷			合	盍	合	盍	末			曷		合	盍	没物
條件	'b'系 一个字	'b'系	'h'系 白	'g'系	'tz'1系	'tz'系	'd'系	'd'系 多数	一个字	'tz'系 一个字	'd'系 一个字	'b'系	'd'系	'tz'系 一个字	'g'系	'h'系	'g'系	'h'系	'b'系
例	八	法襪	瞎白匣白	掐白甲白	札	薩	達	搭	荅	雜	納	潑	脫	撮	渴	曷	蛤磕	合	不佛
古	ʷat	iʷɐp ʷat iʷɐt	at at₂ ap ap₂			at		ap	ap₂	ap	ap₂	uat			at		ap ap₂		uət iuət
國	A (但襪:uA)		iA		A							uo‹			ɤʌ				u:ᵘo‹ (但没o:ɪɪ)
1.宜	a									ə˫									
2.溧	ɑ˧										—	ə	—						ɵ
3.壇白	ɒ								(—)					(—)		ə			
4.丹	a									y	uɛ	ɛ	uɛ	y	ɛ		uɛ		ɐ
5.丹永	A								—		ə˫	A	ə˫	—	ə˫		—	uə˫o‹	ə˫
6.靖	a								(—)					(—)		ə			
7.陰	a													(—)		ɜ˫			
8.常	ɑ˧													(—)		ə˫			
9.錫	a								a白 ət	ə									
10.蘇	ɔ	a˧							a˧,ə	ə˫									
11.熟	ʊ	a								E˧	ʊ						E˧		
12.崑	ə˫	a							ə˫	—	ə˫								

13.赘温	ɛ˧	a						ɛ˧			O˨(但赘=勤)	—	O˨	ɛ˧		
14.赘园	æ˧	a						æ˧			O˨(但赘=勤)	—	O˨	æ˧		
15.浦东	æ						E˧				œ				E˧	
16.上	A							ə								
17.松	æ						æ,ə	ə			(—)ʌ				ə	
18.吴嘉	ȯ	A					ə									
19.吴武	ɔ	ɑ					ə									
20.嘉兴	o	A					ə									
21.湖双	ʊ	ɑ					(—) ə									
22.杭	a˧		ia˧ (=文)	a˧						ə˦	ɔ		ə˦/a˧			ə
23.绍	æ˧(但里:ʌ)							ə˧	ø	e˩	ø (但措:ɪ)		剪割:ɪ; 退:ə˦; 男:e˩		e˩	
24.诸	A						ɔ (但剪:iɛ; 男ə˦)									ə (但借,逃:ø,o)
25.嵊崇	æ˧		—	ɑ	—	æ˧		—	e			—	e		—	e
26.嵊太	æ˧		—	ɑ	—	æ˧		—	e			—	e		—	e
27.姚	ʉ	a (但鸭(小者):ɛ)						ɪ	—	a	ʉ	ɪ				
28.波	æ˧ (但鸭:ɛ)															
29.黄	ɛ˧									ə	ø˨	ɥø˨	iɪ (但埔:ə)			ɛ˧
30.温	ɔ		ɑ				ø (但摇:ai)									æi
31.衢	A							—	(—) ə˧							
32.华	ɐ˦文,uɐ˦白		oɐ˦	—	ɐ˦文,oɐ˦			—	ɐ˦			—	ɐ˦		—	ɐ˦
33.康	ɑ (但臣:ɤə(一釜))			—	ɑ	—	ɤə	—		oə	(—) ɤə					ə˦

（第三表 3）

吳韻	'eq'																'uoq'		
	'eq'10	'eq'11	'eq'12	'eq'13	'eq'14	'eq'15	'eq'16	'eq'17	'eq'18	'eq'19	'eq'20	'eq'21	'eq'22	'eq'23	'eq'24	'eq'25	'uoq'1	'uoq'2	'uoq'3
	'en2'	'en3'	'en4'	'en5,6'			'in6'	'en9'	'en10'	'en11'	—	'en8'	—	—	'en1,2'		'uang1'		'uang2'
廣韻	德			没			陌格麥革				職	緝	櫛	麥革	德		鐸郭		
條件	'd, tz'系	'g'系	'h'系	'd'系	'tz'系 兩个字		'b'系 文	'g'系 文	'tz'系 文	'b'系 文	'tz'系 每一个字			'b'系 文	'm'母	'l'母 一个字	'g'系 兩个字		'h'系 一个字
例	得則	刻	黑	突	猝	卒	厄文	額文	策文	白文	色	澀	瑟	麥文	墨	北	郭	擴	霍
古	ək			uət			ɐk		ɐk₂		i̯ək	i̯əp	ɐt	ʷɐk₂	ək		ɑk		
國	ɣʌ;Ei有些字白			u			ɣʌ			ᵘɔ	ɣʌ文;sze白	ɣʌ		ᵘɔ		ᵘɔ文, Ei白	uɑ		
1.宜	ə˖					ua	ə˖	ɑ(=a)			ə˖			ɑ	o˕		uo˕		o˕
2.溧	ə					ye	ə				—			ə		ɔ	uə		ɔ
3.壇	ə			—		yᵤE˖	—	ə				—		ə		ɔ			
4.丹	ɐ			uɛ,ɛ	—	y	ɛ									o˕	uo˕,uɛ	uɑ	o˕
5.丹永	ə˖			—		io˕	ə˖			(o)	—	ə˖	—	(o)			uə·	uA	o˕
6.靖	ə					I˖	ə			ɔ	ə					ɔ			
7.陰	ɜ˖					I	ɜ˖,ɑ˖入聲				ɜ˖			ɑ	ɜ˖	ɔ			
8.常	ə˖				—	ye˖	ɜ˖（但'b'系文：ɔ字多，ɑ˖字少）							ɔ			uɔ		
9.錫	ə															ɔ	uɔ		ɔ
10.蘇	ə˖													ɑ;ə˖	ə˖	ɔ			
11.熟	E˖															u	uɔ		
12.崑	ə˖										(—)		(—)			—	o˕		

方言点	1	2	3	4	5	6	7	8	9	10	11	12	13	14	15	16	17
13.寳霜	ɛ˗ (但頸文,蓋文:a)											a	ɛ˗	o˕	uo˕	uɔ	ɔ
14.寳羅	æ˗ (但額文,蓋文:a)											a	æ˗	o˕	uo˕	uɔ	ɔ
15.浦東	ə˗			E˗	œ		ə˗	ɑ,ə˗	ə˗		E˗	ɑ	ə˗	o	uɒ		o
16.上	ə						A;ə 少		ə			A	ə	o		uɔ˕	o˕
17.松	ə,ʌ	ə		—		ə	—		ʌ	ə		—	ə	o	ɒ˕	o	ɒ˕
18.吴黎	ə									—			ə	o˕			
19.吴盛	ə													ɔ			
20.嘉兴	(—) ə								—			A	ə	o			
21.湖双	ə (—)						ɑ;ə		ə	—			ə	[illegible]	ʊ	u	
22.杭	ɵ˖				uɵ		ə						ɔ			uɵ	ɔ
23.紹	ə˗ (但對:e˗)			ø			A (但瓦:e˗)		ə˗		ø	A	o		uo		o
24.諸王	ə (但偶,扣:(β)o˗)			—		ə˖	A (=ɐ) (但[illegible]:æ˗)		ə˖			A	o				(f)o
25.嵊崇	e	—	e	—					e	—		ɑ	o	e	ʊ	—	o
26.嵊太	e	—	e	—					e	—		ɑ	e	e	o	—	ɔ
27.姚	I			ɵ			I	a	I		ɵ	a	ɵ		uɔ		
28.波	æ˗											a	ɔ				
29.黄	ɛ˗	ə		ø˕	ɥø˕		ɑ (=ɛ)		ɛ˗		ɥø˕	ɑ	ɔ		uɔ		
30.温	E			ø	æi		ɑ (=ɐ)		E	ɿ上	æi	ɑ	æi		o	uo	o
31.衢	(—) ə˗															uə˗	ə˗
32.華	ɐ˖			—			ɐ˖			—			ɐ˖		uɐ˖	—	o
33.康	əi			—	ə˖		ai (=ɐ)		—		ə	ai	ə˖		oə		

（第三表 4）

吴韻	‘uaq’					‘ueq’							
	‘uaq’1 ‘uen’3	‘uaq’2 ‘uan’1	‘uaq’3 ‘uan’2	‘uaq’4 ‘uon’1	‘uaq’5 ‘uon’2	‘ueq’1 ‘uon’3	‘ueq’2 ‘uon’4	‘ueq’3 ‘uen’1	‘ueq’4 ‘uen’2	‘ueq’5	‘ueq’6 —	‘ueq’7	‘ueq’8 ‘ong’1
廣韻	麥(穫)	黠(滑)	鎋(刮)	末				沒		德			麥(穫)
條件	‘h’系 一个字	‘g’系	‘h’系	‘g, h’系 四个字				‘g’系 各一个字	‘h’系	‘g, h’系 三个字			‘h’系 一个字
例	劃	刮	滑	括	豁	闊	活	骨	忽	惑	或	國	獲
古	ʷɐk₂	ʷat	ʷat₂	uat				uət		ʷək			ʷɐk₂
國	uA			uoˑ				u		uoˑ			u, uoˑ
1.宜	uɑ				o˩	uə			uo	uə			o˩
2.溧	uɑ˧					uə							
3.壇(西)	uɒ				—	uə							ɔ
4.丹	uɑ		uɑ;(v)ɑ	uɑ		uɛ	uɛ;(v)ɛ	uɛ					ɔ
5.丹(永)	—	uA				uo˅		uə˩					
6.靖	uɑ					uə˧				ɔ			
7.陰	uɑ			uз;uɑ 人少	uɑ	uз˩					ɔ		uз˩
8.常	uɔ	uɑ˧				uз˩					ɔ		uз˩
9.錫	ua					ua						(—)	
10.蘇	uɤ˧					uə							ɔ
11.熟	ua˧					uʊ							
12.崑	uɑ					uɐ							

13.常熟	ua					uɛ˧							uo˥
14.常熟	ua					uæ˧	(v)æ˧	uæ˧	(f)æ˧	uæ˧			uo˥
15.浦东	(v)a	uæ	(v)æ	uæ:	(f)æ	uɛ˧	(v)ɛ˧	uɛ˧	(f)ɛ˧	o			
16.上	uɑ					uə			(f)ə uə	o˥			
17.松	(v)A	uæ	(v)æ	uæ	ɒ˨	uə	(v)ə	uə	(f)ə	o			—
18.吴	—	uA		—		uɐ˧				—		uə˧	
19.吴	uɑ					uə							
20.嘉兴	—	uA		—	uA	uə˧							
21.湖	—	uɑ		—	uɑ	uə (—)							—
22.杭	uA				ɔ	uə			ɔ				
23.紹	uo	uæ			o	uɵ˧				uo			
24.諸	(v)A	uA	(v)A	uA	(f)A	o			(f)o	o	(v)ə˧	o	(v)o
25.嵊	—	uæ˧	(v)æ˧	—		ue	—	ue	(f)e	—		ʊ	o
26.嵊	—	uɑ	uæ˧	—		uə	—	ue	ue	—		o˧	o
27.姚	ua					uɐ (但圈:ə)							
28.波	uæ˧									ɔ			
29.黄	uɔ	uɛ˧						uɔ (但圈:ɔ)					
30.温	uɑ	o						ø	yø	(v)æi	(v)ɑ	u,æi	(v)ɑ
31.衢	—	uA		—	ə	uA		uɐ˧					—
32.華	—	uɐ˧文, uoɐ˧白	uɐ˧	uɐ˧文, uoɐ˧白	—	uɐ˧文, uoɐ˧白	uɐ˧	uɐ˧文, uoɐ˧白	uɐ˧	—		uɐ˧文, uoɐ˧白	—
33.康	—	oA	oə	—	oA		uɑ	oə		uəi			—

（第三表 5）

吳韻	'ioq'									'iaq'					
	'ioq'1	'ioq'2	'ioq'3	'ioq'4	'ioq'5	'ioq'6	'ioq'7	'ioq'8	'ioq'9	'iaq'1		'iaq'2	'iaq'3	'iaq'4	'iaq'5
	'iong3,' 'ong6,7'		'iong4'	'iong5'	'iong6'	'ang5'		'iong6'	'iang1'	'iang1'		'iang2,3'	'iang4'	'iang5'	
廣韻	屋六 燭					覺		屋六	覺	藥					
條件	'g'系	'h'系	日母 白	日母 文	'j'系 多數	知徹澄母 多數	知徹澄母 一個字	一個字	'g,h'系 文	l母	'g,h,tz'系	日母	'j'系 知母	'j'系 照系 多數	'j'系 照系 一個字
例	菊局	蓄欲	肉白	肉文	竹屬	桌	鐲	軸	覺文學文	略	腳削	若弱	着	芍	爍
古	i̯uk i̯ʷok					ɔk		i̯uk	ɔk	i̯ak					
國	y		o·u	u	u,o·u 有字白	uo·		u文,o·u白	yɛ	yɛ文,iɑu		ɤʌ,uo·	uo文,ɑu白		
1.宜	io˗			o˗					io(但藥文:ɪ)			o˗			—
2.溧	iɔ(但g,k,gh母:ye)			—	ɔ			—	iɔ	iɑ˧		ɑ˧			
3.壇白	iɔ(但g母:yɥ,ɛ˧)			ɔ					—	iɒ		ɒ			
4.丹	io(但菊:y)			o(但蓄:io)					iɑ				ɑ		
5.丹永	(s)o;io		—		o				iʌ				ʌ		
6.靖	iɔ								iʌ						
7.陰	io			ɔ					iʌ			ɑ			
8.常	iɔ(但蓄:ye˧)			ɔ					iɑ˧(但l母:iʌ)			ɑ˧			
9.錫	iɔ			ɔ					iɔ	iɑ˧		ɑ˧			a
10.蘇	iɔ(但g母:iɔ,ye)			ɔ				iɔ		iɑ˧		ɑ˧			a˧
11.熟	iʊ			iʊ,ʊ					iɔ	iɑ,ia˧		ɔ	ɑ;ɔ		a
12.崑	io			o			io			iɑ		ɑ			

<table>
<tr><td>13.寧</td><td colspan="3">io</td><td colspan="3">o˧</td><td colspan="2">io</td><td>iɔ</td><td colspan="2">ia</td><td colspan="3">a (但惹:ɔ)</td></tr>
<tr><td>14.寧</td><td colspan="3">io</td><td colspan="3">o˧</td><td colspan="2">io</td><td>iɔ</td><td colspan="2">ia</td><td colspan="3">a (但惹:ɔ)</td></tr>
<tr><td>15.浦</td><td colspan="3">io</td><td colspan="4">o</td><td>io</td><td colspan="3">iɑ</td><td colspan="2">ɑ</td><td>æ</td></tr>
<tr><td>16.上</td><td colspan="3">YO(但g母:Yo˧)</td><td colspan="4">o˧</td><td>Yo˧</td><td colspan="3">ia˦</td><td colspan="3">A</td></tr>
<tr><td>17.松</td><td colspan="3">io(但g母:Yo˧)</td><td>—</td><td colspan="2">o</td><td>—</td><td>io</td><td colspan="3">iA</td><td colspan="2">A</td><td>—</td></tr>
<tr><td>18.吳</td><td colspan="3">io˧</td><td colspan="4">o˧</td><td colspan="2">io˧</td><td colspan="2">iA</td><td colspan="3">A</td></tr>
<tr><td>19.吳</td><td colspan="3">iɔ</td><td colspan="4">ɔ</td><td colspan="2">iɔ</td><td colspan="2">iA</td><td colspan="3">ɑ</td></tr>
<tr><td>20.嘉</td><td colspan="3">io</td><td colspan="2">o</td><td>—</td><td>o</td><td>—</td><td>io</td><td colspan="2">iA</td><td colspan="3">A</td></tr>
<tr><td>21.湖</td><td colspan="3">iʊ˦</td><td colspan="3">ᵒu; ʊ</td><td>iʊ˦</td><td>—</td><td>iʊ˦</td><td colspan="2">iA</td><td colspan="3">ɑ</td></tr>
<tr><td>22.杭</td><td colspan="2">iɔ(但蟹:yɤ˦)</td><td>(白文)</td><td colspan="3">ɔ</td><td colspan="2">iɔ</td><td colspan="3">ia˦(但蟹:iɔ,ɔ)</td><td colspan="3">a˦</td></tr>
<tr><td>23.紹</td><td colspan="3">yø(但[illegible]:(n)ø)</td><td colspan="4">o</td><td colspan="2">yø</td><td colspan="2">ia˦</td><td>o</td><td colspan="2">A (但惹:o)</td></tr>
<tr><td>24.諸</td><td colspan="3">iɔo</td><td colspan="3">o</td><td colspan="3">iɔo</td><td colspan="2">iA</td><td>o</td><td colspan="2">A (但惹:o)</td></tr>
<tr><td>25.嵊</td><td colspan="2">io</td><td colspan="7">—</td><td colspan="2">iA</td><td colspan="3">ɑ</td></tr>
<tr><td>26.嵊</td><td colspan="2">io</td><td colspan="7">—</td><td colspan="2">iA</td><td colspan="3">iA</td></tr>
<tr><td>27.姚</td><td colspan="3">yɵ</td><td colspan="4">ɵ</td><td colspan="2">yɵ(但[illegible]:yɔ)</td><td colspan="2">ia</td><td>ɔ</td><td colspan="2">a (但惹:ɔ)</td></tr>
<tr><td>28.波</td><td colspan="3">yʌ</td><td colspan="3">ɔ</td><td colspan="3">yʌ</td><td colspan="4">iæ˦</td><td>æ˦</td></tr>
<tr><td>29.黄</td><td colspan="3">iɔ(但[illegible]:yø;[illegible]:yɔ)</td><td colspan="5">ɔ</td><td>ɔ (一切)</td><td colspan="5">iA</td></tr>
<tr><td>30.溫</td><td colspan="5">[illegible]:iu; 烟:yo</td><td colspan="2">yo</td><td>iu</td><td>o; yo</td><td>iɛ</td><td colspan="4">iɑ</td></tr>
<tr><td>31.衢</td><td>ə˦</td><td>(yə˦)</td><td>yə˦</td><td colspan="3">ə˦</td><td colspan="3">—</td><td>iæ</td><td>iA (但gn母:iæ)</td><td colspan="3">A</td></tr>
<tr><td>32.華</td><td colspan="8">io</td><td>—</td><td colspan="5">io; iɛ</td></tr>
<tr><td>33.康</td><td colspan="2">io</td><td colspan="2">—</td><td>ʊ</td><td colspan="3">—</td><td>AU</td><td colspan="5">iAU</td></tr>
</table>

（第三表 6）

吳韻	'iaq'	'iq'								
	'iaq'6	'iq'1	'iq'2	'iq'3	'iq'4	'iq'5	'iq'6	'iq'7	'iq'8	'iq'9
	'ien$_{5,6}$'	'ien$_4$'		'ien$_1$'	'ien$_2$'	'ien$_3$'	'ien$_4$'	'ien$_9$'	'ien$_{10}$'	'ien$_{11}$'
廣韻	洽 狎	葉	帖	屑薛	屑鐵薛列	帖葉	屑鐵薛列月竭葉業	薛列葉		
條件	'g,h'系 文	'g,h'系 丢一十字		'b'系	'd'系	'tz'系	'g,h'系	日母 白	日母 文	'j₁'系 其餘
例	夾文甲文狹文壓文	捏	協	撇別	跌貼	節接捷	結傑葉業噎歇劫	熱白	熱文	舌摺
古	ap ap$_2$	ịæp	iep	iet ịæt	iet ịæt	iep ịæp	iet ịæt ịɐt ịæp ịɐp	ịæt ịæp		
國	iʌ	iɛ						ɤʌ		
1.宜	ia˂			ɪ˂	屑帖韵:ia˂其餘:ɪ˂		ɪ˂		ə˃	
2.溧	ia˂		—	ie					—	ə
3.壇西	—	iɒ	—	iɛ					ə	
4.丹	ia		ɪ	ɪ						ɛ
5.丹陽	—	iA	—	ɪ		iɪ		—		ə˃
6.靖	iA		—	i			iə			
7.陰	iA		iə	ɪ			iə（促口母:ɪ）		ɜ˃	
8.常	ia˂		iɪ						ə˃	
9.錫	ia˂		iɪ				ie˂		ə	
10.蘇	ia˂	ia˂	ɪ				iə˃		ə˃	
11.熟	ia˂	ia˂	—	ɪ					E˂	
12.崑	ia			ɪ					ə˃	

<table>
<tr><td>13.寶霜</td><td colspan="3">ia</td><td colspan="5">I</td><td colspan="2">ɛ˧</td></tr>
<tr><td>14.寶羅</td><td colspan="3">ia</td><td colspan="5">I</td><td colspan="2">æ˧</td></tr>
<tr><td>15.浦周</td><td colspan="3">iæ</td><td colspan="6">İ (但撇,跌,切,篾,屑,叠:iʌ)</td><td>ɛ˧</td></tr>
<tr><td>16.上</td><td colspan="3">ia˧</td><td colspan="5">I (但gh, gn, y母:ia)</td><td colspan="2">ə</td></tr>
<tr><td>17.松</td><td colspan="3">iæ</td><td colspan="5">I (但迭,撇:iʌ)</td><td colspan="2">ə</td></tr>
<tr><td>18.吴黎</td><td>(iʌ)
(但[illegible]:iɛ˧)</td><td>—</td><td>iɛ˧</td><td colspan="3">I</td><td colspan="2">iɛ˧</td><td colspan="2">ə</td></tr>
<tr><td>19.吴盛</td><td colspan="2">iʌ</td><td>iʌ,iɐ</td><td colspan="3">I (但帖韵[illegible]:iʌ)</td><td colspan="2">iɐ</td><td colspan="2">ə</td></tr>
<tr><td>20.嘉興</td><td>—</td><td colspan="2">iʌ</td><td colspan="5">陰入短式:iɪ, 陰入長式:ie; 陽入:iɛ; 帖韵:iʌ</td><td colspan="2">ə</td></tr>
<tr><td>21.湖雙</td><td>iʌ</td><td colspan="2">—</td><td>i;ie˧</td><td colspan="4">ie˧</td><td colspan="2">ə</td></tr>
<tr><td>22.杭</td><td colspan="2">ia˧</td><td colspan="5">I</td><td>(=文)</td><td colspan="2">ə</td></tr>
<tr><td>23.紹</td><td colspan="3">ia˧</td><td colspan="2">I</td><td colspan="3">ie˩(但屑:ø)</td><td colspan="2">e(但撇泼:ə˧)</td></tr>
<tr><td>24.諸王</td><td colspan="2">iʌ</td><td>—</td><td colspan="6">I</td><td>o</td></tr>
<tr><td>25.嵊崇</td><td colspan="3">—</td><td colspan="4">i</td><td colspan="2">—</td><td>e</td></tr>
<tr><td>26.嵊太</td><td colspan="3">—</td><td colspan="4"></td><td colspan="2">—</td><td>ie</td></tr>
<tr><td>27.姚</td><td colspan="3">ia</td><td colspan="7">I (但贴:ia)</td></tr>
<tr><td>28.波</td><td colspan="3">iæ˧</td><td colspan="6">ie˩(但贴,蝶叠 iɐ)</td><td>ie˩,ye</td></tr>
<tr><td>29.黄</td><td>ɛ˧
(=也)</td><td colspan="9">iɪ</td></tr>
<tr><td>30.溫</td><td>ɑ
(=也)</td><td>iɑ</td><td>ie˩</td><td>ie</td><td>铁迭:ii
贴:ie˩</td><td colspan="5">ie˩</td></tr>
<tr><td>31.衢</td><td>iʌ</td><td>iæ</td><td>—</td><td colspan="2">iɪ</td><td colspan="2">ie˧</td><td colspan="2">—</td><td>ə˧</td></tr>
<tr><td>32.華</td><td>(iɛ)</td><td colspan="2">—</td><td colspan="4">iɛ</td><td colspan="2">—</td><td>ɥyɐ˧
(但[illegible]:ɥyɤã)</td></tr>
<tr><td>33.康</td><td>(ɑ)</td><td>iɑ</td><td>—</td><td>ie</td><td colspan="2">屑帖韵:iʌ;薛韵:ie</td><td>iᵉ (但歇:(k)i,叶:iə)</td><td colspan="2">—</td><td>ie</td></tr>
</table>

（第三表 7）

吴韻	'iq'									
	'iq'10 —	'iq'11 'in4'	'iq'12 'in1'	'iq'13 'in2'	'iq'14 'in3'	'iq'15 'in4'	'iq'16 'in7'	'iq'17 'in8,10'	'iq'18 'in9,11'	'iq'19 'in11'
廣韻	薛悦	陌虢	緝 質日 錫 昔 職							昔文
條件	'l'母 一个字	'g'系 一个字	'b'系	'd'系	'tz'系	'g,h'系	日母 白	文	'j'系 其餘	文
例	劣	劇	必逼	立笛力	習七昔即	吸一極喫益	日白	日文	十失直	尺文石文
古	i̯ʷæt	i̯ɐk	i̯əp i̯ĕt iek i̯æk i̯ək							i̯æk
國	iɛ	y	i（但喫:ʅ）				ʅ			
1.宜	ɪ˧	io˩	ɪ˧					ə˥		ɑ（=白）
2.溧	—	ie						ə		
3.壇西	iE,ə	—	iE					ə		
4.丹	ɪ	ɪ							ɛ	
5.丹永	ɪ	iɪ	ɪ		iɪ		—		ə˥	
6.靖	i	iʌ	i			iə				
7.陰	ɪ	iʌ	ɪ			iə（但口母:ɪ）		ɜ˥		ɑ（=白）
8.常	iɪ	iɑ˧	iɪ					ə˥		
9.錫	iɪ	iɑ˧	iɪ			ie˧		ə		
10.蘇	ɪ	iə˥, ia˧	ɪ			iə˥		ə˥		
11.熟	ɪ	ia˧	ɪ					E˧		
12.崑	ɪ							ə˥		

<table>
<tr><td>13.寶山霜草</td><td>I</td><td>ia</td><td colspan="5">I（但喫,泣：iɛ˦）</td><td colspan="4">ɛ˦</td></tr>
<tr><td>14.寶山羅店</td><td>I</td><td>ia</td><td colspan="5">I（但喫,泣：iɛ˦）</td><td colspan="4">æ˦</td></tr>
<tr><td>15.浦東</td><td>I</td><td>iɑ</td><td colspan="5">緝,質韵：I（但急,及,匹,漆：iʌ）；錫昔,職韵：IΛ（但覓,滴,積：I）</td><td colspan="3">緝,質韻：E˦；職韻：ə˦</td><td>ɑ, ə˦</td></tr>
<tr><td>16.上</td><td>I</td><td>ia˦</td><td colspan="5">I（但gh, gn, y母：ie；喫：iə）</td><td colspan="3">ə</td><td>—</td></tr>
<tr><td>17.松</td><td>I</td><td>iʌ</td><td colspan="5">緝,質韻：I（但急,及,匹,漆：iʌ）；錫,昔,職韵：IΛ（但覓,粒：I）</td><td colspan="3">ə（但食：ʌ）</td><td>—</td></tr>
<tr><td>18.吴黎</td><td>I</td><td>—</td><td colspan="3">I</td><td colspan="2">iE˦</td><td colspan="3">ə</td><td>—</td></tr>
<tr><td>19.吴盛</td><td>I</td><td>iɐ</td><td colspan="3">I</td><td colspan="2">iɐ</td><td colspan="3">ə</td><td>—</td></tr>
<tr><td>20.嘉興</td><td>ə</td><td>io</td><td colspan="5">iɪ; ie; iE（條件同上頁）</td><td colspan="3">ə</td><td>—</td></tr>
<tr><td>21.湖州雙林</td><td>—</td><td>iʌ</td><td>i; ie˦</td><td colspan="4">ie˦</td><td colspan="3">ə</td><td>—</td></tr>
<tr><td>22.杭</td><td>ə</td><td>ia˦</td><td colspan="4">I</td><td>（=文）</td><td colspan="4">ə˦</td></tr>
<tr><td>23.紹</td><td>ə</td><td>ie˩</td><td colspan="2">I（但粒：ə˦）</td><td colspan="3">ie˩</td><td colspan="3">e（但式,食：ə˦）</td><td>ə˦</td></tr>
<tr><td>24.諸王</td><td>ə˦</td><td colspan="6">I</td><td colspan="4">ə˦</td></tr>
<tr><td>25.嵊崇</td><td>—</td><td colspan="5">i</td><td colspan="2">—</td><td>e</td><td>—</td></tr>
<tr><td>26.嵊太</td><td>—</td><td colspan="5">i</td><td colspan="2">—</td><td>ie</td><td>—</td></tr>
<tr><td>27.姚</td><td colspan="10">I（但喫：yə）</td></tr>
<tr><td>28.波</td><td>æ˦</td><td colspan="6">ie˦（但喫：yʌ）</td><td colspan="3">ie; ye</td><td>ie˩</td></tr>
<tr><td>29.黄</td><td>ə</td><td colspan="9">iɪ</td></tr>
<tr><td>30.温</td><td>E</td><td>iæi</td><td>ie˩</td><td>ᶦi</td><td>緝韵：æi；錫昔韵：ᶦi</td><td>iæi</td><td>日：(n)E</td><td colspan="4">緝韵：æi；錫昔韵：ᶦi</td></tr>
<tr><td>31.衢</td><td colspan="2">—</td><td colspan="2">iɪ（但粒：</td><td colspan="3">ie˦</td><td colspan="4">ə˦</td></tr>
<tr><td>32.華</td><td colspan="2">—</td><td colspan="5">iE（但粒：ɐ˦文，ɤə白）</td><td>—</td><td>ɐ˦</td><td>—</td></tr>
<tr><td>33.康</td><td colspan="2">—</td><td>ie; ə˦i</td><td colspan="2">緝質韵：ə˦；昔職韵：əi（但粒：ɤə）</td><td colspan="2">iə˦（但喫：(k)i）</td><td>—</td><td colspan="2">緝韵：ə˦；昔職韵：əi</td></tr>
</table>

（第三表 8）

吳韻	'iueq'										
	'iueq'1	'iueq'2	'iueq'3	'iueq'4	'iueq'5	'iueq'6	'iueq'7	'iueq'8	'iueq'9	'iueq'10	
	'iuon1,2'			'iuin1'	'iuin2'	'iuon3'	'iuin6'	'in8'	—	'iuon6'	
廣韻	屑穴 薛悅 月越			術	物	薛悅	術	緝	鎋刷	薛悅	
條件	'h'系 一个字	'y'母 多數	'h' 'g' 系 系 'h'母	'g'系	'h'系 一个字	'j'1系		日母 一个字	'tz'1系 一个字	'tz'系 两个字	
例	曰	越	血决缺	屈	鬱	拙說	出述	入	刷	絶	雪
古	iʷet i̯ʷæt i̯ʷɐt			i̯uĕt	i̯uət	i̯ʷæt	i̯uĕt	i̯əp	ʷat₂	i̯ʷæt	
國	yɛ（但血白:iɛ）			y（但掘:yɛ）		uo˂	u		uA	yɛ	
1.宜	ya˧		ye		io˩	ye˧			ɑ	ye˧	
2.溧	yɑ˧（但越白:iɔ）		ye		iɔ	ye					
3.壇西	yʮE˧				iɔ	uə			yʮE˧		
4.丹	y							uɛ	y		
5.丹永	—	io˩					—			io˩;iɪ	
6.靖	yA	yø˧			iɔ	yø˧			yA	i	
7.陰	io˩					ɑ˩白，ɜ˩文，人少			ɑ	ɪ	
8.常	ye˧				iɔ	ʮɜ˩			ye˧白，ʮɑ˧文	ye˧	
9.錫	ya		yɵ			ə			iɪ		
10.蘇	ya˧	yɵ				ə˩				ɪ	
11.熟	iɔ	iʊ				E˧				ɪ	
12.崑	yɜ				io˩	ə˩				ɪ	

13.寶	iɔ	io				ɛ˧			ɪ
14.寶	iɔ	io				æ˧			ɪ
15.浦	yœ		yø			E˧ (假読：œ)			ɪ
16.上	Yɵ			Yo˨		ə			ɪ
17.松	Yə˧		Yɵ˨	io	Yɵ˨	ə			ɪ
18.吴	yA	yə˧			—	ə			ɪ
19.吴	yA	yɵ				ə			ɪ
20.嘉	yə˧					ə			ɪ
21.湖	ie˧				—	ə		—	ɪ
22.杭	yE	yɪ˧			iɔ	ɥɵ˧	ə˧	ɥa˧	ɪ
23.紹	yø					é		ɪ	
24.諸	iɔo, iaɒ	iɔo				o (僅站母：ɵ˧)			ɪ
25.嵊	a	y		—		e	—	e	i
26.嵊	a	y		—		ie	—	ie	i
27.姚	yɔ	yʉ				ɪ			
28.波	yʌ,ye	ye	ye;yʌ	yʌ		Ye			
29.黄	yɛ˧		Yø˨		iɔ	ɥø˨	iɪ	ɥø˨	
30.温	yø			y		yø	æi	ø	yø
31.衢	yA	yə˧	ə˧		yə˧	ə˧	—	ə˧	ie˧
32.華	ɥyɐ˧				—	ɥyɐ	iE	ɥyɐ˧, ɥyɤ̃	iɐ˧, iE
33.康	yA		øə˧	—	yə˧	(øə)	ə˧	—	ie

韻母的討論

本篇跟聲母的討論一樣，也是只能就幾種可注意的地方討論討論，不能把全部的分合例，音值，跟古音國音的關係都說全了，否則不如把全表重抄一道還醒目一點。

1. 韻頭

討論韻母影響到聲母的時候，曾經把韻頭分爲開合齊撮四類，大略以 u，i，iu（國際音標[u，i，y]）代表合齊撮，其餘的都算開口。不過在事實上這些音當然没有這末簡單。

有些韻的字，雖然因爲它們的聲母變化近乎開口韻字的變法而叫做開口，其實都是近乎聲化（輔音化）的性質，用等韻的名辭來形容它們，於音理上是差得很遠了。這些韻有四類，就是'm，ng'（嘸，五白），'y'（詩，思），'el'（而，耳文），跟'u_1'（夫，符）。它們的音值的討論見下第 3 節主要元音的頭幾段。

開口韻（第二表 1—5 頁）大致都是跟古開口相當，其中有些不合的依次講起來如下：第二表 1 頁'$o_{1,2}$'（賒，蛇）[①]古音是齊齒，現在除丹，靖，温，華，康，都没有 i 音了。浦東賒讀 sio 好像是保存古音 shia 的 i，但浦東的沙（古音開口 sha）也念 sio，所以前者的 i

① 括弧中表示例字，下仿此。

恐怕是後來新生的，换言之，不是 shia 直接變 sio，乃是齊齒 shia 變開口 sha 變 sa 變 so 又變齊齒 sio。

第二表 2 頁‘$ei_{1,2}$’（悲，梅），3 頁‘an_1’‘b’系（反）‘on_1’（半），4 頁‘en_1’（本），第三表 1 頁‘$oq_{6,8}$’（僕），‘aq_2’（麥白），2 頁‘$aq_{6,7}$’（法），‘$eq_{1,8}$’（潑，不）都是古音唇音合口字，現在在吴語（跟大多數方言），除 u 韻爲本韻音之外，唇音不用 u 韻頭，都變了開口了，所以梅古音合口 muài，現在國音用 mei，吴音用 mai，mei，mé 等等開口韻。不過唇音入聲字在‘oq，eq’兩韻下國音略有合口傾向，例如佛字，音在 fuo，fo 之間。但這也是後來新生的變化（cf. 浦東賒 sio），因爲非但唇音合口字略帶合口，連古開口字也是略帶合口，例如莫（古音 màk）國音在 muo，mo 之間。

還有‘d’系跟‘tz’系的字除 u 韻爲本韻音之外也大都不用合口韻頭。這個包括第二表 2 頁‘$ei_{3\text{-}6}$’（類，歲），3 頁‘$on_{2\text{-}3}$’（暖，酸），4 頁‘$en_{5\text{-}6}$’（嫩，寸），第三表 2 頁‘$eq_{2\text{-}3}$’（脱，撮），3 頁‘$eq_{12\text{-}14}$’（突，卒）。這些字在古音是合口或撮口，現在除溧，壇，丹，丹永，常，嘉，杭，黄，温，華把上述字的一小部分讀成合口或撮口外，其餘照開口讀。這類的字在國音只有‘ei’韻的 n，l 母‘en’韻的一個嫩字讀開口，其餘都讀合口，與吴語大致不合。這類字讀起合口音來並不一定是個有舌根作用的 u 音，因爲‘d，tz’系的聲母既然用舌尖，底下的合口韻往往也是舌尖韻的 ÿ 音，例如溧陽歲字 sÿai 去聲，英文 swipe，國音歲 sÿei 去聲，英文 sway（音 swei），這種中國的韻母跟英文的 w 很不同的。

第二表 3 頁‘ou_2’（鄒），4 頁‘en_8’（森），5 頁‘ang_5’（爽），第三表 3 頁‘$eq_{19\text{-}20}$’（色，澀）‘tz_1’系聲母是古音齊齒韻字。現在把古

音的 i 韻頭失掉了，都變成開口了。又 5 頁'ang_5'(爽)在宜，壇西，丹，常，杭，温，華，康全變成一部分變合口，這是跟國語一樣的。

第二表 3 頁'$áng_6$'(嘗白)，第三表 1 頁'aq_1'(尺白)在古音也是齊齒，在吴語多數變成開口了。

第二表 5 頁'$áng_{3-4}$'江韻照《切韻指掌圖》是叫合口，但它的古音既是一種 o 音，跟一般的合口不同，在現代吴語讀很更開，所以現在當然歸開口。不過'ang_5'的江韻(雙)有的地方讀真的合口，跟上述的陽韻字(爽)一樣。

第二表 5 頁'ong'(公，龍，從等等)第三表 1 頁'oq_{1-6}'(沃，緑，俗等等)在古音都是合口或撮口，在多數吴音都念成一種 o 音，所以歸在開口。它的韻音有時候很像一種 u 音，但舌根並不提高，乃是作 o 音時唇特别並攏一點的 o 音。這些韻裡的'g'系變法平上去(恭，共)不全跟入聲(曲，局)並行。在入聲古撮口變齊撮，在平上去'ong_{4-5}'古撮口變了今開口了。不過温州保存古韻頭的地方多一點。

合口韻大都是古的合口撮口。不合例的如下：

第二表 6 頁'ù'韻的古歌韻本是 a 音，但在現在吴語多數地方跟戈韻變法一樣有些地方連模也一樣，只看聲母是那一'系'而不管古韻，所以現在把它們都擱在一塊兒。這些韻的字不讀合口時大概讀一種不圓唇的 ou 韻，例如[倒 v 加倒 m]，這種音在江蘇部的西半見的最多。

第二表 7 頁'uo'(瓜，花)，第三表 3 頁'uoq'(郭，霍)雖然歸在合口，在好些地方不作合口，以地方論，大概是一半一半，而且看不出哪一區用 uo 的多哪一區用 o 的多。

第二表 7 頁‘ua,uei’(怪,會),8 頁全頁(慣,昏,王),第三表 4 頁全頁(刮,忽)都是‘g,h’系的合口,這個差不多全是很一致的用合口。但一個很有趣的例外就是‘h’系的字(還,滑,昏,忽)的韻頭 u,在實羅,浦上舊,松,諸王,嵊崇,温全變或一部分變成唇齒音,因而 wan 變成 van,hueq 變成 feq,成了開口了,這個可以算是江西湖南派。

第二表 7 頁‘$uei_{5\text{-}6}$’(鬼白,跑白)在一大半地方讀 iu[y]變成撮口了。

齊齒韻大致是古音的齊齒。不合例的如下:

第二表 9 頁‘$ia_{1\text{-}2}$’(下文,家文),‘$iai_{3\text{-}4}$’(戒文,諧文),10 頁‘iau_{1}’(交文,孝文),‘$ien_{5\text{-}6}$’(間文,陷文),11 頁‘in_{6}’(行文),‘$iang_{1}$’(講文),第三表 5 頁‘ioq_{8}’(覺文,學文),‘iaq_{6}’(甲文,狹文),在古音都是開口,在吴語的文言讀法都是齊齒,與官話一樣。但是在温州大部分字只有一種開口讀法,在黄巖永康有一半字是開口讀法,没有文白之分。

第二表 10 頁‘$iau_{3\text{-}5}$’(繞,超),‘$iou_{5\text{-}6}$’(柔,周),11 頁‘$ien_{7\text{-}9}$’(染,扇),‘$in_{7\text{-}11}$’(認,程),12 頁‘$iang_{2\text{-}5}$’(讓,長),‘$iong_{4\text{-}6}$’(絨,中),第三表 5 頁‘$ioq_{2\text{-}4}$’(肉,竹),‘$iaq_{2\text{-}4}$’(若,着),6 頁‘$iq_{2\text{-}9}$’(熱,舌),‘$iq_{16\text{-}18}$’(日,失),都是古音照之,穿昌,牀乘,審式,禪,日齊齒韻的字,這些字在國語都全變開口。在吴語現在姑且跟一部分的傾向歸入齊齒,其實各處也不一致。日母的白話音用‘gn’聲母,韻母也都齊齒。它的文言音就跟其餘的命運一樣。過半數地方倒還是用開口音(用舌尖聲母),在丹(日母文)靖,錫,熟,嵊太,波,黄,温,華,康有一部分字用齊齒,但各處不是一致的,有的這幾韻齊齒，有的那幾韻齊齒，有的只有一兩韻，有的大多數。

第二表 12 頁‘iong’韻都是古撮口，現在列如齊齒，是因爲起頭的韻頭往往不甚圓唇。遇到有幾處的韻頭的確比主要元音的圓唇程度較高的例才用[y]號。例如甯波‘ioq₁₋₂’(局，欲)用真撮口韻頭。

撮口韻(第二表 12，13 頁，第三表 8 頁)也大致是古撮口。不過古照之穿昌等等的字(朱，水，軟，川，春，說之類)，跟上述的齊齒一樣，也是有過半地方讀作舌尖聲母，上述的齊齒改開口，這裡就是撮口改合口。不過這個合口不一定是 u 音，有的地方用一種 ÿ 音(圓唇舌尖元音)，例如上海朱 tzÿ。

‘l’母跟‘tz’系(如徐，慮，絶，雪之類)在表中雖歸撮口，變齊齒的也很多。

‘g，h’系(居，虛)大概都很一致的用撮口，不過吴與雙林根本就没有撮口音，所以連居，捐，決也都念成齊齒了。在作者所知，從南潯望西到湖州城全是這樣的。

2. 韻尾

吴語不大有真複合元音的韻(ua，ia 不算真複合元音，因爲韻頭 i，u 往往是形容性，被收入聲母的身上而仍舊可以成刮，甲那類的入聲字。au，ai 才是真複合元音呐)。所有的少數的元音韻尾歸在下節主要元音裡講。現在先講鼻音韻尾。

吴語的鼻音韻尾大略可以分-n，-ng，跟形容性的半鼻音三種。第三種其實已經是没有韻尾了，不過爲便於跟别種音比較，也叫它作韻尾。

'an,on,uan,uon,ien,iuon'六韻母(古山咸兩攝)的鼻音之有無跟性質都是一同來的。這幾韻在吴語中没有一處是用脚踏實地的-n或-m輔音性韻尾的,除丹陽一處'on,uon'兩韻外也没有一處用-ng輔音性韻尾的,大概不是用半鼻音的元音(法文派)就是用純口音的元音。總計靖,常,杭,紹,嵊,姚,衢,華文用半鼻音。壇西只有'on'韻用半鼻音。錫,浦,波有一部分字似用似不用。其餘的(包括華白)都用純口音的韻音。

'ang,uang,iàng'三韻(古宕攝)多數用一種鼻音。用輔音性ng音作韻尾的有宜,溧,壇西,丹,丹永,靖,常,杭,紹,嵊太,華,康。用一種不完全的ng韻尾,或前半元音不帶鼻音後半帶半鼻音的有陰,錫,蘇,熟,寶,浦,上,松,吴黎,吴盛,嘉,黄,衢。純粹半鼻音(法文派)的有崑,湖雙,諸,嵊崇,姚,波。

'áng,uáng,iang'三韻(庚耕(登)陽)複雜一點。在溧,壇西,丹,丹永,靖,杭,華,康有一部分字的韻讀如'en'的跟國語相近,它的音值就歸下文'en'韻討論。

這三韻不變'en'者,其中用輔音性的ng的,有宜,常,紹,嵊太,華。用不完全的ng或後半部用鼻音者有陰,錫,熟,寶,浦,嵊崇,黄。用純粹半鼻音的有蘇,崑,上,松,吴黎,吴盛,嘉,諸,姚,波,衢。可見在有的地方在'ang'韻雖然用後半鼻音而在'áng'韻用全部半鼻音的。這是兩者不同的地方。'áng','iang'韻用純粹口音者有壇西,丹,温,康(永康用ai,韻尾i是從-ng變來的)。

'ong,iong'(古通攝)兩韻的韻尾差不多全是用輔音性的ng。只有寶,浦,嵊崇的ng似乎讀得不很着實。温州鍾韻字用純口音是特别的。

‘en, uen, in, iuin’(古深臻攝)四韻的韻尾很有趣。古音的-m是没有一處有的。像國音把古 m,n 併爲一類,把 ng 另列一類,這種辨法多數地方也没有的。只有紹與能辨第二表 11 頁‘in_{3-9}’(陳)爲 n 尾,‘in_{10-11}’(程)爲 ng 尾。(甯波雖辨陳程,但是在聲母跟韻元音,韻尾仍都是 ng)。至於音值方面,這類的韻尾大都受下字同化的影響。比方一個心字在吴盛單讀時可以隨便讀 sin 或 sing,讀者也不覺得有 n,ng 的區别,但是後頭連起别的字來就跟着後頭聲母的發音部位同化了,同化最全的是照下例變的:

例語:	門面	京都	鏡子	門檻	親娘	蒸飯	尊姓	芸香	青海	分紅
上字韻尾變:	m	n	n	ng	gn	半鼻音,微作下聲母勢。				

同化幾乎全的有崑,蘇,錫,嘉,吴盛,湖雙,杭,華幾處。

不全同化的有丹,靖,熟,寶,吴黎,紹,諸,黄,衢。用穩固的 ng 尾而絶對不受下字聲母影響者有壇西,陰,常,浦,上,松,姚,波。這幾韻在諸王一律讀半鼻音,也全無同化。在温州有些字用 ng,有些字用純口音,也無同化。這幾韻跟上述的‘ang, áng’諸韻不同的地方就是上述者雖然讀一種不着實的 ng 尾,但不大受下字的同化作用。本節講的這些韻讀單字時倒大都是清清楚楚的一律讀 n,或是一律讀 ng,或是有時 n 有時 ng(聽者跟讀者都不能預測),可是看下字聲母是什末部位,就完全跟着它變。同化作用在語音學上是很平常的事情,但是單字音有時用 n 有時用 ng 而讀者不認爲兩種音,這是音位(phoneme)觀念大受引伸的一個例了。

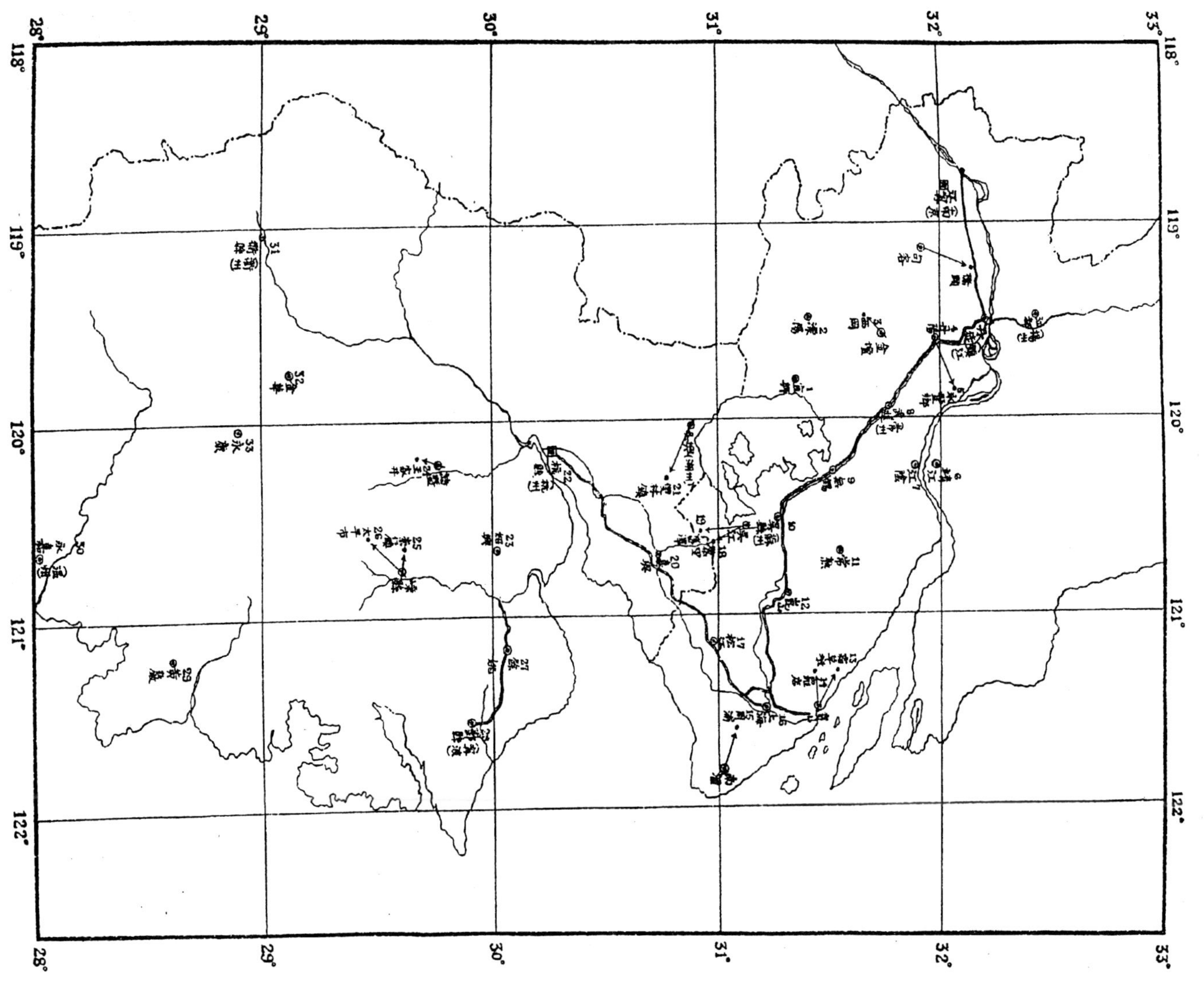

第一圖：調查區域

p,t,k 音。入聲字單讀時除嘉興入聲長讀法
外，其餘的都略帶一點喉部的關閉作用［"耳
處處全有一點，所以第三表中一律省去。但入
不用［"耳朵"］，只作一種短音，例如六是［lo 加
［lo 加"耳朵"加 ko 加"耳朵"］也不是［lokko 加
的"促音"），乃是［loko 加"耳朵"］，第一個字單
讀入聲了。

要元音變得最利害了。本節內只能就其大略
節中把地名全舉出來。

m，ng'兩韻（嘸，五白），都是古音合口字，這類
例如無讀 vu，吾讀 ngu，但在白話就失去了韻
的地方（如崑山）讀成 n 了。魚白字在多數地
作 gniu，yu 的讀法，就是仍照文言讀撮口。

y'韻（試，思）都是從古齊齒韻來的，現在多數
了。但在波，黃，康，溫有一部分字讀齊齒的。
皮，衢一部分字讀成略圓唇的元音，在開撮之
地方分得出知茲，痴雌，但能分這個的就往往
所以跟國語不同。

el'韻（而，耳文）大概是從官話影響而來的文
讀法見第二表 9 頁'i'）。這韻的音值很不一
舌元音，但過半數仍是以 l 邊聲爲主音，所以

就是聲化韻了，它的最清楚的代表是杭州。

第二表 6 頁的‘u’韻(夫，符)，就是‘f，v’聲母碰到了‘u’韻的時候，嘴唇懶得更動位置，就一直保存聲母的唇齒相接的狀態，不再改成‘u’韻所需的兩唇相對的狀態，所以韻母也成了一個 v 音了。這個跟國語也是一樣的。

以上四種可以算是聲化韻母，雖然前三個算開口韻，第四個算合口韻，嚴格説起來可以算是“不列等”的。

第二表 1—2 頁上‘o，a，ai，ei’四韻(巴，敗，來，類)的分類很參差，所以這兩張表上頭没有一條縱線可以從頭畫到底的。粗略説起來‘o’是國音的 a，‘a’跟‘ai’是國音的 ai，‘ei’是國音的 ei。這些音在吴語大都是單元音，用真 ai，ei 複合元音的甚少。

第二表 2 頁‘au’韻(高，老)的分類很整齊。它的音值在過半數的地方也是有單音化的傾向。在江蘇吴語的西半，這個韻的-u 尾變成不圓唇的後元音。

第二表 3 頁‘ou’韻(走，歐)的分類也是很規則的。它的音值可是無奇不有，其中有一大派是用 é，ei 那類的音的，這一派讀法的範圍彷彿在運河的流域似的。

第二表 3 頁‘an’韻(三，班)的分類也很整齊。它的音值大概總是一個單純的前元音 e，ä 之類，而且不定帶半鼻音。

第二表 3 頁‘on’韻(半，南)在國語本大致作 an，在吴語就跟着聲母變，規則甚複雜。它的元音比‘an’當中的元音大都高一點，而且常常帶圓唇。

第二表 4 頁‘en’韻(根，能)的最普通的元音是[倒寫 e]，但常常略偏前一點。

第二表 5 頁‘ang’(桑)與‘áng’(生白)差不多處處能辨,‘ang’的元音後一點‘áng’的元音前一點。

第二表 5 頁‘ong’韻(公,風)的元音最多是用一種特別窄唇的 o,聽起來像一種 u 音,但舌根並不很高,因爲兩唇接近,所以覺得聲音暗。

第二表 6 頁‘u’,‘ù’兩韻(孤,戈)在有些地方跟着古音分的(例如:丹永,嵊),在有些地方跟着聲母變的(例如蘇),所以分起來很參差。它的音值,有的全用 u,有的用一個開口元音起頭,讀成不圓唇的 ou 的意味。

第二表 7—8 頁其餘的合口韻的主要元音跟它們的開口式差不多一樣,例如‘an’是讀 ä 的,那末‘uan’就讀 uä。就是在有幾處,‘en’韻裡頭的[倒寫 e]在開口時元音略偏前,在‘uen’就不偏前了。

第二表 9 頁‘i’韻(衣,西)大都是很緊的一個 i 音,有幾處舌尖伸前而得一種 iz 音,也有地方舌不向前而讀音發生一點摩擦得 ij 音。

同頁上‘io,ia,iai’韻(靴,家文,皆)的分類跟音值的參差大致跟開口一樣。

第二表 10 頁‘iau,iou’韻(小,九)的主要元音也跟開口‘au,ou’差不多。但在‘ou’讀 ei 音的地方,‘iou’或者變開口讀 ei(如常樓 lei,劉 lei),或改韻讀 iou(如陰樓 lei,但劉 liou),没有讀 iei 的。

同頁‘ien’韻(天,咸文)元音與‘an’不發生什末密切關係。它的最普通的音值是一種略開略向後的 i 音。不過在有些地方有一部分字讀如‘an’的齊齒。

第二表 11 頁‘in’韻(心,令)的元音都是一種 i 音,但遇到‘g,h’系的時候(金)在有些地方 i 音被吸入顎化的聲母而韻的元音變成 é 或 e(如蘇銀 gnen)。

同頁跟第二表 12 頁的‘iàng,iang,iong’韻(江文,薑,庸)的元音跟它們的開口韻‘ang,áng,ong’的元音一樣。

第二表 12—13 頁‘iu’韻(居,虛)最普通的就是普通的[y]音,但有的地方加一點摩擦,有地方微帶舌尖作用。但‘iu_7’(朱)在有些地方用 ÿ,另成一韻。

第二表 13 頁‘iuei’韻(吹文,税)的主要元音跟開口‘ei’差不多,但有些地方,撮口的介母雖失去而它的痕跡留在元音的變性中,例如上海吹文音 tsö。

同頁‘iuon’韻(玄,捐)的撮口程度甚小,在好些地方不過是有一個微圓唇的 i 韻頭。但是主要元音是跟‘on’韻相近而不跟‘an’相近。在‘tz’系大都變成齊齒,就跟‘ien’一樣的讀法了,例如上海全‘ziuon’讀如錢 zien。

同頁‘iuin’韻(君,云)的代表音是[yin]而不是北京派的[yn]。除這種讀法之外就是仿‘en,in,iong’的讀法了。

入聲韻的元音不完全與平上去相當,總類數也較少,所以得另外分開來講。

第三表 1 頁‘oq’韻(谷,各)多數地方只有一種 o 音,能分開 o 跟闢 o 的,如熟,寶,姚之類也不全依同一的法則,它的條件一半看是什末古韻,而一半又看是什末聲母。金華用一種 e 音,最特別。永康鐸覺韻用 au,跟國語白話音相近,別的没有用複合元音的(介母不算)。

從'oq'以下一直到第三表3頁終,分類的縱線没有一條可以從頭畫到底的。分的最細的,例如浦東,客白,掐白,渴,磕,刻(a,ä,ö,é,e)都不同的。分的最媽呼的,比方甯波,一律讀成一種ä音。但是大多的地方居兩種極端的當中。音值上面,凡古開口者現在也不外乎些不圓唇的單元音,古合口的有時候有一點o,u那類的音;除介母不計,用複合元音的只有温州跟永康。永康的麥,黑等字用ai,ei音,跟北方白話音一樣,但這種變化有自變的可能,未必有歷史的影響。

第三表3—4頁合口韻比開口簡單些。'uoq'不跟'uaq,ueq'混,但'uaq,ueq'中間有些末韻字很有趣。括豁闊活四字除掉衢,華,康三處把它們一樣看待外,其餘的差不多總是拿括豁當'uaq'類,闊活當'ueq'類。

第三表5頁齊齒韻'ioq'(菊)的韻音没有什末特别,可以跟開口參考。

第三表6—7頁'iq'韻(立,力)的元音大概是有i,ie兩種,但分法有的是跟着聲母變的,例如上海'g,h'系的一部分用ie,其餘用i;有的是要看什末古韻,例如松江(看第三表7頁)。音值用真i的很少,多數地方念成一種[ɪ]音。遇到'j_1'系聲母變開口é,e之類,在講韻頭時已經講過了。

第三表8頁'iueq'韻(屈,説)的元音大半不是用一種e就是用一種ö。有些字改用開口齊齒的那又當别論。

第三章　吴語聲調

凡　例

下列第四表(共兩頁)是吴語聲調的分類跟音值表。

表第一行是古音的平上去入。因爲現在還没有人知道古音聲調的音值,所以只好寫四個類名。

第二行是古聲紐的清濁。聲調的變化與聲母的發音部位全無關係,而與發音方法最有關係,所以這一行差不多就是充分條件了。

第三行是今吴語調類的名稱,有幾格各處不一致的就只寫“見下”。

第四行是例字。

第五行是國語的聲調,入聲都分配在陰平,陽平,賞聲,去聲裡頭去了。國語四聲的音值大略是高微降,中升,低長尾升,高降至低。

表正文每格註類名,聲調線,跟音樂簡譜。這些材料的原來記録大半是照音管所定的絶對音高用有長短的音樂符號寫在調查方式的五線譜上的。但是字調的絶對音高往往跟着人的嗓子,跟臨時的精神變的,這種變化於字在語音上的地位不發生意義的,所以要做比較的時候,得要取發音者當時平均的音高做水平線來量他字調的相對音高。有一樣難處是讀者假如前後不是在同等的精神,假如不一貫,所讀出來的就會不在同一個調(key),那就取平均音高也没有用了。這次所得的江陰跟松江的材料就有點這個毛病。

還有一層是非但絶對音高,連音程(interval)的絶對大小,也看發音者的精神跟脾氣變的。高興的時候或是不怕難爲情的人容易用大一點的音程不起勁或是怕難爲情的時候就會把音程減小(曲線上下擠扁)。關於這層暫時没有想到好法子把材料改成一致的。

總看起來總算是還比較得起來。

長短音除入聲差不多全是特短外,其餘的没有很辨長短。

圖的畫法是這末樣的:先取某處的五線譜的記録,(例如蘇州)取它的最低音(小 f♯)跟最高音(中 c♯)的中點(a 或 a♯)于是乎把這個中點一律叫它做 *do* 或是 *mi* 或是 *sol*。從許多例統計起來,最便利的叫法是管這個中點叫做 *me*(3^b)或是 *ri*($2^♯$)。假如從最低音到最高音當中的半音數是雙數的(例如蘇州 f♯ 到 c♯ 是一共八個半音(bageh bann－in)),那就看大部分的音偏向於哪部分多,就取兩個中音的偏向於那一邊的爲中點(例如蘇州取 a 而不取 a♯)。取定中點爲 3^b 之後,那其餘的 1,2,3,4 簡譜就都可以定了。例如蘇州的陽平是 f♯ b,前音略長,後音略短,那末 a 既然是 3^b,當然 f♯ 就是 1,b 就是 4,所以得相對聲調 1$\underline{4}$。

曲線的畫法是先畫一根横線作爲平均音高,它的音高值就算

是 3^b。横標裡頭(abscissa)就是時間,竪標(ordinate)就算高音,横竪的比例因爲單位的性質不同,本來没有關係,只取其便,只要大多數曲線畫得不太平也不太陡就行了。

曲線局部的長短比例不能很準確,因爲記音的時候也不過是大略以意爲之,或者應該説"以耳爲之",所以畫的時候只要大略表示出各部相對的長短就行了。大概是一個不變的音就用平線(當然略),兩個一様長的音用直斜線,一長一短用平斜折線,三音一様長的用兩段折線,中點在第二個音(三個八分音符上加弧線是表示全長等于四分音的意思,照樂譜寫法弧線下應該寫一個斜體 3 字,現在一律省去),三個音長短不一様的也大略照比例略示不同。聲調的實在曲線本來是漸變的彎線,本來不能用音樂的符號來表示,但是在耳聽記載法跟教學法上最合實用的還是音樂符號,表中所畫的線既有斜度(漸變)已經不合音樂符號所表示的音,所以只能算從五線譜記録推測出來的曲線形狀就是了。

各地每調叫什末名稱大半是没有問題的,不過有時候也得有一點斟酌。比方蘇州的古上去濁母都併作一種讀法,例如有白,右同音,那末倒底還是説陽上(有白)變陽去(右)還是説陽去變陽上呐?單是就蘇州一處論,那就無從解答,兩種説法都對的。假如説看它的聲調音值究竟"是"上還"是"去,那完全是外行話。咱們軋根兒就不知道古調的音值,無從比較起頭,所以不能説像古音上爲上,像古音去爲去。要是拿現在的調查來比罷,那是一處一個様子。不要説天津,重慶的上去音值剛剛掉個"個兒",就是在吴語裡,常熟跟紹興的陽上去就差不多相反。跟諸暨比起來更無從説起,因爲連曲線形狀都根本改變了。調類的定名只有以類比類是有意義的。比方蘇州陽上去的名稱不能定，可以拿别處的歸類法比較。在好些别的地方有陽上的全濁跟陽去同調而陽上的次濁不與陽去混，這些地方當然可以算是陽上一部分“變陽去”的例。但陽去全部變陽上的簡直没有這種地方，所以不論音值上怎末樣，蘇州的陽上算是變陽去。

表的右邊三行表示調類的總數，*do* 的絕對音高，跟發音者的嗓子是成年的男人，男孩，還是女人的嗓子。

第四表：聲調表　　（第四表 1）

聲調／方言：縣名	區域	派別	例字	平：清	平：濁：次濁	平：濁：全濁（文/白）	上：清：全清	上：清：次清	上：濁：次濁文	上：濁：次濁白	上：濁：全濁
古四聲				平			上				
分合條件				清	濁：次濁	濁：全濁（文/白）	清：全清	清：次清	濁：次濁文	濁：次濁白	濁：全濁
今吳音聲調類				陰平	陽平		陰上		陽上（見下）	陽上（見下）	陽上（見下）
例字				江天	來名	同前	懂好	土草	也文永文	有白老	是稻
今國音聲調類			國	陰平	陽平		賞				去
1.宜興	城內		宜	陰平 4	陽平 $2^{\flat}4$		陰上 42		=陰平；=陽上	陽上 $24^{\sharp}$	
2.溧陽	城內		溧	陰平 54	陽平 $3^{\flat}72^{\flat}$		陰上 45，54		陽上 45		
3.金壇	西岡		壇西	陰平 $3^{\flat}4$	陽平 $24^{\sharp}$，17		陰上 24？		陽上 $3^{\flat}1$		=陽去？
4.丹陽	城內		丹	平 $2^{\flat}1$		=去？	陰上 $44^{\sharp}$			=陽去	
5.丹陽	永豐鄉		丹永	平 $2^{\flat}1$			陰上 $1^{\sharp}4$				=陽去
6.靖江	城內		靖	陰平 $3^{\flat}2^{\flat}5^{\flat}$	陽平 13		陰上 $24^{\sharp}$				=陽去
7.江陰	城內		陰	陰平 $5^{\sharp}2^{\sharp}$	陽平 452		陰上 $6^{\sharp}7$（讀音太重）				=陽去
8.武進	城內	"紳談" "街談"	常紳 常街	陰平 4	陽平 73		陰上 5 陰上 35			=陽平	=陽去
9.無錫	城內		錫	陰平 $53^{\flat}$	陽平 $13^{\flat}$		陰上 $2^{\flat}2^{\flat}3^{\flat}$		=陰上；=陰平	陽上 $2^{\flat}3^{\flat}2$	
10.吳縣	城內		蘇	陰平 $44^{\sharp}$	陽平 14		陰上 $41^{\sharp}$		=陰上，=陽去	=陽去	
11.常熟	城內		熟	陰平 51	陽平 12		陰上 $2^{\sharp}2$			陽上 $2^{\flat}7$	
12.崑山	城內		崑	陰平 $2^{\sharp}32^{\sharp}$	陽平 $1^{\sharp}3^{\flat}2$		陰上 $53^{\flat}$		=陰上；=陽上	陽上 $2^{\flat}1$	

13. 14. 富山	⊕霜草墩 ⊕羅店		富(霜)(羅)	陰平 53	陽平 $^{2}31$	陰上 $^{4}35$		=陰上; =陽去	=陽去	
15. 南滙	⊕周浦		浦(東)	陰平 $4^{\sharp}1^{\sharp}$	陽平 14	陰上 $^{4}35$		—	陽上 $^{3b}23$	
16. 上海	城内		上	陰平 41	陽平 13^{b}	陰上 $3^{b}2^{b2}$		=陰上; =陽去	=陽去	
17. 松江	城内		松	陰平 $6^{b}2$	陽平 $13^{b}7$	陰上 432		=陰上; =陽上	陽上 $^{7b}67$	=陽去
18. 吳江	⊕黎里		吳(黎)	陰平 4	陽平 $2^{b}3^{b}2^{b}$	陰上 $4^{\sharp}1^{\sharp}$			陽上 $23^{b}24$	
19. 吳江	⊕盛澤		吳(盛)	陰平 42	陽平 $^{2}31^{\sharp}$	全陰上 51	次陰上 $1^{\sharp}2$	=全陰上 =陽上	陽上 $^{2b}12^{b}$	
20. 嘉興	城内		嘉(興)	陰平 $5^{b}7$	陽平 $12^{b}7$	全陰上 $5^{\sharp}7^{2}$	次陰上 75^{b}	陽上 171		
21. 吳興	⊕雙林鎮		湖(雙)	陰平 $32^{\sharp}$	陽平 $14^{\sharp}$	陰上 $51^{\sharp}$			陽上 $231^{\sharp}$	
22. 杭縣	城内		杭	陰平 $2^{\sharp}1^{\sharp}2$	陽平 $^{\sharp}11^{\sharp}$	陰上 51				=陽去
23. 紹興	城内		紹	陰平 37	陽平 $^{\sharp}27$	陰上 $^{2}13$		陽上 13^{b}		
24. 諸暨	⊕王家井		諸(王)	陰平 $3^{b}1$	陽平 $23^{(1\sharp)}$	陰上 $4^{\sharp}1^{\sharp}$		陽上 $2^{\sharp}31^{\sharp}$		
25. 26. 嵊縣	⊕崇仁鎮 ⊕太平市		嵊(崇)(太)	陰平 53	陽平 $5^{b}13$	陰上 5^{3b}		—	陽上 $23^{b}24$	
27. 餘姚	城内		姚	陰平 $3^{b}4$	陽平 24, $^{\sharp}21$	陰上 435		=陽去		
28. 鄞縣	城内		波	陰平 51	陽平 $241^{\sharp}$	陰上 $54^{\sharp}6^{b}$		=陽去?		=陽去?
29. 黃巖	城内		黃	陰平 324	陽平 212	陰上 $4^{\sharp}24$				陽上 212
30. 永嘉	城内		溫	陰平 $4^{4\sharp}$	陽平 $^{3}41^{\sharp}$	陰上 53^{b}		陽上 241		
31. 衢縣	城内		衢	陰平 $45^{b}5$	陽平 271	陰上 45		=陰去		陽上 $3^{b}5$
32. 金華	城内		華	陰平 2	陽平 $1^{\sharp}72$	陰上 434		—	陽上 42^{3}	
33. 永康	城内		康	陰平 52	陽平 $^{3b}7$	陰上 $^{4}3^{b}4$		陽上 $^{3b}2^{b}4$		

（第四表2）

古	去					入				調類總數	原調絕對音高	發音者資格
條件	清 全清	清 次清	濁 喻匣一部分	濁 其餘濁 全濁	濁 其餘濁 次濁	清 全清	清 次清	濁 次濁匣母	濁 其餘全濁			
吳	陰去 全陰去	陰去 次陰去	(見下)	陽去	陽去	陰入 全陰入	陰入 次陰入	(見下)	陽入			
例	對呌	去太	様換	事大	夢外	不各	脫出	六學	白石			
國	去					冷僻字；普通字文：去多数 普通字白：陰平，陽平；上；去.		去多数	陽平多数	4	一	一
1.宜	陰去 $3^{b}24^{\#}$		陽去 21			陰入 4		陽入 $3^{b}4$		8	1=F#	成
2.溧	陰去 $42^{b}3^{b}$		陽去 $3^{b}7$			陰入 4	=陽入	陽入 $1^{\#}2^{\#}$		8	未記	成
3.壇西	陰去 $3^{b}24$		=陰上？			陰入 5		陽入 $3^{b}2$		7？	1=F#	成
4.丹	陰去 $1^{\#}3$		陽去 $1^{\#}3$			入 5^{b}或$1^{\#}3$				5?	1=f#	女
5.丹永	去? 24 ?=?		陽去 $34^{\#}$			陰入 $4^{\#}$		陽入 $34^{\#}$		5?6?	1=C	成
6.靖	陰去 $34^{\#}2$		陽去 $3^{b}42^{\#}$			陰入 $4^{\#}$		陽入 23		7	1=F	成
7.陰	陰去 $6^{b}57^{b}$		陽去 $54^{\#}7^{b}$			陰入 2		陽入 $5^{\#}7^{b}$		7	1=A♭	成
8.常紳街	陰去 $51^{\#}2^{\#}$		陽去 24			陰入 5		陽入 24		7	1=F	成
9.錫	陰去 $3^{b}4$		陽去 $2^{b}73^{b}$			陰入 4		陽入 $1^{\#}4$		8	未記	成
10.蘇	陰去 $51^{\#}2^{\#}$		陽去 $41^{\#}$			陰入 $4^{\#}$		陽入 $2^{\#}3$		7	1=f#	女
11.熟	陰去 $3^{b}24$		陽去 $2^{\#}13$			陰入 4		陽入 $1^{\#}2^{\#}$		8	1=G#	童
12.崑	陰去 $2^{\#}1^{\#}3$		陽去 $21^{\#}2$			陰入 4		陽入 $1^{\#}2$		6?7?8	1=F#	成

	阴去	阳去	阴入	阳入			
13.14.寶	陰去 ═ 44#	陽去 ²1#4	陰入 ═ 44#	陽入 3b5	7	1=F#	成
15.浦東	陰去 25	陽去 3b5	陰入 ═ 4	陽入 23	8	1=G	成
16.上	陰去 ²2b3	陽去 13b	陰入 ═ 4#	陽入 23	7(6)	未記	成
17.松	陰去 135	陽去 62	陰入 4# 5#	陽入 71	8,9?	1=c	成
18.吴	全陰去 513；次陰去 21#3	=全陰去；陽去 73b	全陰入 6b；次陰入 45	陽入 2#3	10	1=f#	女
19.吴	全陰去 412；次陰去 ²13b	=全陰去；陽去 13b	陰入 ═ 4	陽入 23	10	1=e	童
20.嘉	陰去 21#3b	陽去 73b	陰入 3. 4#71	陽入 171	9	1=f#	女
21.湖	陰去 3b24	陽去 3b4	陰入 ═ 4	陽入 2#3	8	1=c#	童
22.杭	陰去 2#	陽去 1#2#	陰入 ═ 5	陽入 12	7	1=f	女
23.紹	陰去 3b2	陽去 2(1#)	陰入 3#b3	陽入 3b4	8	1=f#	童
24.諸	陰去? 21(=陰平)	陽去 2#31#2	陰入 ═ 4	陽入 1#2#	7,8?	1=eb	成
25.26.嵊	陰去 ³2#4	陽去 1#4#	陰入 3b4	陽入 1#2#	8	未記	成
27.姚	陰去 123, 3b2b	陽去 13b	陰入 ═ 4	陽入 34#	7	1=F#	成
28.波	陰去 32#3	陽去 72	陰入 ═ 5	陽入 2#3	7,8?	1=A	成
29.黄	陰去 ═ 5	陽去 1#5	陰入 ═ 4	陽入 1#2#	8	1=G	成
30.温	陰去 41	陽去 2b13b	陰入 32#4#	=陽去	7	1=e	女
31.衢	陰去 54	陽去 3b2；=陽上	陰入 ═ 4	陽入 1#2#	8	未記	成
32.華	陰去 51#	陽去 2b3b7	陰入 3	陽入 1#71#	8	1=F	成
33.處	陰去 54#	陽去 1#5	陰入 =陰上?	陽入 =陽上?	6,8?	未記	成

聲調的討論

吴語的聲調大致有兩派。一派平上去入看聲母的清濁各有陰陽兩類，一共八聲；一派把陽上歸入陽去，只有七聲。

陰陽平兩類的分法最整齊。除丹，丹永只有一種平聲外其餘都是一樣的分兩類。陰平的音值降的多，升的少。陰平跟下字相連起來，在江蘇是先高後低的多，在浙江是先低後高的多。（但從單字聲調上推測不出來這種傾向）。陽平的音值大多數是低升，或低高低。

上聲的清音字都是陰上。但吴盛跟嘉興次清字又分出一類，共有兩種陰上。上聲次濁字文言音在江蘇往往讀成陰平或陰上，因此喻母字，也念的像影母字念法。在浙江没有遇到這種例。上聲次濁大都成陽上一類，但在丹永，靖，陰，常街也併入陰上。上聲全濁在宜，溧，錫，熟，崑，浦東，吴黎，吴盛，嘉興，湖雙，紹，諸王，嵊，黄，温，衢，康是陽上，在其餘的變陽去。但有一層要注意的是全濁字陽上陽去之分不是全跟古上去一樣的，大概有三分之一的字剛剛跟古上去相反，所以叫它做上叫它做去是看大多數的傾向，而且上述的各地對於某字屬上某字屬去也不一致的。衢州的上聲次濁全併入陰去是很特别的。上聲的音值没有什末一致的傾向，至於陰陽上的比較末，陰上大概總是比陽上高一點。

去聲清音字都成陰去，濁音字都成陽去，這兩類是很清楚的。不過吴黎，吴盛又把清音依全清次清的區别分作兩類。這兩處的喻匣母一部分又歸入全清去裡去，音值上頭是陰去比陽去大都高一點。

入聲清音字都成陰入，濁音字都成陽入。但溧陽的次清字也歸陽入，丹陽不分陰陽入，吴黎次清另成一種陰入，嘉興，湖雙次濁歸陽入，外人形容嘉興人説“六塊肉”的聲音就是因爲六肉讀陰入。温州的陽入跟陽去一樣，因爲它的音很長，所以算它併入陽去。入聲的音值倒很一致，陰入大都是一個高而短的平音，陽入大都是一個低而短的升音。不讀極短音者有嘉興的陽入，它的陰入第二式，金華的陽入，跟温州的陰入。温州的陽入變陽去，陰入雖不是短音，但不跟任何平上去相同，而自成一類，所以仍叫它陰入，彷彿長沙的入聲字雖不短促，而仍舊自成一類，所以還是入聲。

各調的陰陽比較起來，除掉前者較後者略高之外，曲線的形狀陽調比陰調也較複雜一點。這大概是因爲發聲母時濁音影響聲帶的狀態，因而使音高的變化複雜一點。

第四章　聲韻調總討論

各地的特點

溧. ‘n’母中有字讀 l。‘$on_{3,5}$’（酸，蠶）讀撮口（shiuo，zhiuo）。入聲次清字（鐵，策）歸陽入。

壇西. ‘n’母全歸‘l’。‘$on_{3,5}$’（酸，蠶）讀撮口。‘iang’（涼，張）讀 ie，ä（lie，tzä）。

丹. 並定羣等全濁母平聲字有文白兩種音，文言近官話，白話近其餘的吳音。‘h(u)’不變 f，但‘w’變 v（影母合口也用 v）。‘on’韻（看，南，安）用 ung，有輔音性韻尾。‘iang’韻（良，張）讀 ie，ä（如壇西）。‘iuon’跟‘iou’混（捐＝鳩，遠＝有）。平聲似不分陰陽，入聲不分陰陽。

丹永. ‘zh，z’母讀音幾乎全不帶音（純用 s），後略加[彎頭 h]。‘o，a，ai’（沙，敗，海）只分兩類，分法與國語 a，ai 分法相近。前者的音值是（倒寫草體 a）。‘$on_{3,5}$’（酸，蠶）讀撮口。平聲不分陰陽。

靖. ‘$v_{4,6}$’微母文言上聲（尾，武）讀 f，‘$zh_{3,6}$’日母文言上聲（忍，乳）讀 s，sh[平鈎 c]。‘$iang_{1-2}$’與‘ien’同音（央＝煙，良＝

連),上聲分類仿國語辦法。

陰. ‘$v_{4,6}$’微母文言上聲(尾,武)讀 f,‘$zh_{3,6}$’日母文言上聲(忍,乳)讀 s,sh[平鈎 c]。‘$a_{3,5}$’(街白,敗白,泰白)不讀 a 而讀 ä。‘uon’多數人讀開口 ö(官＝干)。上聲分類仿國語辦法。陽去字跟下字相連時(被頭,電話)有一種特別的“江陰腔”。

常. 有些開齊字(猜,尋,蒼蠅)讀合撮。聲調分紳談,鄉談截然不同的兩派。紳談陽上白話變陽平(我白＝鵝),文言變高平的陰上。街談上聲一律讀中升的陰上(近江陰),其餘聲調單讀時雖一樣,連起來也不同;兩字相連,第一字是陽平(黄佬)的時候,紳談第一字低平,街談第一字往往變中升。第一字陰去(睏來)的時候,紳談第一字往往高平,街談第一字降,跟去聲單字讀法一樣。

錫. ‘y’母(有,摇)讀法摩擦極多,前半也不全帶音。‘z’母(尋,遂)差不多全讀 dz。‘o_{3-6},a_1,uo,u_{4-6}’都不分(家白＝瓜＝姑)。‘u,ù’韻大部分字讀一種不圓唇的 ou 音[倒 v 加 8 字上口開],所以有的無錫人讀注音字母ㄅㄆㄇㄈ爲ㄅㄡ,ㄆㄡ,ㄇㄡ,ㄈㄡ。但‘f,v’母‘u’韻仍讀(唇齒性的)u 音,外人學無錫人讀無作 vöu 是不對的。陰上字(好,走)聲調特别。陰平字單讀時不特别,兩字相連上字是陰平時(香山,標標),兩字的全調類似一個上聲字,也成平常所謂無錫腔。

蘇. ‘j’系字(張,穿,船)老年人大都能跟‘tz’系字辨。講究唱曲的也辨得很清。年輕人只有少數能辨。‘au’韻字(好,俏)女人多數用 ä,男人用近似 ä 略偏後的音。這是一個外頭人特别注意的音。‘a’韻幾乎成開 o,與南京一樣。‘ai,ei,an’

全同韻(來＝雷＝蘭)。‘u,ù’韻‘b’系字大半念 u,其餘的 u 音前加一個 e[倒寫 e],也是蘇州味兒的音。陰去是特別蘇州調。

熟. ‘j’系讀舌尖後[北京派]音,它的‘zh’母裡又有破裂摩擦音,別的地方不是缺那樣就是缺這樣,所以只有常熟一處兼有兩點而成一種 dj 音[d 加暨鉤 z 吐氣](成,傳)。‘o,uo,u’一部分合併(暇＝花＝呼)。‘on_{6-8}’併入‘en’(南＝能,庵＝恩)。‘oq_{2-4}’(谷),‘eq_{1-5}’(渴)讀一種 uq 音。陰平聲調有一點特別。聲調分類極整齊,陰陽平上去入八類差不多恰恰是古清濁母的平上去入。(就是上聲次濁文言讀陰上)。

崑. ‘iou’併入‘ien’(劉＝連,九＝簡)。

寶. ‘o_{2-6}’(啞,茶),‘on_{2-5}’(安,看)讀成一種不圓唇的 ou 音[倒寫 v 加 8 字上開口]。‘ei’(梅),‘ou’(謀)讀成[倒 v 加大寫 i]。

浦. ‘b,d’母(飽,東)用真帶音的[b,d]音,因爲是陰調,所以聽起來好像不“濁”。‘h(u)’,‘f’(荒,方)常混。‘w’,‘v’(胡,無)常混。‘$o_{2,5}$’讀齊齒,與‘iau’混(捨白＝小,沙＝消)。聲調分類甚規則。入聲的主要元音最富,共有八種,哭殼客白掐磕刻渴(o,ò,a,ä,é,e,ö)七字全不同音。

上. 有新舊派,新派分類近似蘇州,舊派近似浦東,(兩派人以“蘇州音”,“浦東音”互相指斥),但許多人攙雜兩種。舊派來＝雷≠蘭,新派雷≠來＝蘭。舊派‘on’(暖,南)有的字讀 é 有的讀 ö,新派一律作 ö,舊派‘h(u),f’常混(忽＝拂),‘w,v’常混(王＝房),新派不大混。舊派分兩種 oq(各,谷),新派不分。兩派陽平上去單讀時都不分(陽＝養＝樣),在詞句中陽平跟上去不同。(按本書中所謂舊派恐怕已經是混合派,真正的舊派,大概還能辨全濁上去,'b,d'兩母用真濁音,等等)。

松. 'b,d'兩母(飽,東)跟浦東一樣。富于雙唇摩擦音[phi,beta]。'áng,iang'韻字(硬白,陽)的元音舌位比一般的讀法高的多,是[半鼻音的草體大寫 e]。入聲清音'iq'韻字似較其餘清音入聲字高一個整音。

吴黎. 'a'韻(家白敗白)極'暗',跟蘇州南京一樣。'au'幾乎是單純的中性 a 音(比較比較英國 Cockney 音把英文 *out* 的 au 音讀成 a)。'ou'韻齊齒(侯＝油)。'ai,ei,an'(來,雷,蘭)與蘇州同。有三種去聲,三種入聲一共十聲。

吴盛. 'ng'母開口變'hh'(眼白＝咸白)。'ai,ei,an'與黎里一樣。'ou'也變齊齒。'uang'韻一律開口(王＝杭,光＝剛)。有三種上聲,三種去聲,一共十聲。

嘉興. 'ng'母開口變'hh'(眼白＝咸白)。'uang'韻一律開口(王＝杭,光＝剛)有三種上聲,一共九聲。陰入有長短兩種讀法,陽入音曲長。入聲次濁跟匣母字都歸陰入,所以外人聽嘉興人說"六塊肉"的聲音特別。嘉興的陽平音值,'ou'韻跟'on'韻的音值近似常熟,所以乍聽嘉興音有點像常熟音。

湖雙. 'an,on'(難,南)全併爲 é,這次所研究的别處吴語没有這樣的。'ang'(康)元音甚高,用一種開 o 的半鼻音。'uei'韻用[u 加倒寫 m 加横杠 i]。'uang'大半開口(光＝剛,但王≠杭)。没有撮口韻母(居=基,玄=嫌,決=結)。入聲没有類似 o 的音。入聲次濁跟匣母都歸陰入。

杭. 别處有文白兩讀的字(家,間,交,江,櫻,角,甲,耳等等),在杭州大都一律取文派的音,白話中取白派音的字甚少。'y'母的喻匣似有一點區别,但不敢決定。'tz'系的齊撮字(先,須)有少數人用舌尖音,多數人用北京派的顎化音,但仍舊不跟'g'系齊撮(掀,虚)混。'uan'韻併入'uon'(關=官)。上聲仿官話辦法,但俟,士,市,柿,是,似,已另成陽上,音值極像陽去。

杭州'ou,on,ien,ang'(歐,安,煙,剛)韻的音值跟常州音很相近,而不用白派的讀音,所以杭州人説話頗有點像常州人讀國語白話文。

紹. 'a'韻用[a]。'en'韻的讀音跟分法很複雜,能辨'$in_{8,9}$'跟'$in_{10,11}$'(陳,程)。富於半鼻音韻音。'gnien'字韻音在平上(年,輦)用半鼻音的 i,但在去聲(驗,念)必讀開了用 iä 帶半鼻音。四聲全憑古清濁分陰陽,比常熟還更規則。

紹興,甯波等處有一種階級叫"墮民",前清時不許入場考試,清末解放過後他們也可以進學堂。紹興的同仁學校是專門爲他們設的。他們的語音跟所在地一般的語音不同,在紹興者名叫"凡音字眼"。但是因爲這種學校的教員都是普通人,所以他們的"凡字眼"也漸漸的失掉了。據普通階級人所説,跟同仁學校學生局部的證明只得到一種發音特别的地方,就是'tz'系齊撮(西,須)不變顎化音(紹興普通音都變,西=希,須=虚)而仍讀舌尖音,如蘇州,上海。有沒有別種特別的地方，沒有調查出來。

諸王. ‘h(u)，f’混(荒＝方)。‘w，v’混(魂＝墳)。‘en，uen，in，iuin’(根，困，丁，巡)(古臻深攝)四韻全用半鼻音，這次所研究的别處吴語没有這樣的。‘en’韻的音跟南京先韻字的韻音相似。陰平陰去好像不分。

姚. ‘z’母齊撮白話併‘y’母(袖＝右)。‘en_{6-7}，uen_{1-2}，$iuin_{1,3}$’(寸，困，君)用 gn 韻尾。‘ang’韻用[半鼻音倒寫 c]，比一般用的元音舌位高。入聲有好些字(谷，突，北)用一種圓唇高混元音[横杠大寫 u]。陽上去併。

波. ‘on_1’韻(半，盤)用半鼻音 u，其餘‘on’都用口音。‘ang’韻用[半鼻音倒寫 c]，比一般用的元音舌位高。‘i，ien’(衣，煙)兩韻有人全分，有人一部分字混。入聲開口只有 o，ä 兩韻；哭，殼都是 oq；客白，掐白，磕，刻，渴都是 äq(cf. 浦東)。陰平陰去不易分。陽平陽去起音低，所以有一種特别“濁重”的“甯波腔”。

黄. 撮口‘g’系不顎化，所以雖然‘iu_6’讀[y]音而居，朱不混。但‘ou，on，eq’韻變齊齒時，‘g，h’系都全顎化了，所以幹＝見，蛤＝劫。祭韻‘j’系(試)讀 i。‘el’韻讀 y 韻[前舌尖韻]。‘iu，iuei’(許，暑，水)一律讀 iu[y](微帶舌尖)。‘ou，iou’(鈎，鳩)雖全變齊齒，但韻音不同，絶不相混。牛白是‘ngou’讀 gnieö，牛文是齊齒‘gniou’讀 gni·u。上聲次濁字(有，老)歸陰上。上聲字單讀時(尤其是陽上)，當中喉頭關一關，作一個[耳朵]音，把字切成兩個音節似的。

温. ‘on’改撮口時‘g，h’系音(干)也全顎化。‘y’韻一部分(支，池）讀 i[上小字大寫 i 加 i]。‘au’韻的豪韻近似無錫‘au’，但與肴韻不混，因爲肴韻近似上海‘au’。其餘的吴語没有能辨豪肴的。‘an’併‘a’（歎＝泰），跟宜，溧一樣。‘$on_{4,5}$，uen_2’一部分讀撮口（安，昏）。‘ang，áng’跟它們的合齊撮（江唐陽，庚耕韻）用純口音的元音[倒寫草體 a，大寫草體 e]全無鼻音。入聲韻有些字用真複合元音 ai 的。陰入不短，陽入併陽去（木＝墓，石＝謝）。

華.　‘b，d’有少數幾個字的白話音（半白，打白）用 m，n（cf. 康）。‘o’韻一部分（家白）讀 uö。‘au，ou’韻音近官話。‘ei，an，on，ù，uo，uan，uon，$ien_{3,11}$，iuon，aq’一部分，uaq，ueq 一部分，幾韻（梅，三，安，多，瓜，千等等）在别處都没有文白之分的，在金華都有文白兩種讀法。

衢.　‘an’韻是半鼻音的[a]，與‘áng’一樣（杏白＝限白）。上次濁歸陰去，去次濁歸陽上。

康.　‘b，d’在口音韻尾的韻（巴，單），讀真帶音的[b，d]，而且音很長，在鼻音韻尾的韻（邦，登）變作 m，n（但聲調方面仍屬陰類）。‘g’系齊撮只半顎化，只到德文 geben，Kiel 的 g，k 的程度，不在很前，也不變破裂摩擦音。‘y’韻（知，試）一部分讀 i。‘a’韻（買，敗）大半變讀 ia。‘au，ou’韻（老，口）複合音甚清楚，近國音。庚耕陌麥韻一律讀 ai。‘ua’（瓜）讀撮口。覺鐸藥韻讀 au，昔職德韻讀 ei，所以古-k 尾字大半變-u，-i 尾。（比較國語白話音）。上入聲調不容易分。

吴語全部的公共點

吴音國音古音的比較當然只能看表才可以知道它們當中確實的關係:現在只能很攏統的説一説,假如有少數幾處不合例的,就不提了。

聲母方面吴音有並定羣澄牀從等濁音平(上)去入皆跟清音有別,合古音分類,不合國音。澄牀禪從邪讀破裂摩擦還是純摩擦,内部不一致,與古音不合,與國音也不合。微日兩母白話用鼻音(近古音),文言用口音(近國語)。見曉系齊撮顎化,去古音遠,跟國音近。但在山庚江那些韻的白話讀音不顎化,跟古音近。n,l不混,跟"上江話"不同。

韻母比國音"高化",例如麻韻古前a,在國音變後a,在吴語變o;歌韻古後a,在中部官話o,在吴音u,或不圓唇的u。複合元音大半變單元音,例如ai,ei,au,ou往往變成ä,é,ò,e,這是去古音很遠的。

'j'系字有一大半地方讀開合,跟國音相近,跟古音不同(因爲'j'系字,除沙,山、齋等類少數字外,都是古音齊撮)。

没有m韻尾,也没有一致辨-n,-ng韻尾的。古山咸攝字往往全失去鼻音。臻深攝字韻尾最容易跟下字起音部位同化。通宕梗攝字的-ng有時讀得不很着實。這幾點跟上江方言差不多,跟北方南方音不同,跟古音更不同。

有入聲而没有-p,-t,-k韻尾。

聲調最普通的是有八聲，或七聲（陽上歸陽去），跟古音近，離國音遠。聲調的區別没有官話清楚，陽平上去尤其易混。

音韻分類上（不是講音值）也有比國音更合古音的（例如打白讀 dáang，鳥白讀 deau），也有不如國音合古音的（例如有幾處秦，尋讀撮口），但通算起來還是吴音的分類跟《切韻》所代表的古音近一點。

從《廣韻》的觀點，來統計吴音一切“不規則”的字音（例如全濁上去對换，牀禪對换，括豁闊活異韻之類），就可以看出來古今音“叔祖姪孫”關係的一班。這個統計還没做出來，本書暫不列入。

吴語範圍的大小要跟着吴語的定義而定的，吴語的定義又是要看跟著哪個點或哪幾個同變的點而定的。現在暫定吴語爲江蘇，浙江當中並定羣等母帶音，或不帶音而有帶音氣流的語言。這樣就包括這次所寫的 33 處方言，不過在這一點上，丹陽要算在邊界上了。定義本來無所謂對不對，只有好不好。將來這一帶的語言調查得更清楚之後，大概還有更好的定義，因而把吴語觀念的範圍也改變了也未可知的。

第二部　吴語

第五章　詞彙

凡例跟索引

吳語詞類的材料甚繁複，現在暫取最常用的詞，還有吳語跟別處特別不同的若干詞，以國語爲綱，列成比較表。還有只一兩處兩三處特有的詞，另外列成各地特別詞的表。

國語註音用國語羅馬字，吳語註音用註音羅馬字（它們的音值見第一章凡例甲表跟第二章凡例乙表），假如是註音類而不註音就用單引號‘　’，例如杭州樓字注音是 lei，註類是‘lou’。

寫詞不能不寫聲調，聲調拼法如下：

平：無號

上：單元音雙寫

韻頭有 u 者改 o，例如廣 goang

韻頭有 i 者改 e，例如兩 l*e*ang

韻尾有 u 者改 o，例如好 ha*o*

韻尾有 i 者改 e，例如海 ha*e*

（以上四條遇 u，o 或 i，e 相連，仍用雙寫法，例如 uo

上聲作 uoo 不寫 oo,以避與 o 上聲相混)

去:韻尾 i,u,n,ng,l 改為 y, w, nn, nq, ll。没有這類韻尾的加一個 h

入:元音後加一個 q

輕聲:在字母前加一點

陰陽調不註。凡是 b, d, g, j, tz, p, t, k, ch, ts, f, h, sh, s, 清音聲母字或不寫聲母的(古影母字或喻匣字改讀陰上陰入等等)都是陰調類。[①] 凡是 bh,dh,gh,dj,dz,v,hh,(y,w),zh,z,m, n,l,ng,gn 濁音聲母字都是陽調類。有次陰去的(例如吴黎)從聲母上也看得出來。假如濁音念陰調的就在聲母後加一撇(國語加 h),例如蠻陰平作 m'an。

詞的漢字寫法是知道字就寫字。不知道字就寫音。寫音的最要緊的條件是以本地字註本地音(聲調也在内),從第一至第四音表上就可以查出來這個詞確實是念甚麽音。切不可用别處的字音來寫本地的詞,那末寫就全無價值了。用漢字註音的時候假如明知道不是那個字,就在旁邊寫一個小"音"字,假如一連幾個字都是音,就在末了寫"皆音"兩個字,假如有幾個詞式(用撇隔開的)都是音就寫"全皆音"。聲調寫"平,上,去,入,輕"字樣。假如所用的字的聲調本來是對的,或是有些方言字向來當輕音字用的,就不必註聲調。

詞的次序是大略照通用的程度。為便於檢查,列一個國語索

① 國語羅馬字遇清音陽平的時候把韻頭 i,u 寫成 y,w,例如平 pyng,黄 hwang,巡 shyun。

引如下：

國語		次第	國語		次第
bahba	爸爸	57	herngsh	横是	74
bairtian	白天	41	hertaur	核桃	63
bu	不	24	howtian	後天	49
chiuhnian	去年	50	igeren	一個人(代.)	10
chyantian	前天	45	jehge	這個	12
daa hachiann	打呵欠	67	jehhoel	這火兒	13
daa shaan	打閃	68	jehlii	這裡	14
deanshin	點心	54	jehme	這麽(程度)	15
deenghoel	等火兒	52	jehme	這麽(方法)	16
-diaw	-掉	34	jeyge	這個	12
dihfang	地方	38	jintian	今天	47
dongshi	東西	37	lea	倆	11
erltz	兒子	59	maashanq	馬上	75
ge	個輕	9	meiyeou	没有(無)	25
geei	給(動.)	35	meiyeou	没有(未)	26
geei	給(介.)	36	mha	媽	58
gen	跟(連.)	30	mingnian	明年	51
gerjy	胳肢	69	mingtian	明天	48
hair	還(副.)	29	naa-ige	哪一個	21
hala	哈辣	70	naal	哪兒	22
hann	和(連.)	30	naalii	哪裡	22
heen	很	27	nahge	那個	17

國語		次第
nahlii	那裡	18
neeige	哪一個	21
neu-erl	女兒	60
neyge	那個	17
nii	你	4
niimen	你們	5
pwutaur	葡萄	64
pyiba	琵琶	65
pyiba	枇杷	66
-shanq	-上	33
sheauharl	小孩兒	61
sheir	誰	20
sherme	甚麽	19
shyifel	媳婦兒	62
shyrhow	時候	39
ta	他	6
tamen	他們	7
tay	太	28
tian	天	44

國語		次第
tsay	菜	71
tzang	髒	72
tzangtuu	髒土	73
tzaochi	早起輕	40
tzao deanshin	早點心	54
tzaofann	早飯	55
tzarmen	咱們	3
tzay	在	31
tzaynall	在那兒	32
tzeeme	怎末	23
tzwotian	昨天	46
tzyhjii	自己	8
woan	晚	53
woanfann	晚飯	56
woanshanq	晚上(晚飯後)	42
woanshanq	晚上(夜間)	43
woo	我	1
woomen	我們	2

第五表:30處75詞的詞彙

國	1. woo 我	2. woomen 我們	3. tzarmen 咱們
宜	nguu 我	nguudoq 我篤音	
溧			
壇西			
丹	ng'oou 我	ng'oudji 我齊音	
靖	ng'oou 我	ng'oumen 我們	
陰	ng'oou 我	ng'oouga 我家白	hää-gn'ii 喊音你,ng'oou ||我||
常紳	ngou 俄音(cf.第四表1)	ngougo 俄音家白	haq・gni 哈音你輕,|| go 哈音你輕家白
常街	ng'oou 我文	ng'oougo 我文家白	haq・gni 哈音你輕,|| go 哈音你輕家白
錫	ngoou 我	ngooulii 我俚	nan・gni 難音你輕
蘇	ngow 餓音,now 怒音,少,ngh 五白音,更少	gnih 伲去音	
熟	ngoou 我	ngooulii 我俚	
崑	ngoou 我	ngooulii 我俚	
寶	nguu 我,nng 五白音	nng-ni 五白㇋	
浦	nguu 我	gnii 伲上音	
上	nguu 我,aqlaq 阿辣皆音,甚少	gnii 伲上音,nguu・gnii 我伲輕音	
松	n-nong 唔儂皆音	n・na 唔平音那輕音	

國	1. woo 我	2. woomen 我們	3. tzarmen 咱們
吴黎	nng・nou 五白音奴輕音	nng-gnii 五白伲輕皆音	同左，又 nngta 五白音他文音(＝'我與你')
吴盛	nng・nou 吾白音奴輕(續下)	nng•gni 五白伲輕皆音	nng•li 五白俚輕皆音(續下)
嘉興	nng 五白音，nng・nou 五白奴輕皆音	nng・nga 五白牙輕皆音	
杭	ng'òò('ngao')傚陰上音	ng'òòmen 我白們	
紹	ngoo 我，ngooloq 我落音	ngaalaq ㄫㄚ上辣音	
諸王	ngoou 我	ngaabä ㄫㄚ上班音	
嵊崇太	ngoa 我白	ngaalaq ㄫㄚ上辣音	
姚	ngoo 我白	hhaqlaq 匣白辣音	
波	ngoo 我白，ngoonoq 我白諾音	aqlaq 阿辣皆音	
黄	ngoo 我	ngooté 我推音	
温	nng 五白音	nnglé 五白音來音，五白音大文家白(續下)	
衢	nguu 我，nguu・neng 我能輕音	nguudhé 我隊輕音	
華	nga 我白	ngaliang 我白良音	
康	ngoe 我白	ngoelöhnong 我白亂音儂音(人字)	
續吴盛	wuu・nou 吾文上奴輕皆音，少(在王江涇 Yànggangjin 多)	wuu・lii 吾文上俚輕皆音，少(在王江涇多)	
續温		又可加 kaq 客音在多數代名前，後加人白例如，客五白皆音大文家白人白 kaq-nngdhahgoneng	

國	4. nii 你	5. niimen 你們	6. ta 他
宜	gnii 你	gniidoq 你篤音	to 他
溧			to 他
壇西			ta 他
丹	nng 五白音	nngdji 五白音齊音	ta 他
靖	gn'ii 你	gn'iimen 你們	ta 他
陰	gn'ii 你	gn'iiga 你家白	ta 他
常紳	gni 你白(伲音)	gnigo 你白(伲音)家白	dha 他濁
常街	gn'ii 你文	gn'iigo 你文家白	dha 他濁
錫	gnii 你	gniilii 你俚	dho ㄉ'ㄛ(他字)
蘇	néh'倷',nh'唔'止格,少	nhdoq'唔篤',néhdoq'倷篤'甚少	l'i '俚'陰平,｜·né｜'倷'輕
熟	neeng 能上音	neengdoq 能上篤皆音	ghé('ou'韻)溝濁音(cf. 康)
崑	nenn 能去音	nndeq 唔得皆音	yi 夷音
寶	nong 儂音	nndeq 唔得皆音	yi 夷音
浦	nong 儂音	naa 那上音	yi 夷音
上	nong 儂音	naa 那上音	yi 夷音
松	zeqnong 雜儂皆音	zeqna 雜那輕皆音	zyhdji 自其皆音

國	4. nii 你	5. niimen 你們	6. ta 他
吴黎	n'a 那陰平音	nn-naa 唔那輕皆音	i・nou 伊奴輕皆音
吴盛	n-neq 唔音納音,n'a 那陰平	nngna 五白那輕皆音	i(nou)伊(奴輕)皆音
嘉興	néé'倷'	néélaq'倷'辣輕音	i 伊
杭	n'ii 你	n'iimen 你們	ta 他
紹	noq 諾音,|loq|落音	naaloq 那上落皆音,naa 那上音,少	yi 夷音
諸王	gnii 你	gniabä 虐平班皆音	dji 其*
嵊崇太	noong 儂上音	noonglaq 儂上辣皆音	yi 夷音
姚	nong 儂音	naq 捺音	ghé 該濁音
波	nng 五白音,|noq|諾音	nn-naq 唔捺皆音	dji 其*
黄	nn 唔上音	nnté 唔推皆音	ghé 該濁音
温	gnii 你	gniilé 你來音,你大文家白	ghi 其*
衢	gnii 你,|•neng|能輕音	gnii・dhé 你隊輕音	ghi,dji 其*
華	noong 儂上	noong(a)liang 儂(阿)良皆音	ghoq 谷濁音
康	nn 唔音	nnlöhnong 唔亂儂(人字)皆音	ghou 溝濁音

國	7. tamen 他們	8. tzyhjii 自己	9. ge 個輕(一丨,這丨)	10. igeren 一個人(E. alone)
宜	togo 他家白		geq 葛音	
溧	togo 他家白		geq 葛音	一葛音人白
壇西			geq 葛音	
丹	tadji 他齊	dzyhgo 自家白	geq 葛音	一葛音人白
靖	tamen 他們	zyhgo 自家白	geq 葛音	一葛音人白
陰	taga 他家白	zyhga 自家白	geq 葛音	一葛音人白,一干音'仔',一獨自
常紳	dhago 他濁家	zyhgo 自家白	geq 葛音	一葛音人白
常街	dhago 他濁家	zyhgo 自家白	geq 葛音	一葛音人白
錫	dholii 他字'俚'輕	zyhgu 自家白	geq 葛音	一葛音人白
蘇	l'idoq'俚篤'	zyhga 自家白	geq 葛音	一干音'仔'
熟	ghédoq 溝濁篤皆音	zyhga 自家白	gow 個	一干則皆音
崑	yidheq 夷特皆音	zyhga 自家白	gheq 搿音	一干音'仔'
寶	yideq 夷得皆音			
浦	yi・lah 夷賴輕皆音			一干音'仔'
上	yi・lah 夷賴輕皆音	zyhga 自家白	gheq 搿音	一干音'仔'
松	zyhdji・lah 自其賴輕皆音		gow 夠音	一干音'仔'

國	7. tamen 他們	8. tzyhjii 自己	9. ge 個輕(一|，這|)	10. igeren 一個人(E. alone)
吴黎	i・lah 伊賴輕皆音	zyhga 自家白	ghé 該濁音	
吴盛	i・l'a 伊賴輕皆音	zyhga 自家白	geq 葛音	一干音'仔'，一家頭(sic!)
嘉興	i・lah 伊賴輕皆音	zyhga 自家白	géh 夠音	一夠音人白
杭	tamen 他們	zyhjii 自己	goq 各音	一各音人文(-zen)
紹	yaloq 爺落，yilaq 夷辣全皆音	zhih 自字	géq 革文音	一革文音人白
諸王	djia 茄音|bä|班音	zhih 自字	gé 該音	一該音人白
嵊崇太	yilaq 夷辣皆音			
姚	ghiqlaq巜'丨辣	yih 異音(自字)	göq 谷音	一谷音人白
波	dji(q)laq 其平，人辣皆音	zhih 自字，|go|家白	ghoq 谷濁音	一谷濁音人白
黄	ghété 該濁推皆音	zyhjii 自己	gé 該音	一該音人白
温	ghilé 其* 來音，其* 大文家白	zyh 自	gé 該音	一該能(人字)皆音
衢	ghi-，dji-dhé 其* 隊輕音		gheq 葛濁音	
華	ghoq (a) liang 谷濁(阿)良皆音			
康	ghoulöhnong 溝濁亂儂(人字)皆音		goe('gùh')個	

國	11. lea 倆代	12. jeh-, jeyge 這個	13. jehhoel 這火兒
宜		geqgeq 葛葛皆音	
溧	兩葛音人白	geqgeq 葛葛皆音	
壇西		geqgeq 葛葛皆音	葛音日白光
丹	兩葛音人白	geqgeq 葛葛皆音	葛音歇候(-hey)
靖	兩葛音人白	tzyhgow 志音個	志音歇
陰	兩葛音人白，兩家白頭	jihgeq 記葛皆音	記音歇
常紳	兩葛音人白	tzyhgeq 志葛皆音	志音歇
常街	兩葛音人白	tzyhgeq 志葛皆音	志音歇
錫	兩家白頭	ihgeq 意葛皆音	意音歇，||亭音(辰字)光
蘇	兩家白頭	gégeq 該葛皆音，égeq 哀葛皆音(續下)	姑音歇(續下)
熟	兩家白頭	ligow 離音個	離音歇辰光||恩音|
崑	兩家白頭	gähgheq 鑑白艞皆音	鑑白音歇
寶		dhihgeq 第葛皆音	第音歇
浦		dhiqgheq 迭艞皆音	迭音歇，姑音歇
上	兩家白頭	dhiqgheq 迭艞皆音	迭音歇
松	兩家白頭	dhiqgow 蝶夠皆音	蝶音歇，夠入喜皆音

國	11. lea 俩代	12. jeh-,jeyge 這個	13. jehhoel 這火兒
吴黎	两干音'仔'(sic!)	geqgeq 葛葛皆音,低高	
吴盛	两葛音人白,两家白頭	geqgeq 葛葛皆音	葛音歇
嘉興	两夠音人白	giqgéh ㄍㄧ夠音	葛音歇
杭	两各音人文(-zen)	geqgoq 葛各皆音,jiqgoq 結各皆音	結音歇
紹	两革音人白,两家白頭	géqgéq 革革皆文音	革音文歇
諸王	两該音人白	geqgeq 葛葛皆音	葛音歇,街白希皆音
嵊崇太			
姚	两谷失落聲母(öq)人白	giqgöq 葛谷皆音	葛音歇,一葛皆音時光
波	两家白頭	dhònggiqghoq 蕩ㄍㄧ谷濁皆音	(用'現在')
黄	两該人白	gaqgé 甲白該皆音	腔去音,甲白腔去皆音
温		geqgéㄍㄜ該音,高,低降升	公音,中升
衢		geqgeq 葛葛皆音,高低	
華		geqgeq 葛葛皆音,低高	
康			
續蘇		geqgeq 葛葛高低,皆音,泛指	葛音歇低高,葛軒皆音

國	14. jehlii 這裡	15. jehme 這麼(程度)	16. jehme 這麼(方法)
宜	街白音頭	ianq 樣陰去音	ianqlao 樣陰去佬皆音
溧		jianqgeq 降文葛皆音	
壇西			
丹	葛音裡	gäh-n-tzoong 蓋音 ㄋ 種(又同右)	geqtzoong 葛音種
靖	志音塊	gann 鑑白音	tzyh-gnienn 志驗皆音(‘這恁樣’?)
陰	jeàngkuey□記黨切塊(續下)	zeqgánq 實梗白去音	(同左),又記音種樣式
常紳	茲盔皆音,蕩音塊	gann 鑑白音,|種	鑑白種,||樣則音,鑑白爹葛皆音
常街	茲盔皆音,蕩音塊	gann 鑑白音,|種	鑑白種,||樣則音,鑑白爹葛皆音
錫	意搭,意頭	zheq-nng-hhaw 實五白號,五白號全皆音	
蘇	該搭,哀搭(續下)	zeqgháng 賊梗濁去,zánq 盛白,盛白能輕,全皆音	
熟	離搭,||家白,離頭全皆音	záq · gah□介白,||能輕,賊介白,||能輕,席介白,||能輕,全皆音	
崑	鑑白搭皆音,鑑白音面	ghäh · neng 鑑濁白能輕;gäälädhei 減白蘭頭,全皆音(指情形)	
寶	第音面,第搭皆音	zeqgháng 實梗濁白去皆音	
浦	迭搭皆音,迭音塊	zeqgháng 實梗白去皆音	
上	迭搭皆音	gah 介白音,zeqghah 實介濁白皆音,||能輕皆音	實介白能輕皆音,葛能輕皆音樣子
松	蝶音面,蕩音邊,蕩音面	zaqghah 若介濁白皆音,||能輕音	

國	14. jehlii 這裡	15. jehme 這麽(程度)	16. jehme 這麽(方法)
吴黎		zeqghah 實介濁白皆音	
吴盛	葛搭皆音,葛音裡,葛浪	zeqgah 實介白皆音	
嘉	葛塔皆音	gah 介白音,(又同右)	zeqgaq 實介白皆音
杭	結音裡	gah ㄍㄚ, zaqgah 若音ㄍㄚ,葛音様	zaqgah 若音ㄍㄚ
紹	革文音裡	gah 介白音,(又同右)	zeqghéq 實革濁文皆音,革文音様,‖子
諸王	géqdho 葛音ㄉ'ㄛ	gah 介白音,(又同右)	介白葛皆音,葛音様,‖子
嵊崇太	葛音裡	zeqgah 實介白皆音	
姚	一單皆音裡	gah 介白音,(又同右)	葛音様子
波	蕩音頭	gah 介白音	格莫格皆音,格音相貌
黄	甲白搭,甲白堂你文輕(oni)全皆音	gaqtii 甲白體皆音	
温	geqliiㄍㄜ裡	geq · nengㄍㄜ能音	
衢	葛音裡	geql'eng-葛冷陰平皆音様	
華		geqsang 葛生白皆音	
康		go-hai('gu-háng')孤亨皆音	saiyanq 生音様('那様':彀音様)
續陰	記蕩,記搭,□搭,全皆音		
續蘇	葛搭,葛面,葛字低,全皆音,泛指		

國	17. nahge，neyge 那個	18. nahlii 那裡	19. sherme 甚麼
宜	dohgogeq□家白葛音	過音邊	dih('dienn')店音(底音異)
溧			dii 底，丨葛音
壇西	laqgeq 辣葛皆音		dii 底，丨葛音
丹	gowgeq 過葛皆音	過音裡	digoh 底告音，高低升
靖	gowgow 過音個輕	過音頭，過音塊	digò 低高皆音，diò 刁音
陰	gowgeq 過葛皆音	過頭，過蕩，過搭全皆音	dawtzeq 到則皆音，到音(形.)
常紳	gowgeq 過葛皆音	鍋盔	dia 爹音，丨葛音
常街	gowgeq 過葛皆音	過塊輕，全皆音	dea 爹上音，丨葛音
錫	gowgeq 過葛皆音	過搭，過頭全皆音	shaa 啥，丨葛音
蘇	guégeq 歸葛皆音	歸搭，歸首全皆音	shah 啥，丨葛音
熟	gowgow 過個皆音	過喊，過搭介白，全皆音	shah 啥，丨個音
崑	géqgheq 夠入㹎皆音	géqdaq 夠入搭皆音	saa 啥，丨㹎音
竇	geqgeq 葛葛皆音		saa 啥，丨葛音
浦	igheq 伊㹎皆音		saa 啥，丨㹎音
上	igheq 伊㹎皆音	伊音面，伊音頭	saa 啥，丨㹎音
松	zyhdjigow 自其皆音個		saa 啥，丨夠音

國	17. nahge，neyge 那個	18. nahlii 那裡	19. sherme 甚麼
吴黎	giqgeq巜丨葛音		saa 啥，丨葛音
吴盛	giqgeq巜丨葛音	伊音面，記音面	saa 啥，丨葛音
嘉興	gégé 夠夠皆音高低	gihmienn巜丨面	saa 啥，丨西
杭	l'aagoq 喇谷皆音	laalii 喇音裡	saa 啥
紹	hánqgéq 亨白去革文，皆音，亨白去各皆音	亨白，去音裡，丨頭	soo 啥，soshi 啥西
諸王	meigeq 梅葛皆音	meidho 梅ㄉ'ㄛ	hhaatzeq 鞋上則皆音
嵊崇太		bhanqkuéh 傍音塊	hhaughéq 毫音巜'ㄝ
姚	ghánqgöq 梗音白去谷皆音	ghánqdanlii 梗濁白去單裡皆音	söq 宿音，丨谷音
波	giqghoq巜丨谷濁音	giqté巜丨推音，巜丨面，巜丨頭	soo 啥
黄	gaagé 解白該皆音	解白地皆音	zawdeq 造得皆音(形.)(續下)
温	hégé 海平該皆音	bhòdaq 旁搭	ghaqgnié 格濁白娘皆音
衢	bheqgeq 撥濁葛皆音，旁葛皆音		saa 啥
華	meqgeq 末葛皆音	末音裡	day 戴音
康		gowdaq 彀搭皆音	dziagoe(‘dzaiguh’)豺？個皆音(形.)(續下)
續黄			gaa-m 解白‘嘸’降升(名.)
續康			dziasiéq 豺音？□(名.)

國	20. sheir 誰?	21. naa-ige, neeige 哪(一)個?
宜	loogo 落上音家白	
溧	loogo 落上音家白	
壇西		loogeq 落上音葛音
丹	loogeq 落上音葛音; oogeq 啞白葛皆音, 低音告音人白	loogeq 落上音葛音
靖	l'aagow 喇音個	l'aagow 喇音個
陰	l'aageq 喇葛皆音	l'aageq 喇葛皆音
常紳	logeq 落平葛皆音, 爹音人白	langgeq 郎葛皆音
常街	l'oogeq 落陰上葛皆音, 啥上音人白	l'aanggeq 朗陰上葛皆音
錫	loogeq 落上葛皆音, 啥人白	looliigeq 落上裡葛皆音
蘇	lohgeq 落去葛皆音, 啥人白	lohliigeq 落去裡葛皆音
熟	啥人白	hhaaliigow 鞋土音裡個
崑	啥人白	hhaaliighéq 鞋上音裡夠濁入音
寶	啥人白	looliigeq 落上音裡葛音
浦	啥人白	hhaaliigheq 鞋上音裡搿音
上	啥人白	hhaaliigheq 鞋上音裡搿音
松	啥人白	hhääliigow□裡夠音

國	20. sheir 誰？	21. naa-ige，neeige 哪(一)個？
吴黎	啥人白	hhoodéhgeq 華上担葛皆音
吴盛	啥人白	hhoodéhgeq 華上担葛皆音
嘉興	啥人白	hhooľiigiqgé 華上裡《丨夠音
杭		l'aa-iqgoq 喇一各皆音
紹	啥(soo)人白，hhaazy 鞋上時皆音	hhaaliigeq 鞋上裡革文，皆音
諸王	hhaagé 鞋上該皆音	hhaaleqgé 鞋上勒該皆音
嵊崇太	nahnong 那儂(人字)皆音	
姚	宿音人白	hhaaliigöq 鞋上裡谷皆音
波	zÿÿnoq 汝音諾皆音，啥(soo)人白	aqliighoq 阿裡谷濁皆音
黄	gää-n 減兒皆白音	
温	ghaqneng 格濁白音人白(續下)	gniau-iq-gé 紐平一該皆音
衢		
華	l'aageq 喇葛皆音	l'aageq 喇葛皆音
康		
續温	ghaqzhi 格音誰，zhineng 誰人白	

國	22. naalii 哪裡，naal 哪兒	23. tzeeme 怎末	24. bu 不
宜	落上搭皆音	na -gniang 難娘皆音（'哪恁樣'?）	feq 勿
溧		laageq 喇葛皆音	feq 勿
壇西			feq 勿
丹	落上音裡，ㄛ上裡	nuunggeq 暖葛皆音	feq 勿
靖	喇音裡	tzieen-gnienn 剪念皆音（'怎樣'?）	beq 不
陰	l'aalii 喇音裡 l'äälii 懶音裡，懶搭皆音	n'áang-háang□亨白陰輕	feq 勿
常紳	郎盔皆音	nan-gaan 難減白皆音	feq 勿
常街	朗陰上盔皆音	n'aan-gaan 難陰上減白	feq 勿
錫	落上裡搭皆音	naqháng 捺亨白，捺亨白五白號全皆音	feq 勿
蘇	落去裡搭，落搭全皆音，啥場化	naqháng 捺亨白皆音，náang□	feq 勿
熟	鞋上裡，||搭音，喇音裡，||搭音，啥場化	naaneng 哪上能輕皆音	feq 勿
崑	喇搭皆音	naaneng 哪上能輕皆音，捺亨白，少	feq 勿
寶	鞋上音裡，六上音裡，啥場化，啥戶蕩	naaneng 哪上能輕皆音	v'eq 物陰入音，feq 勿少
浦	鞋上音裡，||搭音，哈場化，啥戶蕩	naaneng 哪上能輕皆音	
上	鞋上音裡搭音，啥場化，啥戶蕩	naaneng 哪上能輕皆音	v'eq 物陰入音
松	hhäälii□裡，啥戶蕩	naaneng 哪上能輕皆音	v'eq 物陰入音

國	22. naalii 哪裡，naal 哪兒	23. tzeeme 怎末	24. bu 不
吴黎	華上担皆音	naqhah 捺蟹去皆音	feq 勿
吴盛	華上裡担皆音	naqhaq 捺哈入皆音	feq 勿
嘉興	華上裡灘皆音	naqhah 捺蟹去皆音	feq 勿
杭	喇音裡	jiqgaq 結音《丫	béq 不
紹	鞋上裡	naqgéq 捺革文皆音	véq 物音
諸王	hhaadho 鞋上ㄉ'ㄛ	hhaatzeqgah 鞋上則介白皆音	feq 勿
嵊崇太		naagah 哪上介白皆音	
姚	鞋上裡登皆音，色谷皆音地方	dzaqgöq 宅白谷皆音，||浪音	v'iq 物陰入音
波	soo-usé 啥烏賽皆音，啥地方	dzaa□，|maq□襪音（續下）	feq 勿，veq 物音（續下）
黄		tzeq-n 則兒白音音	feq 勿
温	(zy)gniaudhò(是)紐平蕩	tzy-na 茲那皆音，低低	fuq□
衢	啥地方	haqdeengyanqtzyy 哈等皆音樣子	
華		laahang 喇亨白皆音，高低	
康		saisai（'sángsáng'）生生皆白音，高低	
續波		dzaameq-hhánqtzyy □末杏白子皆音（'怎末樣子'?）	m'eq 没陰入音，用在形.前

國	25. meiyeou 没有(無)	26. meiyeou 没有(未)	27. heen 很
宜			
溧	m-m'eq 嘸没陰入皆音		
壇西	mbeq 嘸不，mdeq 嘸得全皆音	veqzhing 物音□(曾字)	
丹	ntzeq 唔則 mtzeq 嘸則少，全皆音	feqdzeng 勿曾	m'ä 蠻陰平音 shi 希音
靖	meqdeq 没得	beng 奔不曾切	m'an 蠻陰平音
陰	mbeq 嘸不皆音	feng 分音	m'ä 蠻陰平音，shi 希音
常紳	mbeq 嘸不，mdeq 嘸得人少，全皆音	venq 份音	shi 希音，zenq 甚，oq 惡音
常街	mbeq 嘸不，mdeq 嘸得人少，全皆音	venq 份音	shi 希音，zenq 甚，oq 惡音
錫	mbeq 嘸不皆音	feqdzin 勿秦音	m'an 蠻陰平音，man 蠻音
蘇	mbeq 嘸不皆音	fen 分音	m'é 蠻陰平音
熟	mbeq 嘸不皆音	feng 分音	m'ä 蠻陰平音，häwäh 哈患皆音
崑	mbeq 嘸不，ndeq 唔得少，全皆音	feng 分音	m'ä 蠻陰平音
竇	mbeq 嘸不皆音	feqzeng 勿曾，v'eqzeng 物陰入音曾	m'é 蠻陰平音，交文闗
浦	m-meq 嘸没皆音	v'eqzeng 物陰入曾	m'an 蠻陰平音
上	m-meq 嘸没皆音	(同左)，又 v'eqzeng 物陰入曾	m'é 蠻陰平音，交文闗
松	m'-meq 嘸陰平没皆音	v'eqzeng 物陰入曾	m'é 蠻陰平音

國	25. meiyeou 没有(無)	26. meiyeou 没有(未)	27. heen 很
吴黎	mbeq 嘸不皆音		
吴盛	mbeq 嘸不，mdeq 嘸得全皆音	feqgnin 勿甯音	m'é 蠻陰平音
嘉興	mbeq 嘸不皆音	feqzeng 勿曾	m'é 蠻陰平音
杭	meq-eou 没有陰上		m'an 蠻陰平音，交關(-guon)
紹	gn -iou 广(無元音)有皆陰平音	(同左)，veqzhing 物尋白皆音	m'an 蠻陰平音
諸王	m-maq 嘸襪皆音	feqyong 勿容音，fenin(半鼻音)	man 蠻音
嵊崇太			
姚	m'gneou 嘸陰平紐皆音	m'deq 嘸陰得皆音	
波	m'm'eq 嘸没皆陰調音		mä 蠻陰平音
黄	meqyeou 没有		m'é 蠻陰平音
温	n'-nou ろ耨皆音	méh 末音(cf. 第四表 2)	m'a 蠻陰平音
衢	meq-eou 没有陰上	venq 份音，aqvenq 阿份皆音	
華	m 嘸音	mi 中升□(未白?)	m'an 蠻陰平音
康			

國	28. tay 太	29. hair 還(＝尚,猶)	30. gen 跟,hann 和	31. tzay 在	32. tzaynall 在那兒
宜			哈入音		
溧			同	勒音	勒過皆音頭
壇西		ä 晏白平音	同		在葛音頭
丹	太		同白	在	
靖		wan 還	同,搭		
陰	忒,｜嫌,｜覺白音	wä 還	喊去音;勒音	勒音	勒鑑白皆音
常紳	忒,｜煞	wan 還	搭,哈入音;勒音	勒音	勒音頭
常街	忒,｜煞	wan 還	搭,哈入音;勒音	勒音	勒音頭
錫	忒嫌	an 晏白平音	搭,｜則音;勒音	勒音	來娘皆音
蘇	忒,｜煞	ué 彎音,hhé 鹹白音	搭,搨音,｜仔;勒音	勒音,辣音	勒浪皆音
熟	忒,｜嫌	wä 還文,ä 晏白平音	搭;納音	勒音	勒浪辣裡全皆音
崑		wä 還文,hhä 鹹白平音	搭;勒音	勒音	
寶	忒	wé 還文,é 晏白平音	搭,忒音;勒音	勒音	勒浪皆音
浦	忒煞	wé 還文,é 晏白平音	搭是音;'佬'		勒浪,辣裡全皆音
上	忒,｜殕音	wé 還文,é 晏白平音,hhé 鹹白音	得音,得是皆音;'佬'	辣音,辣辣皆音	辣辣皆音
松		é 晏白平音	搭;'佬'	辣音,立辣皆音	立辣皆音

國	28. tay 太	29. hair 還(=尚,猶)	30. gen 跟,hann 和	31. tzay 在	32. tzaynall 在那兒
吴黎		hhé 鹹白音	搭	勒音	勒賴皆音
吴盛	忒,|生白音	wé 還文,é 晏白平音,hhé 鹹白音	得音;lò	來音(?)	勒辣皆音
嘉興	忒	é 晏白平音	搭音	在	勒黑皆音
杭	太	won 還文,an 晏白平音,hhan 鹹白音	同;勒	來音,在	在喇音裡,辣哈入皆音
紹	忒	wan 還文	同	來音,來搭皆音	來東,來亨白去,全皆音
諸王		wé 還文	得音;勒音	來音	來客白皆音
嵊崇太			tzöq 竹音,竹音仔		
姚	忒	waq 滑音	搭	來音	來浪皆音
波	唾音	wä 還文	同,得音	來音	來東,東全皆音
黄	太	wé 還		在	在格
温		va 還	kau 敲	是音,在	是候皆音,zou□
衢				在	在那陰上裡
華					
康					

國	33. -shanq -上	34. -diaw -掉	35. geei 給 (動.)	36. geei 給 (介.＝爲)	37. dong-shi 東西	38. dibfang 地方	39. shyr-how 時候
宜					東西		
溧		-辣音					
壇西							
丹		-到音	baa 把文音	替	東西	地方	時候
靖	-上	-掉,-脱	baa 叭上音	替	東西		時候,辰光
隂	-冷白去音(浪音異)	-落,-脱	baa 叭上音	替	末音事	地方,塲化	辰光
常紳	釀音	-落	baq 八音	替	東西	地方	辰光
常街	-釀音	-落	baq 八音	替	東西	地方	辰光
錫	-釀音	-落	beq 撥音	替,搭音	末音事	地方,塲化	辰光
蘇	-浪音,-向音	-脱	beq 撥音	替,搭音,忒音	末音事	塲化,地方	辰光
熟	-浪音,-向音	-脱	beq 撥音	替,搭音,忒音	末音事	塲化,地方	辰光
崑	-浪音	-脱	beq 撥音	搭音	末音事	塲化	辰光
竇	-浪音	-脱	beq 撥音	替,搭音,忒音	末音事	塲化,地方	
浦	-浪音		beq 撥音		末音事		
上	-浪音,-向音	-脱	beq 撥音	替,忒音	末音事	塲化,地方	辰光,時候
松	-浪音	-脱	beeng 本音	teeng 氽音	末音事		辰光,時候

國	33. -shanq -上	34. -diaw -掉	35. geei 給（動.）	36. geei 給（介. =爲）	37. dong-shi 東西	38. dibfang 地方	39. shyr-how 時候
吴黎	-冷白去音	-脱			末音事		
吴盛	-lò□	-脱	beq 撥音	忒音	末音事	場化，地方	辰光，時候
嘉興	-浪音	-脱	beq 撥音	塔音	東西	地方	辰光
杭	-上	-了	baa 把音	把音	東西	地方	時候
紹	-上	還文音，-的音	béq 撥音	撥音	東西	地方	時候
諸王	-記音	-掉	tzeq 則音	得音	東西	地方	
嵊崇太						東西	
姚	-下白音，-登音	-掉，-慢音	tzöq 竹音	竹音	東西	地方	時候，辰光
波	-上	-掉，-落，-彎音	beq 撥音	搭音	東西	地方，烏賽皆音	時候，辰光少
黄	-上	-嚎音	beq 撥音	代	末音事	地方	時候
温	-來音，-以音	-hhò 杭音			末音事	地方，戶蕩皆音	
衢							
華							
康							

國	40. tzaochi 早起	41. bairtian 白天	42. woanshanq(E. evening)晚上	43. woanshanq (E. night)晚上	44. tian 天
宜					
溧					
壇西	早起		黄昏時候		
丹	早起頭	日白裡	黄昏頭	夜裡	日白,天
靖		日白裡	黄昏頭		天
陰	早起	日白裡向	黄昏頭,又同右	夜裡向	日白
常紳	早起頭	晝間白頭	黄昏頭,又同右	夜頭	日白
常街	早起頭	晝間白頭	黄昏頭,又同右	夜頭	日白
錫	空朝頭	晝間白頭,日白裡向	黄昏頭,又同右	夜裡向	日白
蘇	朝浪音,朝晨頭	日白裡向	黄昏頭,又同右	夜陰去裡向	日白
熟	朝晨頭	日白裡向	黄昏頭,又同右	夜裡向	日白
崑	朝了(晨字)頭	日白裡向	黄昏頭,又同右	夜裡向	
寶	朝晨	日白裡向	黄昏頭,又同右	夜裡向	
浦	朝晨,||頭				
上	朝晨,||頭	日白裡向	黄昏頭,||裡,又同右	夜裡向	日白
松	朝晨,||頭				

國	40. tzaochi 早起	41. bairtian 白天	42. woanshanq(E. evening)晚上	43. woanshanq (E. night)晚上	44. tian 天
吴黎					
吴盛	朝晨頭，莽音頭	日白裡，||向	黄昏頭	夜裡，||頭，夜頭	日白
嘉興	朝晨	日白裡	黄昏頭	夜裡	日白
杭	朝晨，||頭	日文裡，||頭	黄昏頭，夜裡，||頭	同左	天，日文
紹	早起頭，天亮	日白裡	黄昏頭	夜裡	日白
諸王	五更頭	日白勒	黄昏	夜勒音，夜頭	日白
嵊崇太		日白裡，||向			
姚	早間白藤音，天亮頭	日白裡||向	晚白(maan)頭(續下)	夜裡，||向	
波	天亮	日白裡向	晚白(mää)頭(續下)	夜裡向	日白
黄	枯(空字?)心皆音頭	日白得音	黄坤音，||頭，又同右	夜得音	
温	天光		hhashiuö 鹹音昏，||頭		
衢					
華					
康					
續姚			晚白藤音，夜到，夜裡		
續波			完歡皆音(黄字昏字)時候，夜裡，夜頭		

國	45. chyantian 前天	46. tzwotian 昨天	47. jintian 今天	48. mingtian 明天	49. howtian 後天
宜					
溧					
壇西		za -ngo-dhei ㄙ ㄚ ㄫㄛ頭	今牙白音頭	萌音朝	
丹	先音日白則音	dza-ngㄗ'ㄚ五白音	根音朝	萌音朝	後朝
靖	先音日白子	za-yah ㄙ'ㄚ夜	今朝	萌音朝	後朝
陰	前日白則音，前夜頭	zadhei 社平音頭，zoyahdhei 昨平夜頭	今朝	萌音朝	後朝
常紳	前夜則音	zodhei ㄙ'ㄛ頭	基音夜	萌音朝	後朝
常街	前夜則音	zodhei ㄙ'ㄛ頭	基音夜	萌音朝	後朝
錫	前日白則音	zadhei ㄙ'ㄚ頭	今□(ngah)	萌音朝	後日白
蘇	前日白子	zoqgnih 昨 藝 音，昨日白子搭音	今朝，針音朝	萌音朝	後日白
熟	個日白子	zoqgnihdhei 昨 藝 音頭	今朝	萌音朝	後藝音
崑	前日白子	zoqgniq 昨 日 白，昨夜頭	今朝	萌音朝	後藝音
寶	前日白子	zoqgniq 昨 日 白，昨頭，昨夜頭	今朝	萌音朝	
浦	前日白子	zoqgniq 昨 日 白，昨夜頭	今朝	萌音朝，明朝	
上	前日白子	zoqgniq 昨 日 白，昨夜頭	今朝	萌音朝，明朝	後日白
松	前日白子	zoqgniq 昨上日白	今朝	萌音朝	後日白

國	45. chyantian 前天	46. tzwotian 昨天	47. jintian 今天	48. mingtian 明天	49. howtian 後天
吴黎					
吴盛	葛音日白子	zoognihtzyy 昨 藝音子	今朝	萌音朝	後藝音
嘉興	前日白	zoqgnih 昨藝音	針音朝	萌音朝	後藝音
杭	前日文子	dzatzyy 查音子	今朝	明朝	後日文
紹		zaqnga-gnitzeq □□宜則皆音	今朝	明朝	後日白
諸王	前日白子	zanqgniqtzyy 上音日白子	今朝	萌音朝	後日白
嵊崇太					
姚	前(yen)日白子	zanqgniq 上音日白	基迷皆音子	嘸音朝	後日白，||子
波	前日白子	zoqmää 昨晚白	級襪皆音，今朝	明朝	後日白
黄	前日白	zoqgniqng 昨日白五白，輕音	今日白五白輕音	天醸(亮字)	後日白
温		zo-yih 昨平異音	généh 該内皆音	萌音朝	
衢					
華					
康					

國	50. chiuhnian 去年	51. mingnian 明年	52. deenghoel 等火兒	53. woan 晚	54. (tzao) deanshin (早)點心	55. tzao-fann 早飯
宜				晏白 'ann'		
溧				晏白		
壇西				晏白		
丹	舊年	萌音年		遲,晚白 'maan'	早飯	中飯
靖	上年	開年		晏白		
陰	舊年	萌音年		晏白	朝飯	飯
常紳	舊年	開年	晏白點	晏白	早飯,點心	晝飯,夜飯少
常街	舊年	開年	晏白點	晏白	早飯,點心	晝飯,夜飯少
錫		開年	晏白點,晏歇	晏白	朝飯	飯,晝飯
蘇	舊年	開年	晏白歇,阿軒皆音	晏白	粥	飯,中飯
熟	舊年	開年	晏白歇	晏白	點心	飯
崑	舊年	開年	晏白歇點,等歇點	晏白	粥	飯
寶	舊年	開年	晏白歇	晏白	早飯	中飯
浦		開年		晏白		
上	舊年	開年	晏白歇	晏白	早飯	飯,中飯
松		開年			早飯	

國	50. chiuhnian 去年	51. mingnian 明年	52. deenghoel 等火兒	53. woan 晚	54. （tzao）deanshin（早）點心	55. tzao-fann 早飯
吴黎			晏白			
吴盛	舊年	開年	晏白歇，晏白軒入音	晏白	粥	點心，飯
嘉興	舊年	開年	晏白歇	晏白	粥	點心（續下）
杭	舊年	開年	晏白歇，歇葛音歇，歇一歇	晏，遲	早飯	中飯
紹		明年	等歇，呆（ngé）一歇	遲	早飯	晏白音飯
諸王		萌音年	等孟白音(mánq)歇，‖氣，緩點	遲	早飯	晏白音飯，中飯
嵊崇太						
姚	舊年	耐平音年	藤音一腔音	晏白	朝飯	晏白音飯
波	舊年	明年，開年，南音(né)年	藤音上，藤音一上	晏白	天釀音(亮字)飯	晝過飯
黄	舊年	明年	慢底音五白輕	晏白	枯音(空字?)心飯	藝音晝飯
温			等翁上音添		天光	日白晝
衢						
華						
康						
續嘉						下午點心叫小點心

國	56. woan-fann 晚飯	57. bahba 爸爸	58. mha 媽	59. erltz 兒子	60. neu-erl 女兒
宜				ngogni 娃白兒白	
溧		爹爹			
壇西		爹爹	m'ma 姆陰平媽輕		
丹	夜飯		m'a 媽,gnie 娘	gnitzeq 兒白則音	
靖	夜飯		gnienx 娘娘		女兒文
陰	夜飯	爹爹	gniangx 娘娘	gnitzeq 兒白則音	女兒文
常紳	夜飯	爹爹	gniangx 娘娘	gnitzeq 兒白則音	女女
常街	夜飯	爹爹	gniangx 娘娘	gnitzeq 兒白則音	女女
錫	夜飯	爹爹	gniangx 娘娘		no-gni ‘囡’伲音
蘇	夜陰去飯	爹爹	m'• méh 姆陰平妹輕音	gnitzyy 兒白子	nö-ng ‘囡’五白輕
熟		爹爹,伯伯少	aqgniang 阿娘,姆陰平媽少,好娘少	gnitzyy 兒白子	‘囡’
昆	夜飯	爹爹,阿伯少	m'• ma 姆陰平媽輕		‘囡’
寶	夜飯	爹爹	m'• ma 姆陰平媽輕	gnitzyy 兒白子	‘囡’
浦			m'• ma 姆陰平媽,阿媽陰平		
上	夜飯	爹爹,阿伯少	m'• ma 姆陰平媽輕	gnitzyy 兒白子	‘囡’,‘囡’五白輕
松		爹爹	gniang 娘		

國	56. woan-fann 晚飯	57. bahba 爸爸	58. mha 媽	59. erltz 兒子	60. neu-erl 女兒
吴黎					
吴盛	夜飯	阿伯	m'・ma 姆陰平媽輕	gnitzyy 兒白子	'囡五白輕'
嘉興	夜飯	阿平爹	m'・ma 姆陰平媽輕	ng-tzyy 兒白子	'囡'五白輕
杭	夜飯	爸陰平爸	m'・ma 姆陰平媽輕,(續下)	ltzyy 兒文子	女兒文
紹	夜飯	爹爹,阿伯	m'o 媽陰平,gn'iang 娘陰平	gnitzeq 兒白則音	"囡"
諸王	夜飯	爹爹,阿伯	m'・ma 姆陰平媽輕,aqméh 阿妹音	gnitzyy 兒白子	'囡'
嵊崇太					
姚	夜飯	爹爹,阿伯少伯伯少	m'・mo 姆陰平媽輕	ngtzyy 兒白子	'囡'
波	夜飯	阿伯,爹爹少阿爹少	aqm 阿姆高低(續下)	ngtzyy 兒白子	'囡'
黄	夜飯	伯	aqyi 阿姨音,高低	ntzyy 兒白子	nhé'囡'
温	鞋音(黄字)昏	阿大白,阿伯	n'a 那陰平	séh-ng 舍音兒白	
衢					
華					
康					
續杭			gn'・gniang 广陰平娘輕		(注:各處'囡'字作爲屬'non'類。)
續波			女僕:阿姆低高		

國	61. sheauharl 小孩兒	62. shyifel 媳婦兒（妻俗稱）	63. hertaur 核桃	64. pwutaur 葡萄	65. pyiba 琵琶
宜					
壇西	小把戲				
丹	小五白輕音	老媽（-moo）（女僕曰'鄉下人'）		葡萄	琵爬音
靖	小五白輕音	阿媽（-moo）	蒲音桃	孛音萄	琵爬音
陰	小瓦白音兒	阿媽（-m'o）	蒲音桃	孛音萄	琵爬音
常紳	小佬輕	婆則音，女佬	蒲音桃	孛音萄	琵爬音
常街	小佬輕	婆則音，女佬	蒲音桃	孛音萄	琵爬音
錫	老小	屋（ueq）裡人白	胡桃	孛音萄	琵爬音
蘇	小幹音，|| 五白輕音	家白小，家白主婆	胡桃	孛音萄	琵爬音
熟	小幹音，小人白	家白主婆，娘則音，屋（ueq）裡人白	蒲音桃	孛音萄	琵爬音
崑	小幹音	娘子，家白主婆	蒲音桃	孛音萄	琵爬音
寶	小'囝'	娘子，家白主婆，家白小，老婆		孛音萄	琵爬音
浦	小'囝'，小幹音	娘子，家白主婆，家白小，老婆			
上	小'囝'	娘子，家白子音婆，家白小	蒲音桃	孛音萄	琵爬音
松	小'囝'	女人			

國	61. sheauharl 小孩兒	62. shyifel 媳婦兒(妻俗稱)	63. hertaur 核桃	64. pwutaur 葡萄	65. pyiba 琵琶
吴黎					
吴盛	小人,小把入戲	家白婆	蒲音桃	孛音萄	琵爬音
嘉興	小人白	家白婆	蒲音桃	孛音萄	琵爬音
杭	小牙文音兒	老婆	核桃	葡萄	琵爬音
紹	小人白	老婆,太娘	胡桃	葡萄	琵爬音
諸王	小人白	老媽(-m'o)	核(hhoq)桃	孛音萄	琵爬音
嵊崇太					
姚	小人白	老媽(-m'o),老人白	核(wöq)桃	葡萄	琵爬音
波	小彎音,小'囡'	老人白,老婆,家白小,屋裡人白	胡桃	紫胡桃	琵爬音
黄	小人白	老媽(音煙)	核桃	葡萄	琵爬音
温	碎細兒白皆音	老銀音,老安(冤同音)	核桃	葡萄	琵爬音
衢					
華					
康					

國	66. pyiba 枇杷	67. daa hachiann 打呵欠	68. daa shaan 打閃
宜			
溧			
壇西			
丹	別爬皆音	daa hoshienn 打文蝦白音獻音	daa huaqshienn 打文豁音扇音
靖	別爬皆音	daa hoshiuonn 打文蝦白音暄音去	
陰	別爬皆音	daa hoshienn 打文蝦白音獻音	daa hoqshienn 打文霍音獻音
常紳	別爬皆音	daang huoqshienn 打白霍音獻音	(同左)
常街	別爬皆音	daang huoqshienn 打白霍音獻音	(同左)
錫	別爬皆音	dáang hushienn 打白蝦音白獻音	dáang hoqshienn 打白霍音獻音，打||
蘇	別爬皆音	dáang hoshienn 打白蝦白音獻音	hoq hoqshieen 霍霍險皆音，打||
熟	別爬皆音	dáang huhenq 打白呼音很去音	dáang huoqshienn 打白霍音獻音
崑	別爬皆音	dáang hoqshienn 打白霍音獻音	hoqshienn lä tzä 霍音獻音來哉音
寶	別爬皆音	dáang hoshienn 打白蝦白音獻音	dáang hoqshienn 打白霍音獻音
浦			
上	別爬皆音	dáang hoshienn 打白ㄏㄛ獻音	dáang hoqshienn 打霍音獻音
松			

國	66. pyiba 枇杷	67. daa hachiann 打呵欠	68. daa shaan 打閃
吴黎			
吴盛	別爬皆音	dááng hoshienn 打白蝦白音 獻音	dááng hoqshienn 打霍音 獻音
嘉興	別爬皆音	dááng hoshienn 打白蝦白音 獻音	hoqshienn lé li 霍獻皆音 來哩
杭	別爬皆音	daa hashienn 打文哈平音獻音	daa heqsonn 打文赫音扇音
紹	別爬皆音	dááng hohenq 打白蝦白音 很去音	dááng hoqsénn 打白豁音 扇音
諸王	別爬皆音	dááng ho-hon 打白蝦白音 罕平音	dááng foqsö 打白霍音扇音
嵊崇太			
姚	皮音爬音(同左)	dááng ho-hénn 打白蝦白音 漢音	séén huaq sénn 閃豁音 扇音
波	皮音爬音(同左)	dááng ho-hénn 打白蝦白平音 漢音	shieendjianq 閃杖音
黄	皮音爬音(同左)	dááng chingkoh 打白清音 可去音	
温	皮音爬音(同左)		
衢			
華			
康			

國	69. gerjy 胳肢(動)	70. hala 哈辣	71. tsay 菜(飯)	72. tzang 髒
宜				
溧				
壇西				tzang 髒
丹	ho 蝦白音			laqsaq 垃圾
靖		哈平媽皆音氣		
陰	hotsyx 蝦白雌雌皆音	蒿音	小菜	oqtsoq 齷齪
常紳	hotsy 蝦白雌皆音	蒿音	菜	naqdaq 捺搭皆音
常街	hotsy 蝦白雌皆音	蒿音	菜	naqdaq 捺搭皆音
錫	hulowchÿhx 花路處處皆音		小菜	oqlah 惡賴皆音
蘇	hotsi 蝦白妻皆音	蒿音，軒音	小菜	oqtsoq 齷齪
熟	hu . . . cheql'ioux 蝦白(某人之)撤溜溜皆音	軒音人白音氣	小菜	òtzò 凹糟皆音
崑	hognioqtsi 蝦白肉白妻皆音	軒音	小菜	leqseq 垃圾
寶		軒音	小菜	oqtsoq 齷齪
浦				òqtsòq 齷齪
上	ho . . . yeangtsix 厂乙(某人之)癢妻音妻音	蒿音	小菜	oqtsoq 齷齪
松			小菜	oqtsoq 齷齪

國	69. gerjy 胳肢(動)	70. hala 哈辣	71. tsay 菜(飯)	72. tzang 髒
吴黎				
吴盛	hogeqtzy 蝦白音胳肢	蒿音	小菜	lasi 垃圾皆平
嘉興	hogeqtzy 蝦白音胳肢	蒿音	小菜	lasi 垃圾皆平
杭	hu... eang 呼音(某人之)癢	蒿音	下文飯	fong 封音, leqseq 垃圾
紹	hoyeang 蝦白音癢		下白飯	fong 俸音
諸王		軒哈平人白皆音	菜,菜虚音(蔬)	oqtsoq 齷齪
嵊崇太				
姚	ho ... laangtsyx 蝦白(某人之)冷白雌雌皆音	麻人白	下白飯	fong 封音,封封皆音
波	ho ... yeangchÿx 蝦白陰平音(某人之)癢吹白音吹白音	麻口	下白飯	oqtsoq 齷齪, òtzò 凹糟皆音
黄	tzoq... guoqyeang 捉(某人之)骨癢	shiencheou 酣音□	菜酒席上;菜蔬碟中;羹碗中	oqtsoq 齷齪
温		蒿音	菜,菜蔬	etze, ‘autzau’ 凹糟皆音
衢				
華				
康				

國	73. tzangtuu 髒土	74. herngsh(yh)橫是音	75. maashanq 馬上
宜			
溧			
壇西	leqseq 垃圾		
丹		vengsuh 橫白豎	moozäh 馬上
靖	öqsöq□□	hhongzhiuh 紅音豎，wáng 橫白豎	m'oozhianq 馬上
陰	leqseq 垃圾	wángzhiuh 橫白豎	m'oozánq 馬盛白音
常紳	leqseq 垃圾	wángdoon 橫白短音	moogniang 馬白讓白音
常街	leqseq 垃圾	wángdoon 橫白短音	m'oogniang 馬陰上讓白音
錫	leqseq 垃圾	wángshÿ 橫白書音	m'azhánq 媽音上文
蘇	leqseq 垃圾	uángshÿ 橫白陰平書音	m'azhánq 媽音上文
熟	leqseq 垃圾	wángdjeng 橫白成音	m'azhánq 媽音上文
崑	leqseq 垃圾	wángshÿ 橫白書音	m'ozanq 麻陰平上白
寶	leqseq 垃圾	wángsÿ 橫白書音	m'ozanq 麻陰平上白
浦	laqsiq 垃入屑音，(續下)	wángsiu 橫白書音，鹹白書皆音	m'ozanq 麻陰平上白
上	lasi 垃圾皆平	wángsÿ 橫白書音	m'azánq 媽盛白皆音，moo-馬盛白音
松	oqtsoq 齷齪		m'oozánq 馬陰上盛白音

國	73. tzangtuu 髒土	74. herngsh(yh)横是音	75. maashanq 馬上
吴黎			m'aazánq 媽陰上盛白音
吴盛	lasi 垃圾皆平	wángsÿ 横白書音横白竪	m'aazánq 媽陰上盛白音
嘉興	lasi 垃圾皆平	wángshÿ 横白書音	m'ozánq 馬陰平上
杭	leqseq 垃圾	hhendzÿh 横柱音	m'aazanq 媽陰上上
紹	étzau 哀糟皆音	wángjiuh 横白柱音	moozanq 馬上白
諸王	laqzaq 辣音□	wángzhiuh 横白竪	moozanq 馬上白
嵊崇太			
姚	leqseq 垃圾	wángsÿ 横白書音	moozanq 馬上
波	ähtzò 晏白糟皆音	wangzhiuh 横白竪	moozanq 馬上
黄	leqseq 垃圾		liqkeq 立刻
温	benqseq ㄅㄥ圾		ziuseou〔zysiu〕随手
衢			
華			
康			
續浦	l'òqsòq 落陰入朔皆音		

特別詞小字除註音外都是用國語註的詞義。

宜：　奔音，搬。　帶攙，如手|手。　‘lienjienn’連見皆音，泥，髒，如手上髒。

溧：　loqsu 落蘇皆音，茄子。

壇西：hhei weq 侯惑皆音，是阿，是的嘔。　hhei lao 侯佬皆音，是的。（單呼詞變成形容詞）

丹：　diax 爹爹伯父。　進娶。　bou 波音，行走。　ley 漏落下。　姑娘未嫁者。　小姐已嫁者。　（sic!）。舅爹母兄。　舅舅母弟。　djiowm’ää 舅鸞上，母兄妻。　djiow-ng 舅兀母弟妻。　鄉下人女僕。　枵音，掀。　堂前堂屋。　痰音。　吐唾沫。　梨瓜甜瓜。　樣範樣子。　yi-m’ää 姨鸞陰上，母姊。　姨娘母妹。

靖：　耳篤耳朵。　村音。　立，站站。

陰：　ihsyy 意死皆音，潮溼。　漏落下。　棧音，陡。鍋箸鍋巴。　觸目寒塵。　論則皆音，結巴。　tziaqm’áång□□螞蟄。　耳文他睬他。　撩鈎調羹。　打雞蛋臥雞子。　鋪平音。雞蛋打碎烹法（sic!）。　正是是的。　是得是。

常：　奔音，搬。　斷音。銅汗音，俗，錢。　出來（早晨）起來。　鍋貯鍋巴。　ihsyy 意死皆音，潮溼。　lahgeqbau 癩格包蛤蟆。　觸目寒塵。　毒恨。　張張候候。　甕音，壞（形.）。　別音，追。　測音，舊布紙爛兒。男女音。　家白，男人。　女娘家白，女人。　波音，行走。　逃跑。　細小。　大文音，趟。　厭音。在已經…（豈可再…）。　納音，費，如穿鞋太|。

锡：杩薄。　揜比。　意暑皆音。usqseq□□潮溼。　出來(早晨起來)。
焦飯貯鍋巴。　觸目寒塵。　黇音線針。　相，標音，瞅，瞧。
細小。　丁心皆音，蜻蜓。

蘇：(只取不常見於蘇白書的)白白落落白鐃。　diq的音，如|衣裳搗衣，|背搥背。　棧音，陡。　特音，落下。　反脚反倒，副。　硬襯做鞋梆的哥(音)巴。　gong拱平音，ghong共平音，如狗|開門。　gháng更白濁音，擠，人|過去。　灘音，只。　甚音，殺淹死。　酒靨酒窩兒。　夾白喇子下白，夾肢窩。　謝音菜薺菜。　作孽痛苦。　測音，舊布紙爛貌。角白猛白，螞蚱。　蹤去，跳。　力音，捏(加害)。　的音，捏(不加害)。褙去，泥，如手上|。　合爬人(趴)着。　合撲東西面向下放着。
螃蟹(蟹音eq，hhö，weq，haa)。　活音嚨嗓子。　páng澎音，雨落窗上。
亨文音，撕。　台甫(台去聲)。　坐起，中間白，堂屋。　偷珠眼|針|。
差得懸音浜音，差得遠之(音)呐(音)。　凳，|子凳子，椅子。　靠背椅子。

熟：鑑白難去皆音，橄欖。　搭脚瘸子。　geengdhei敢去音頭蓋兒。
酒瘺酒窩兒。　力音，轉(他動.)。　正是是的。　hhei weq後□皆音，是阿。　六音浴洗澡。

崑：飛算架白皆音，翅膀。　göhdhei敢去音。頭蓋兒。　血頭，發鬆可笑。zah-nn丈母皆字，丈母。　酒靨酒窩兒。　勒音子栗子。　噴砌音，噴嚏。減白蘭頭這末樣子。

寶：冰塊雹子。　飯貯鍋巴。　zah-nn，zah-ng丈母皆字，丈母。　葛洛皆音，夾肢窩。　bhaqzoq白白勺調羹。　抵當平，料想。

浦：teq忒音，都(副.)。　génndhou敢去音。　頭蓋兒。　飯貯鍋巴。
ueqsaq□殺淹死。nan拈，dan丹音，拿。

上：(只取不常見于書的) 飯是音，鍋巴。　葛則洛皆音，夾肢窩。　碌音起來(早晨)起來。　雲耳白，木耳。　喊平音頭那兒，如在他||。　拉海，來全皆音，在裏頭(等于 Fr，*en*)。　迭當碼子這個傢伙(等于 Am."this guy")。　葛佬皆音，所以。　發霧下霧。

松：laqchih 拉氣皆音，到裏頭，如扔|||。　拿(陰平)拿。　'dan'單音，拿。　soong 悚音(十音沙五白切)，十五。　介白佬皆音，所以。

吴黎：ziaw 笑濁音，不要。　順右。

吴盛：得死文，得很。　指爪指甲。　阿拉(阿是字阿)，是吧。

杭：paq□掰。　biòh 標去音，不要。　dji-l 茄兒茄子。　倒霉丢臉(sic!)。不音焦鍋巴。　seeipaang 手胖上音，骼臂。　tzaq 札眨。　ku-erl 耳環。tsenn 櫬音，賺。　打呃得打冷膈。　iqjiaqgoqtzyy 一角文角白子。　單音，拿。　照音末吶末(于是)。　帕兒手絹兒。　篆拾。　時道時興。　回，臺趟。　順右。　dei 兜舀。　tae 胎上音，性情懶。

名詞加'兒'字者：紙，衫，叉，花，刀，杯，梨，桶，領，帶，壺，襪，套，帽，蓋，底，帕，析，瓶，畫，棒(但棍子)，罐，盤(但盆子)，荳，條，柄，茄，袋，鐲，鈴，鴨(但雞無兒)，鳥，簍，ku(耳環)，糙音(綽號切)，一滴，肉圓，酒窩，鬧鬧，打架，眼鏡，戲法，木人頭，馬褂(兒或子)。

加'子'字者：桌，椅，凳，窗，房，鏡，櫃，鞋，靴，扇，袍，桃，李，栗，橘，褥(但被無子)，帳，對，盆(但盤兒)，簿，棍(但棒兒)，轎，車，片，岔，燕，驢，呆(痴人)，繩，兒，餡，筷，袖，裡，角白，啞叭(或不加'子')。

紹：別裡別處。　窗門窗戶。　鏺焦鍋巴。　手胖上音，骼臂。　綁身坎肩兒。　人白客白，客人。　各異兩樣。　㨶音，拿。　裡那兒（如來東夷裡）（在他那兒）。　zéh 是字，是。　篆音，拾。　新的才（如昨天才來）。　才至才（如明天才來）。　才至新的才（過去將來都可用）。　相唤作揖。

諸王：別勒堂別處。　鑊焦鍋巴。　湊隊一塊兒。　虎蟻螞蟻。　㨶音，拿。　照音末呐末（于是）。

姚：包子（鹹的）。　饅頭（甜的）。　挖音起來（早晨）起來。　翼梢膀翅膀。　蹺脚瘸子。　布襴裙子。　dzau-朝舌吵架。　郎心釘槌。　倒霉丢臉（sic!）。　游河泅水。　鑊焦鍋巴。　寄拜爹乾爹。　同隊，贊齊白，一塊兒。　浸殺，沃殺淹死。　各異，各樣兩樣。　交文夫皆音，螞蟻。　嘸高音，没甚麽。　結煞谷音，末了兒。　馱音，拿。　相唤作揖。　花绿促音，傍晚。　大媽母姊。　兀娘母妹。

波：鼻頭鼻涕。　老老常常。　造孽吵架。　滑脱是誤以爲。　惶恐害臊。　聚隊都（副.）；一塊兒。　幽過躲。　手骨胳臂。　馱音，拿。　huä 還文，清音，乖（小孩兒丨）。　老闆營業東家。　阿大白，經里。　温音，蘸（丨醬油）。　插着拾到。　酒潭音，酒窩兒。　人白客白，客人。　bhow 婆去音，繁。　各樣兩樣。　完歡皆音，螞蟻。　嘸高音，没甚麽。　尼姑尼姑。　司姑帶髮修行者。　忖想。　時道時興。　盧臺皆音，梯子。　打白恭作揖。　hoa 歪（上聲）。　烏音，煨。　薰聞（鼻丨）。　爲啥，丨丨行（hhang）當爲甚麽。　苦膽膽兒。　缺少。

黄：曉音，不要。　撻窗窗戶。　baajiaq ㄅㄚ脚跛脚。　太醫大夫。　逢見嚎不見了。　倒霉丢臉（sic!）。　suenq 峻陡。　ghuen□蹲。　鑊團鍋巴。　湊得好像。　俊坤後頭，後來。　火螢哥（gé）丨丨蟲。　套次，回。　騎音，站。　欠欠幾乎。　丁香耳環。　蟢蜘蛛。　望看

(如|書)。 箸筷子。 嫂,燒火老媽子。 老安人白,老婆兒。 火姆皆音,螞蟻。(女僕以地名稱,如來自甯波的就稱他爲"甯波",來自台州的就稱他爲"台州")。 ghann□餡。 相唤作揖。 奪音,煨。 雁鵝(ngé)大雁。

温: yuöjiu-ng媛姐兀小姐。 tsyh刺看。 刺著看見。 捉拿。 吃天光吃早點心。 吃日白晝吃午飯。 吃黄昏(hhashiuö)吃晚飯。

第六章　語助詞

凡例跟舉例

中國方言的文法，在句子的結構上差不多是全國一樣，像官話跟吴語的“你到哪裡去”跟閩粵的“你去哪裡”這種小小的區别已經是例外的了，所以講中國方言的文法差不多就是講語助詞。中國的語助詞非但是表示口氣的輕重信疑的態度，有好些更具體一點的關係像領格，過去，程度，假設等等關係也是必須用或可以用語助詞表示的。所以下列語助詞表的材料，一半是文法性質，一半也是詞彙的性質。因爲語助詞大半是輕音，大半又是没有字，所以在這個表裡凡有應當用小“輕”字或是“音”字的地方，都一概省去不用。

表第一横行略説每類的功用。第二行註文言中大略相當的語助詞。這一行是隨便加入作爲幫助解釋用的。並没有什末統計的根據。第三第四兩行是從作者在《清華學報》寫的一篇文章①裡札出來的。第四行的號數就是原報上的號數。因爲讀者未必

① “北京，蘇州，常州語助詞的研究”，《清華學報》三卷二期，第 865—917 頁，1926 年 12 月。

查得到原報，並且本篇裡有點改動的地方，所以再給每種功用舉一兩個例來解釋（每行頭上的是國語語助詞）。

de 的　1A，1B，領格；前置形。　蘇：我葛書；好看葛花。

de 的　1C，後置形。　蘇要一朵紅葛。　宜：要一朵紅佬。

le 了　2C，過去。　蘇：我昨日去看戲葛。

de 的　1D，事類。　蘇：是葛，我鞋要去葛。　溧：是佬，我也要去葛。

de 的　1E，副。　蘇：好好叫走。

de 的　1 I，連。　蘇：四胡葛六胡末，十胡惑；三尺葛六尺末，九尺惑。

de 得　1F，動結果，性。　蘇：俚走得慢。　宜：他（to）走則慢。　文：其言也善。

de 得　1H，可能。　蘇：吃得落。　宜：他走得動勿煞？

de 得　1G 動結果，量。　蘇：倦得（來）眼睛鞋張勿開葛哉。

hao…！好…！—贊歎。　蘇：該格水清得拉（或得來）！

le 了　2A，起事。　蘇：勿好哉，要死（sii）哉！　陰：勿好留，雨來留！（還未來）！

le 了　2B，設想結果。　蘇：再勿去就晏哉！　陰：再勿去就晏留！

le 了　2D，敘事過去。　蘇：後來我就去睏哉。　常：到後來他（dha）又來祭。

le 了　2C，完事。　蘇：飯開好哉。　上：飯開好才。

le 了　2C，完事，重。　蘇：飯開好葛哉，　上：飯開好賴才。

le 了　2F，時間附詛。　蘇：吃仔飯再去。

le 了　2G,假設附謳。　蘇:我死(sii)仔倷那亨!

le 了　2H,設想正句。　蘇:晏歇弄壞脱仔!　錫:晏歇弄壞了(或則)!

le 了　2H,命令。　蘇:走好仔啊!　波:吃飽 *hhei*!

j'着　7B,分詞。　蘇:坐仔比立仔適意。

j'着　7B,方法分詞。　蘇:騎仔馬尋馬。

ne 呢　3C,假設附謳。　蘇:萬一勿成功呢,格末只好就算哉。

ne 呢　3A,特指問。　蘇:俚會唱,倷(會啥)呢?

ne 呢　3B,起頭問。　蘇:葛是何必再去呢?

ne 呢　3A,特指問。　蘇:陳先生家文?陳先生來葛哉。

ne 呢　3B,起頭問微重。　蘇:葛末倷爲啥去家文?　錫:葛末你爲啥去吶?

ar 阿　8C,問事問微重。　蘇:啥人家文?做啥家文?　錫:啥人啥?做啥啥?

ma 嗎　4A,是非問(中性)。　蘇:倷何去家文?

ba 吧　6B,是非問(中性)。　蘇:倷何去家文?

ne 呢　3E,申明有。　蘇:十葛篤,闊得野篤。

ne 呢　3A,延長動。　蘇還覅完勒。

ma 嗎　4B,反詰是非。　蘇:倷想騙我阿?　宜:你想騙我得罷?

a 阿　8A,設問。　蘇:倷勿肯阿?　溧:你勿肯惑?

a 阿　8D,稱呼。　蘇:阿三阿!　溧:老三乁(ei)!

a 阿　8F,感歎。　蘇:倷葛葛人阿!

a 阿　　8I，暫頓。　蘇：阿三阿，我告愬倷阿，我想阿，昨日阿，歸格人阿，俚說葛葛句閒話阿，倷勿必相信得俚葛。

a 阿　　8J，重假設頓。　蘇：倘使俚嫁撥仔俚倷啊，葛是“也好”哉！

a 阿　　8H，警告。　蘇：我並覅答應阿！

a 阿　　8L，提醒。　蘇：本生應該是俚葛阿。　上：本來是夷搿拉。

a 阿　　8L，勸聽。　蘇：嫑哭，阿！乖點，阿！

ar 阿陽平　8M，試定問意見。　蘇：該葛倒嘸啥，鞋？倷想那亨？

a 阿　　8H，提醒。　蘇：本生是俚葛呀。　常：本來是他(dha)葛辣。

南京 ei乁11A，反對。　蘇：勿是，勿是，勿是葛呀！　常：勿對，勿對，勿對惑！

me 嚜　5B，你應知特指。　蘇：該葛要拿滾水沖葛呀。諸王：要滾水沖該拉。

me 嚜　5A，你應知泛指。　蘇：我曉得勿對惑。　諸王：我曉得勿成功及。

lo 咯　10A，公認。　蘇：總算勿差哉惑。

me 嚜　5A，你應知泛指。　蘇：我曉得勿對末。　錫：我曉得勿對諾。

me 嚜　5C，暫頓。　蘇：先末吃飯，吃完仔末揩面；唔篤末先去，伲末慢慢叫末哉。

me 嚜　5D,假設暫頓。　蘇:倘使落雨末,我就勿去哉。

ba 罷　6A,勸令。　蘇:來罷(bhah),吃點罷。　宜:來罷(bhah)。

ba 罷　6C,試定。　蘇:勿見得罷(bhah)。　宜:勿見得罷(bhoh)。

ba 罷　6D,假設逗,指行爲。　蘇:勿對俚説罷,鞋勿大好。上:勿對夷話呢,鞋勿大好。

a 阿　8E,命令微重。　蘇:來娘!嫑怕娘!　常:來三!來sueq(色惑切)!

ne 呢　3D,感歎帶贊歎。　蘇:葛倒危險葛娘!

ne 呢　3F,'還没有'。　蘇:覅完勒。

bale 罷了,就是了。　限制。　蘇:必過説説罷哉。

同上,derle 得了。　任聽。　蘇:讓俚去希末哉。

bale 罷了。　催勸。　蘇:答應仔俚哉惑!

第六表:22處56用的語助詞

用法	領格;前置形	後置形	過去	事類	副	連
文言	之	之	曾…;〇	也;〇	而;然;〇	〇;與
國語	de 的音得	de 的音得	le 了音勒	de 的音得	de 的音得	de 的音得
學報	1A,1B,	1C	2C	1D	1F	1I
宜	geq 葛	lao 佬	geq 葛	geq 葛	tzeq 則	geq 葛
溧	geq 葛	lao 佬	geq 葛	lao 佬,葛	tzeq 則	geq 葛
壇西	geq 葛	lao 佬	geq 葛	geq 葛	tzeq 則	geq 葛
丹	geq 葛	gow 個	geq 葛	geq 葛	tzeq 則	geq 葛
陰	geq 葛	geq 葛	geq 葛	geq 葛	li 哩	geq 葛
常	geq 葛	lao 佬	geq 葛	geq 葛	tzeq 則	geq 葛
錫	geq 葛	geq 葛	geq 葛	geq 葛	li 哩	geq 葛
蘇	geq 葛	geq 葛	geq 葛	geq,giq 葛	jiaw 叫	geq 葛
熟	gow 個	gow 個	gow 個	gow 個	neng 能	jiaw 個
崑	ghé 溝濁	ghé 溝濁	ghé 溝濁	ghé 溝濁	jiaw 叫	ghé 溝濁
上	gheq 搿	gheq 搿	gheq 搿	gheq 搿	jiaw 叫,neng 能	gheq 搿
松	gow 個	gow 個	gow 個	gow 個	jiaw 叫	——
吴黎	gheq 搿	gheq 搿	gheq 搿	gheq 搿	——	——
吴盛	geq 葛	geq 葛	ie 煙	e 厄	jiaw 叫	——
嘉興	géq 夠入	géq 夠入	géq 夠入	géq 夠入		
杭	diq 的	diq 的	diq 的	diq 的	jiaw 叫	diq 的
紹	géq 革文,gheq 搿	géq 革文,搿	géq 革文,搿	géq 革文,搿	li 哩	——
諸	gé 該	gé 該	gé 該	gé 該	tzyy 仔	gé 該
姚	göq 谷	göq 谷	göq 谷	göq 谷	jiaw 叫	——
波	ghoq 谷濁	ghoq 谷濁	ghoq 谷濁	ghoq 谷濁	jiaw 叫	——
黄	gé 該	gé 該	gé 該	gé 該	zy 時	——
温	gé 該	gé 該	bha 罷	gé 該	neng 能	gé 該

用法	動結果,性	可能	動,結果量	贊歎	起事,設想結果
文言	也	能	至;直;竟	哉!	——
國語	de 得	de 得	de 得	好…! 真…!	le 了音勒
學報	1E	1H	1G	——	2A,B
宜	tzeq 則	deq 得	dawtzeq 到則	dawtzeq 到則	li 連(哩音異)
溧	tzeq 則	tzeq 則	dawtzeq 到則	dawtzeq 到則	lieq 咧
壇西	tzeq 則	tzeq 則	dawtzeq 到則	deqhhan 得鹹白	lieq 咧
丹	tzeq 則	tzeq 則	tzeq 則	deq-a 得啊	lé□
陰	deq 得	deq 得	deqlä 得來,到||	deqlä 得來	liou 留
常	tzeq 則	tzeq 則	dawtzeq 到則	dawtzeq 到則	li 哩
錫	tzeq 則	tzeq 則	deq 得,daw 到,到則	jinq...deq 竟…得	'leau'了
蘇	deq 得	deq 得	deqlé 得來	deqla 得拉,deqlé 得來	tzé 哉
熟	deq 得	deq 得	deqlä 得來	deqlä 得來	tzä 哉
崑	deq 得	deq 得	deq 得,deqla 得拉	deqlä 得來(lä)	zä 才
上	deq 得	deq 得	deq 得,得來(lé)	deq 得,得來(lé)	zé 才
松	——	——	——	——	tzé 哉
吴黎	deq 得	deq 得			dhé 枱
吴盛	deq 得	deq 得	deq 得	lé 來	léq 來入
嘉興	——	——	——	——	li 哩
杭	deq 得	deq 得	deq 得,deqlei 得ㄌㄟ	deq 得,得ㄌㄟ	deqlei 得ㄌㄟ
紹	dhéq 代入	dhéq 代入	daw 到	la 拉	tzé 哉
諸	dheq 特	dheq 特	dheq 特	——	hha 鞋
姚	daq 搭	daq 搭	daq 搭	vaqnaq 乏捺	tzé 哉
波	léq 來入	léq 來入	léq 來入	lé 來	léq 來入
黄	deq 得	deq 得	deq 得	deq máang a 得猛阿	hhau 嚎
温	ge 該	deq 得	shiq 些	tzaq zeq...é 扎實…哀	bhé□

用法	敘事過去	完事	完事,重	時間附逗；假設附逗	設想正句；命令	分詞
文言	——	矣	矣	既…,○…則	——	
國語	le 了音勒	le 了音勒	le 了音勒	le 了音勒	le 了音勒	j 着音之
學報	2D	2C	2C	2F,G	2H	7B
宜	‘lien’連（哩音異）	‘laolien’佬連	‘laolien’-ou 佬連痾	tzeq 則	tzeq 則	tzeq 則
溧	lieq 咧	lieq 咧	lieq 咧	tzeq 則	tzeq 則	tzeq 則
壇西	lieq 咧	lieq 咧	tzeqlieq 則咧	tzeq 則	tzeq 則	tzeq 則
丹	geq 葛	lé□	lé□	tzeq 則	tzeq 則	tzeq 則
陰	geq 葛	tzò 糟,葛留	tzò 糟,葛留	tzeq 則	tzeq 則	tzeq 則
常	tzi 祭	geqli 葛哩	geqli 葛哩	tzeq 則	tzeq 則	tzeq 則
錫	‘leau’了	‘leau’了	‘geqleau’葛了	tzeq 則	tzeq 則	tzeq 則
蘇	tzé 哉	tzé 哉	geqtzé 葛哉	tzeq 仔	tzyy 仔	tzyy 仔
熟	tzä 哉	tzä 哉	geqtzä 個哉	tzeq 則	tzeq 則	tzeq 則
崑	zä 才	zä 才	gheqzä 搿才	zyh 是	zyh 是	zyh 是
上	zé 才	zé 才	lazé 賴才	zyh 是	zyh 是	zyh 是
松	——	——	——	zyb 是	——	——
吴黎	dhé 枱	——	——	zyh 是		
吴盛	leq 勒	lé 來	e 厄	tzyy 仔	tzyy 仔	laq 拉
嘉興	li 哩	li 哩	li 哩	zyh 是	zyh 是	zyh 是
杭	deqlei 得ㄌㄟ	deqlei 得ㄌㄟ	deqlei 得ㄌㄟ	l’eò 了	leiㄌㄟ’□	l’eò 了
紹	tzé 哉	tzé 哉	tzé 哉	dhéq 代入	dhéq 代入	dhéq 代入
諸	hha 鞋	hha 鞋	hha 鞋	lé 來	lé 來	leq 勒
姚	tzé 哉	tzé 哉	göqtzé 谷哉	tzyy 仔	tzyy 仔	tzyy 仔
波	léq 來入	léq 來入	diqléq 的來入	léq 來入,tzyy 仔	léq 來入 hhei□	léq 來入仔
黄	hhò 嚎	hhò 嚎		hhò 嚎	——	deq 得
温	hhòhbhé □□	bha 罷	bha 罷	hhò□	hhò□	le 老

用法	方法分詞	假設附謳	特指問	起頭問	特指問	起頭問 微重	問事問 微重
文言	…而	也	——	哉？	——	哉？	也？
國語	j 着音之	ne 呢音呐	ne 呢音呐	ne 呢音呐	ne 呢音呐	ne 呢音呐	a 阿
學報	7B	3G	3A	3B	3A	3B	8C
宜	tzeq 則	neq 呐	neq 呐	neq 呐	——	saq 煞	saq 煞
溧	tzeq 咧	neq 呐	neq 呐	neq 呐	neq 呐	neq 呐	la 拉
壇西	tzeq 則	nä 難	nä 難	nä 難	——	nä 難	a 阿
丹	tzeq 則	ni 呢	ni 呢	ni 呢	neq 呐	ni 呢	sä 三
陰	tzeq 則	neq 呐	neq 呐	neq 呐	——	neq 呐	a 阿
常	tzeq 則	neq 呐	neq 呐	neq 呐	neq 呐	san 三	san 三
錫	tzeq 則	nan 難	nan 難	neq 呐	難	呐	sha 啥
蘇	tzyy 仔	gni 呢	gni 呢	gni 呢	jia 家文	jia 家文	jia 家文
熟	tzeq 則	neq 呐	neq 呐	neq 呐	neq 呐	jiaq 脚	jiaq 脚
崑	zyh 是	gniq 呢入	gniq 呢入	gniq 呢入	gniq 呢入	ia 呀	ia 呀
上	zyh 是	niq，gniq 呢入	(g)niq 呢入	(g)niq 呢入	(g)niq 呢入	(g)niq 呢入	a 阿
松	——	——	——	——	——		
吴黎							
吴盛	zyh 是	né 奈	né 奈	——	leq 勒	a 阿	a 阿
嘉興	zyh 是	nä 奈	nä 奈	——	——	——	——
杭	l'eò 了	gni 呢	gni 呢	gni 呢	——	gni 呢	a 阿
紹	dhéq 代入	gni 呢，néq	gni 呢	gni 呢	gni 呢	jioq 覺，	djioq 局
諸	deq 得	gnin 呢 半鼻音	gnin 呢 半鼻音	gnin 呢 半鼻音	——	lé 來	a 阿
姚	tzyy 仔	gni 呢	gni 呢	gni 呢	jiah 戒文	jiah 戒文	la 拉
波	léq 來入，仔	ngi 呢几丨	ngi 呢几丨	ngi 呢几丨	ngi 呢几丨	la 拉	la 拉
黄	——		ni 呢 neq 呐，leq 勒		leq 勒	（末韻略長）	a 阿
温	le 老	né 耐	né 耐	né 耐	——	né 耐	a 阿

用法	是非問(中性)	是非問(中性)	是非問(中性)	申明有	延長動
文言	乎?	否?	否?	焉;○	焉
國語	嗎?	吧?	…不…阿?	ne 呢音吶	ne 呢音吶
學報	4A	6B		3E	3A
宜	faq 法	feqsaq 勿煞	feqsaq 勿煞	deq-hhou 得河	deq 得
溧	faq 法,vaq 乏	faq 法,乏	faq 法乏	dou 多	deq 得
壇西	feq 法,feqsaq 勿煞	faq 法,勿煞	faq 法,勿煞	deq 得	deq 得
丹	feqsä 勿三,m'ä 蠻陰平	feqsä 勿三,蠻陰平	feqsä 勿三,蠻陰平	dou 多	dou 多
陰	hou 火…,|…拉,iq 抑…,|…拉	hou 火…,|…拉,抑…,|…拉	hou 火…,|…拉,抑…,|…拉	leq-é 勒せ	leq-é 勒せ
常	faq 法,veqzan 物饞	faq 法,物饞	faq 法,物饞	deq 得	deq 得
錫	aq 阿…,aq 阿…sha 啥	aq 阿…,阿…啥	aq 阿…,阿…啥	deq 得	deq 得
蘇	áq 阿…jia 家文('脚')	áq 阿…家文('脚')	áq 阿…家文('脚')	doq 篤	leq 勒,lé 來
熟	aq 阿…jiaq 脚	aq 阿…脚	aq 阿…脚	doq 篤	lä 來
崑	aq 阿…ia 呀	aq 阿…呀	aq 阿…呀	dheq 特	lä 來
上	vaq 唔,|拉	vaq 唔,|拉	vaq 唔,|拉	laq 辣	léq 來入
松					

用法	是非問（中性）	是非問（中性）	是非問（中性）	申明有	延長動
文言	乎？	否？	否？	焉；〇	焉
國語	嗎？	吧？	…不…阿？	ne 呢音吶	ne 呢音吶
學報	4A	6B		3E	3A
吴黎					
吴盛	aq 阿…	aq 阿…	aq 阿	leqhoh 勒化	li 哩
嘉興	vaq 唔	vaq 唔	vaq 唔		
杭	ba 吧，…不…	ba 吧，…不…	ba 吧，…不…	leiㄌㄟ	leiㄌㄟ
紹	…勿…，□□[①]，…勿…拉	…勿…，□□，…勿…拉	…勿…，□□，…勿…拉	dnog 東	lé 來
諸	…勿…拉	…勿…拉	…勿…拉	kaq 客白	leq 勒
姚	vaq 唔	jiah 戒文	jiah 戒文	lanq 浪，diqlé 的來	lé 來
波	vaq 唔	vaq 唔	vaq 唔	lei 雷	lei 雷
黄	vaq 唔	vaq 唔	vaq 唔	a 阿（口氣略異）	——
温	a 阿…vaq 低音	a 阿…ma 嗎	…fuq…阿	naq 捺	捺，哀 é

① 光把動詞説兩遍就算問話式，如“諸要要去？”等于“你要不要去？”

用法	反詰是非設問		稱呼	感歎	暫頓	重假設頓	警告
文言	乎	歟	也;○	也	也	也	也
國語	嗎	a 阿	a 阿	a 阿	a 阿	a 阿	a 阿
學報	4B	8A	8D	8F	8I	8J	8G
宜	deqbho 得罷	a 阿	a 阿	a 阿	a 阿	a 阿	a 阿
溧	a 阿	weq 惑	ei乀	a 阿	a 阿	a 阿	a 阿
壇西	deqmo 得嗎	uaq 挖	ei乀	a 阿	——	——	——
丹	ä 晏白	ä 晏白	a 阿	a 阿	a 阿	a 阿	a 阿
陰	hhò 豪	hhò 豪	hha 阿 陽輕	hha 阿 陽輕	a 阿	a 阿	a 阿
常	a 阿	a 阿	a 阿	a 阿	a 阿	a 阿	a 阿
錫	a 阿	a 阿	a 阿	a 阿	a 阿	a 阿	a 阿
蘇	a 阿	a 阿	a 阿	a 阿	a 阿	a 阿	a 阿
熟	○	○	a 阿	a 阿	a 阿	——	——
崑	ä 哀	ä 哀	a 阿	a 阿	ä 哀	ä 哀	ä 哀
上	a 阿	a 阿	a 阿	a 阿	a 阿	a 阿	a 阿
松							
吴黎							
吴盛	a 阿	a 阿	a 阿	a 阿	a 阿	——	——
嘉興							
杭	a 阿	a 阿	a 阿	a 哦	a 阿	a 阿	a 阿
紹	a 阿	a 阿	a 阿	hho□	a 阿	a 阿	a 阿
諸	a 阿	a 阿	a 阿	a 阿	a 阿	a 阿	a 阿
姚	a 阿	阿,戒文	a 阿	hho 下白	hho 下白	hho 下白	laq 拉
波	a 阿	a 阿	hhä 鹹	hha 鞋,hhò 號	hha 鞋,號	a 阿	laq 拉
黄	a 阿	a 阿	a 阿	a 阿	a 阿	a 阿	a 阿
温	a 阿	a 阿	a 阿	a 阿	a 阿	a 阿	a 阿

用法	提醒	勸聽	試定問意見	提醒	反對	你應知特指
文言	也	——	何如？	也	也	也
國語	a 阿	,a 阿	,ar 阿陽平	阿	南京 ei乁	me 嚜
學報	8H	8L	8M	8H	11A	5B
宜	a 阿	,a 阿	,hha 鞋	weq 惑	weq 惑	weq 惑
溧	a 阿	,a 阿	,hha 鞋	weq 惑	weq 惑	weq 惑，得惑
壇西	——	——	——	weq 惑	meq 末	——
丹	a 阿	,a 阿	,a 阿	vé□	vé□	vé□
陰	a 阿	,a 阿	,hha□	la 拉	la 拉	la 拉
常	a 阿	,a 阿	,hha 鞋	laq 辣	weq 惑	weq 惑
錫	a 阿	,a 阿	,a 阿	weq 惑	weq 惑，gueq 骨	weq 惑
蘇	a 阿	,a 阿	,a 阿	iàq 呀	iàq 呀	iàq 呀
熟	——	,a 阿	——	iaq 呀	iaq 呀	iaq 呀
崑	——	,a 阿半鼻音	,a 阿半鼻音	ä 哀	ia 呀	ia 呀
上	a 阿，辣	,a 阿	,a 鞋	ia 呀	ia 呀	ia 呀
松						
吴黎						
吴盛	——	——	——	——	——	——
嘉興						
杭	a 阿	,a 阿	,hha□	meq 末	meq 末	（用尾降調）
紹	a 阿	,hha 鞋	,hha 鞋	laq 拉	laq 拉	laq 拉
諸	——	,a 阿	,hha 鞋	——	——	laq 拉
姚	laq 拉	,hha 鞋，hho 下白	,bha 鞋，下白	laq 拉	laq 拉	laq 拉
波	laq 拉	,hho 何	,hha 鞋	laq 拉	laq 拉	laq 拉
黄	a 阿	（不用）	（不用）	——	——	——
温	——	——	——	ia 呀	——	é 哀

用法	你應知泛指	公認	你應知泛指	暫頓	假設暫頓
文言	也	矣	也	也;而	也
國語	me 嚜	lo 咯	me 嚜	me 嚜	me 嚜
學報	5A	10A	5A	5C	5D
宜	weq 惑	‘lienweq’連惑	weq 惑	meq 末	meq 末
溧	weq 惑	weq 惑	weq 惑	meq 末	meq 末
壇西	weq 惑	——	meq 末	meq 末	meq 末
丹	vé□	lé□	beq 不	bä 扮,meq 末	bä 扮,末
陰	weq 惑	——	meq 末	meq 末	meq 末
常	weq 惑	liweq 哩惑	weq 惑	meq 末	meq 末
錫	weq 惑,gueq 骨	‘leauweq’了惑	noq 諾	meq 末	meq 末
蘇	weq 惑(‘啘’)	tzéweq 哉惑	meq 末	meq 末	meq 末
熟	weq□	tzäweq 哉□	weq□	meq 末	meq 末
崑	wö 啘	wö 啘	meq 末	meq 末	meq 末
上	ia 呀	——	meq 末	meq 末	meq 末
松					
吴黎					
吴盛	——	——	——	meq 末	meq 末
嘉興	weq 惑				
杭	no 諾	weq 惑	meq 末	meq 末	meq 末
紹	laq 拉	lo 咯	tzégheq 哉穿	meq 末	meq 末
諸	djiq 及	geq 葛	geqdjiq 葛及	meq 末	meq 末
姚	——	——	meq 末	meq 末	meq 末
波	laq 拉	——	——	meq 末	meq 末
黄	——	a 阿	veq 物	veq 物	veq 物
温	m 嘸	——	muq 木	méq 末	méq 末

用法	勸令	試定	假設諠指行爲	命令,微重
文言	——	——	——	也
國語	ba 罷	ba 罷	ba 罷	a 阿
學報	6A	6C	6D	8E
宜	bhah 罷	bhoh 罷	bhah 罷	saq 色
溧	shiò 蝦文	bhoh 罷	bha 罷	seiㄙㄟ
壇西	shioq 蓄	bhoh 罷	bhoh 罷	seiㄙㄟ
丹	bhoh 罷	bhoh 罷	bhoh 罷	a 阿
陰	ma 媽陽輕	ma 媽陽輕	ma 媽陽輕	leqweq 勒惑
常	bhah 罷	bhah 罷	bhah 罷	san 三,sueq 色惑
錫	bhah 罷	bhoh 罷	bhah 罷	ma媽陽陰,sha 啥
蘇	bhah 罷	bhah 罷	bhah 罷	gniang 娘(‘嚯’)
熟	bhah 罷	neq 吶	——	neq 吶
崑	bhah 罷	——	meq 末	gniaq 嚯
上	bhah 罷,vaq 唔,waq 滑	bhah 罷,唔,滑	(g)niq 呢	hha 鞋
松				
吴黎				
吴盛	bhah 罷	bhah 罷	——	a 阿
嘉興				
杭		bhah 罷	ia 呀	ia 呀
紹	djiaq 脚濁	o 啞白	djiaq 脚濁	djiaq 脚濁
諸	——	呢半鼻音	呢半鼻音	jiaq 脚
姚	vaq 乏	vaq 乏	gni 呢	a 阿
波	vaq 唔	vaq 唔	——	hhä 鹹
黄	vaq 唔	vaq 唔	a 阿	a 阿
温	é 哀	bha	méq 末	é 哀

用法	感歎帶 贊歎	‘還没有’	限制	任聽	催勸
文言	——	尚未…	耳,而已,而已矣	可也	——
國語	ne 呢音吶	ne 呢 音吶	bale 罷了,jiowshle 就是了	同左 derle 得了	罷了
學報	3D	3F			
宜	neq 吶	zai 才	‘lienweq’連惑,就 是連	‘haolien’ 好連	‘lienweq’連惑
溧	neq 吶	lai 來, zai 才	liqweq 咧惑 zhio- wzyhliq 就是咧	liq 咧	liqweq 咧惑
壇西	deqnä 得難	zai 才	zhiowzyhliq 就是咧	dii 底	liqweq 咧惑
丹	dou-a 多阿	dou 多	beqlé 不□,behlé 罷 □,就是□	——	lévé ㄌㄝㄪㄝ
陰	neq 吶	leq 勒	bhahliou 罷留,就 是留	meqtzò 末糟	tzòweq 糟惑
常	neq 吶	leq 勒	liweq 哩惑,就是哩	liweq 哩惑	liweq 哩惑
錫	noq 諾	lé 來,得 來	‘bhahleau’罷,就 是了	bhiaq□,|惑	bhiaqweq□惑
蘇	同左; noq 諾	leq 勒	bhahtzé 罷哉,就 是哉	meqtzé 末哉	tzéweq 哉惑
熟	——	leq 勒	bhahtzä 罷哉,就 是哉	meqtzä 末哉	tzäweq 哉惑
崑	gniaq 嚌	lä 來	bhahzä 罷哉,就是才	meqzä 末才	zäweq 才喴
上	ya 爺	léq 來入	bhahzé 罷哉,壽是才	meqzé 末才	meqhòòzé 末好才
松					

用法	感歎帶贊歎	‘還没有’	限制	任聽	催勸
文言	——	尚未…	耳，而已，而已矣	可也	——
國語	ne 呢音呐	ne 呢音呐	bale 罷了，jiowshle 就是了	同左 derle 得了	罷了
學報	3D	3F			
吴黎					
吴盛	——	li 哩	bhahleq 罷勒	——	——
嘉興					
杭	niㄋㄧ	leiㄌㄟ	bhahl'eò 罷了，就是得ㄌㄟ	hòòdeqlei 好得ㄌㄟ，拉倒ㄌㄟ	hòòdeqlei 好得ㄌㄟ，拉倒ㄌㄟ
紹	noq 諾，gnioq 玉	lé 來入	gheqlo 𤞣咯，hhétzé 害哉，||𤞣	hhétzé 害哉	hhétzé 害哉
諸	——	hha 鞋，leq 勒	lö-a 亂阿	hao-hha 好鞋	hao-hha 好鞋
姚	——	lé 來	yowzyhtzé 就是哉	mtzé 嘸哉	zyhtzé 是哉
波	(用語調)	lei 雷	sonnlei 算雷，就是雷	hòòlé 好雷	hòòlé 好雷
黄	a 阿	leq 勒	zhiowzyh 就是	veqzyh-hhò 物事嚎	veqzyh-hhò 物事嚎
温	diq 的	naq 捺	mu 爾	ni 呢，是呢	ni 呢，是呢

附録

蘇州話"北風跟太陽"的故事

這一段故事記了十九處地方的說法。現在先寫出一個來做個樣子。所記的大半都沒有註語調。但是下列的蘇州話是有語調的。(1)是漢字文;(2)是國際音標,每音節前註的是語調跟字調的代數和(resultant)。一個點子有示輕音,但輕音也有高低;(3)是方音羅馬字,只拼字調,不註語調;(4)是吴語音韻羅馬字,只寫聲韻調的類别,不問音值,一看上去好像是一種混合的江浙讀音,其實在前第一,二,三表蘇州行的音值中按類查下去,查出來就是的的刮刮的蘇州音。

(1) 漢字文北風搭太陽(蘇州閒話)

有一轉北風搭太陽恰白恰白勒浪爭白論啥人白葛本事大白;講勒講來仔一葛走路葛人白,身浪着仔一件厚襪。俚篤兩家白頭就商量好好說,啥人白能先叫葛葛走路葛人白脫脫俚葛襪啊,就算啥人白葛本事大白。好,北風就用起仔勁來儘管吹白儘管吹白。落去聲哩曉得俚吹白得越利害,歸葛人白就拿襪裹得越緊;到後來北風嘸不法子,只好就算哉。一歇歇太陽就出來刮喇喇一曬,葛葛走路葛人白嗎上文就拿襪脫仔下白來。所以北風勿能勿承認白到底還是太陽比俚本事大白。

(2) 國際音標

·pɔ ˊfoŋ ·ta ¯tʻɒ ˍiã

(¯sɜu ¯tʂᵒʏ ·ɦᴇ ɦo)

·ɦʏ ·ɪ ˍtʂø ·pɔ ˊfoŋ ·ta ¯tʻɒ ˍiã ˉkʻa ˉkʻa ·lə ·lõ ¯tsã ¯lən ˎʂɒ ·ɲən ·kə ˋpən ·zɿ ˍdʻɜu; ˋkõ ·lə ·kõ ˍlᴇ ·tsɿ ·ɪ ·kə ˋtsᵒʏ ˍlɜu ·kə ˍɲən, ¯ʂən ¯lõ ˉtʂɒ ·tsɿ ·ɪ ˎdʑiɪ ˍɦʏ ¯mø. ¯li ·tɔ ˍliã ¯kɒ ·dᵒʏ ·zᵒʏ ¯sõ ·liã ·hæ ·tsɿ ˉʂə, ˎʂɒ ·ɲən ˍnən ¯siɪ ·tɕiæ ·kə ·kə ˉtsᵒʏ ˎlɜu ·kə ˍɲən ˉtʻə ·tʻə ·li ·kə ¯mø ·ɐ, ˍzᵒʏ ˍsø ˎʂɒ ·ɲən[1] ˋpən ·zɿ ˍdʻɜu. ˋhæ, ·pɔ ˊfoŋ ·zᵒʏ ˍɦioŋ ·tɕʻi ·tsɿ ˎtɕiən ·lᴇ ˋtsiŋ ·kuø ¯tʂʻʮ, ˎtsiŋ ·kuø ¯tʂʻʮ. ˊlɔ ·li ˋɕiæ ·də ¯li ˉtʂʻʮ ·tə ˊɦyə ˍli ·ɦᴇ, ¯kuᴇ ·kə ˍɲən ·zᵒʏ ·no ¯mø ˋkɜu ·tə ˊɦyə ˋtɕiən; ·tæ ˍɦy ·lᴇ ·pɔ ˊfoŋ ˍmpə ˉfa ¯tsɿ, ˉtsə ˋhæ ·zᵒʏ ˎsø ·tsᴇ. ·ʔɪ ·ɕɪ ·ɕɪ ¯tʻɒ ˍiã ·zᵒʏ ˎtʂʻə ˊlᴇ ˉkua ˉla ˉla ·ʔɪ ˎso, ·kə ·kə ˉtsᵒʏ ˍlɜu ·kə ˍɲən ¯mɒ ¯ʐã ·zᵒʏ ·no ¯mø ˉtʻə ·tsɿ ·ɦo ·lᴇ. ˎsɜu ·i ·pɔ ˊfoŋ ·fə ˊnən ·fə ˍʐən ɲən ¯tæ ˋti ˍɦuᴇ ·zɿ ¯tʻɒ ˍiã ·pi ¯li ˋpən ·zɿ ˍdʻɜu.

---

① 依漢字文,此處缺"·kə",疑誤。——編者註

(3) 注音羅馬字 Boqfong daq Tàhyang (Soujöi hhé-hhoh)

Yöy iqjöh Boqfong taq Tàhyang kaqx leqlànq tzanglenn shàhgnin geq beenzyh dhow; gààng leq gààng lé tzyy iqgeq tzöelow geq gnin, shen lànq jaq tzyy i-jieh hhöy m'ö. L'idoq lianqgàdöi zöy sàngliang hää tzyy sheq, shàhgnin nen sie jiäh geqx tzöelow geq gnin teqteq l'igeq m'ö a, zöy söh shàhgnin① beenzyh dhow. Hää, Boqfong zöy yonq chii tzyy jinn lé tziinguöö chÿ tziinguöö chÿ. Lohlii sheädeq l'i chÿ deq yueq lih-hheh, guégeq gnin zöy no m'ö goou deq yueq jiin; däh hhöylé Boqfong mbeq faqtzyy, tzeq hää zöy söh tzé. Iqshiqx Tàhyang zöy cheqlé guaqlaqx iq soh, geqx tzöelow geq gnin m'àzhanq zöy no m'ö teq tzyy hhohlé. Soou-ii Boqfong feq nen feq zhengninn dähdii wézyh Tàhyang bii l'i beenzyh dhow.

(4) 吴語音韻羅馬字 Boqfong daq Tahyang (Sujiou hhanwoh)

Yeou iqjiuonn Boqfong daq Tahyang kaqx leqlanq tzánglenn sohgnin geq beenzyh dhuh; gaang leq gaang lai tzyy iqgeq tzoou-luh geq gnin, shin lanq jiaq tzyy iq-ghieen hhoou m'on. L'idoq leanggadhou ziow sangliang hao tzyy shiueq, sohgnin nen sien

① 依漢字文,此處缺"geq",疑誤。——編者註

giaw geqx tzoouluh geq gnin teqteq l'igeq m'on a，ziow sonn soh-gnin[①] beenzyh dhuh. Hao，Boqfong ziow yonq kii tzyy ginn lai tziinguoon chiu tziinguoon chiu. Loolii heaudeq li chiu deq yueq lih-hhay，guangeq gnin ziow no m'on guu deq yueq giin；daw hhowlai Boqfong mbeq faqtzyy，tzeq hao ziow sonn tzai. Iqhiqx Tahyang ziow chiueqlai guaqlaqx iq soh，geqx tzoouluh geq gnin m'azhianq ziow no m'on teq tzyy hhohlai. Suu-ii Boqfong feq nen feq zhin-gnin dawdii wanzyy Tahyang bii l'i beenzyh dhuh.

① 依漢字文，此處缺"geq"，疑誤。——編者註

我的語言自傳*

本文講的語言自傳有兩方面：先講我所用的語言，換言之，就是我說的各種中國話跟外國話；然後再講到我研究語言學的經過，不過越講到後來恐怕就漸漸的越不如第一方面那麼有意思了。

我是生在天津的，可是還没到會說話就搬到别處去了。我們原籍是江蘇陽湖，後來民國時候一城幾縣的都歸并爲一縣了，我就變成了武進縣的人了，平常當然還是用舊名稱就說我們是常州人。①

我們一家子三代都跟着祖父（諱執詒）在直隸省（現在的河北省）各處住。祖父有差事的時候就在磁州、祁州、冀州各處做官。等差事的時候就住在那時的省城保定，所以我們住保定的時候倒是不少。我們家裏上兩輩都說常州話，可是跟我們孫子輩就說一種南邊口音很重的北京話。可是大家用的陰、陽、上、去四聲都很準，只是較冷較文一點的入聲字就還是念（吴語派）的入聲。凡是聽見天津的低陰平或是保定的下轉的去聲，我們都覺得哼的不得了。

---

* 原載《"中央研究院"史語所集刊》，第 43 本，1971 年。本次出版附録此文，以見作者語言學研究的歷程。——編者註

① 關於常州話較詳細的描寫，參閱 Yuen Ren Chao，"The Changchow(Kiangsu) Dialect"，Mary Haas 慶祝論文集，*Journal of the American Oriental Society*，90. 1. 45—56(1970)。

我小時候説的話有下列的幾點跟那時候的京話不同的：[1]

第一是我們小孩子們有些音根本不會念。凡是咸山攝的字，國音收ㄢ韻，我們把尾音的-*n* 都丢掉了，例如“三、天、完、全”我們就念成[sæ，tʻiɛ，wæ，tɕʻyɛ]。我們并不是不會發韻尾的鼻音，比方像“剛、更、公、孤”那些收[-ŋ]音的字讀起來一點兒没有困難。那麽常州音雖然把國音ㄣ韻字(古深，臻攝)都念成ㄥ韻，仍不失掉鼻音。記得有一次看見猫在堂屋桌上把我的一碗湯面不的兒不的兒的吃了，我就叫：“猫雌我的滅!”因爲我既不會發ㄓ、ㄔ、ㄕ、ㄖ的捲舌音，又不會發ㄢ、ㄧㄢ、ㄨㄢ、ㄩㄢ的尾音-*n*，所以“吃”變了“雌”(陰平)，“面”變了“滅”了。

我母親(馮氏諱萊蓀)的北京話説的比較純正；也許是因爲這個緣故，我在兩個堂房姊姊(詵、蓮)，跟一個哥哥(元成)姊妹(ㄗˇ·ㄇㄟˋ)四個當中最先學會了“安、烟、彎、冤”的發音。有一天我説：“咱們不應該説元[yɛ˧]，寒[ɤæ˧]，應該説[yɛn˧]，[ɤæn˧]。”我説的時候，還特别把尾音-*n* 説的很重。我哥哥聽了氣的不得了，他説，什麽“運”，“恨”！干麻學老媽子説話的聲音？因爲他自己不會説出ㄩㄢˊ、ㄏㄢˊ的音，可是又要學我説的那種聲音不好聽，所以變成了“運”、“恨”了。

對於這種不肯學老媽子的話的態度，不但我們家裏有這種偏見，後來過了許多年碰見傅孟真，他也是有類似的經驗。我是在一九二四年在柏林第一次認得他的。那時候好幾個中國同學雖然多數都不是從北京來的，但是説話差不多全是國音的陰、陽、

---

① 參閲 Yuen Ren Chao，*Readings in Sayable Chinese*，第一册，頁 60—96，San Francisco 1968。

上、去四聲。就只有孟真老是他的“閃董料秤”(山東聊城)的聲調。談起來才知道他并不是不會説,是不屑説北京話。因爲他上北京大學念書,一家子就全搬到北京去住了。那麼用人當然也都是當地的人了。他入了北大没多久就學了一口的北京話。可是家裏聽他改的滿口京腔,就笑他説:“你怎麼説起老媽子的話來了?”他們這麼一笑就把他的北京話給笑了回去,把他本來的“閃董料秤”的話又笑回來了。不記得我從前在保定住的那麼久,并且常看我的周媽是保定人,可是我并没學上了保定話,是不是有人笑過我,現在想不起來了。

我們這一輩説京話説的不準確的第二個來源是因爲我們上一輩説的話都是常州話的底子。上文説的我們把捲舌音ㄓ、ㄔ等念成舌尖音ㄗ、ㄘ等,一半是因爲我們還小,一半是因爲我們上輩除了我母親以外都不會發捲舌音。還有一種南邊的影響就是對於ㄣ、ㄥ韻的字雖然會發鼻音,但是分不出哪些字收ㄣ,哪些字收ㄥ。這是長江流域從成都到上海大概有千把公里寬地方的一個很大的同音區。關於這一點連我母親都分不大出來。到很遲很遲,一直到我“回”了常州,到南京念書,又回到北京,差不多十年過後才覺到有分辨的必要,然後再開始把所有那類的字一個個的重新學過一道。例如“斤、親、心、痕”收ㄣ,“經、青、興、恒”收ㄥ。這是在我會説了兩三種吴語以後才注意到的事情。有時候從諧聲上可以看出來一點兒,例如“親”收ㄣ,“新”也收ㄣ,“青”收ㄥ,“清、情、静”也收ㄥ。不過也有些例外的,比方“經”收ㄥ,“勁旅”的“勁”雖然收ㄥ,可是“用勁”的“勁”收ㄣ。反正從不分到分是必得一個字一個字的學。從分到合就只須記得一條規則就可以一律通用了。例如廣東話分雙唇跟舌尖鼻音的韻尾。學北方話只要記得凡是-*m* 都改成-*n* 一條規則就够了。我大概到十幾二十幾歲才把ㄣ、ㄥ的字分得出來,可是到今天説話説急了的時候有時還會把"因∶英"或是"恩∶鞥"説混了。

還有一點我的口音跟京音不同的就是在前高元音ㄧ、ㄩ之前的舌尖音ㄋ都念成舌面音ㄬ,例如"你、女、年、娘"那些字都用像法文 *compagnie* 的 *gn* 音做聲母。這 *ni*,*gni* 的差别雖然在法文分的很清,可是在中國方言當中很少分的。甚至在某美國大學當遠東系主任的,因爲他是河北南部來的,他一律把ㄋㄧ、ㄋㄩ讀成ㄬㄧ、ㄬㄩ,一點兒不覺得有什麼不同。在我所知,中國只有一處方音裏ㄋㄧ、ㄬㄧ并存的,就是杭州話的"你"字用ㄋㄧ,"擬"字用ㄬㄧ。這"你"字的讀法可能是南宋時候從北方帶來的影響。

上文提到我們説話的陰、陽、上、去四聲都是京音的高、揚、起、降的四種調值,可是關於什麼字歸什麼類,特别是南邊話入聲字的讀法,我們還是説的不大準。我們家裏大人除眼面前的入聲字,例如"一、七、八"念陰平,"十"念陽平,"六"念去聲,此外碰到較冷一點的字就只會按常州音念成短促的入聲。可是我們聽得出來這不是北邊話,所以跟了四周圍的用人咧,街上的人咧,他們要用到那些字的時候我們也跟着學了。例如"鯽魚"叫"幾魚";"不必"説"不比";"會客室"叫"會客史",這里頭的些入聲字北京念去聲,可是我們在河北(那時候叫直隸)南部的保定、祁州那些地方住的最多,所以就跟着他們念上聲了。要是説"蛐·蛐兒"那個蟲名我會説,可是看見"蟋蟀"兩個字就只會用入聲念成ㄙㄧɔ ㄙㄜɔ了。

我小時候除了説不很純粹的京音以外,總喜歡學説各處不同的方言。保定話從帶我的周媽差不多學會了,例如 *Hah .ge dong .si teou .lie tyan .shia*(˩˩) *.lie* 就是"那個東西掉了地下了"的意思。不過那種話我連對周媽都不好意思説。我學的第一種别處的話不是我們本鄉的常州話而是江蘇常熟話。比方説"叫其走去拿一條魚給其"就説成[kɔ g‘ɛ b‘ɔ k‘ɛ nu idiɔ ŋɛ pə g‘ɛ]。這裏頭的"其、去、魚"念成[g‘ɛ,k‘ɛ,ŋɛ]是從最早收-*g* 尾音變成-*u*,而 *ou* 韻在運河一帶都念成 *ei*,[ɛ]之類,所以聽着這麽怪。其實常熟話大部分没那麽怪。懂蘇州常州話的人聽起常熟話來都不太難懂。我怎麽還没會説自己家鄉的常州話,倒先學起常熟話來呐?這是因爲我的姑母嫁給了常熟楊家,到北邊來歸寧,跟着一些小孩兒跟用人只會説常熟話。我要跟兩個表弟玩兒就非得學他們的話不行,所以我很快就學了説"我俚,能篤,其([g‘ɛ])篤,好來!海外好篤!"就是説:"我們,你們,他們,好咑,海外好呐","海外好"就是"好極了"的意思,横是什麽字都喜歡加上一個"海外"。這是我生平學全了的第二種話。

我學常熟話學的這麽容易是有幾個緣故:第一是小孩子跟小孩子學話比跟大人學的快。定寶(后來叫楊蓬士)比我大概只小一歲,我們一天到晚一塊兒玩兒,所以容易學。第二是我一小兒對於各種口音向來留心,所以什麽聲音一學就會。第三是那時候我們已經起頭兒念書了。我們念書是完全用常州音念的,所以只須稍爲把聲音憋一點兒就憋成常熟音了。這樣子麽,我五歲的時候説一種不頂純正的北京話,説一種地道的江蘇常熟話,可是念書就只會用江蘇常州音念。現在回想想那是一種相當怪的方式,可是當時覺着是很自然的事情。

說到念書,我差不多四歲就開蒙了。最早是我母親教我認方塊兒字,一面兒寫一個大字,反面就畫一個畫兒,例如"人"字反面畫個人,"樹"字反面畫一棵樹。可是抽象一點兒的字,例如"有"字、"好"字,還有些虛字像"之、乎、者、也"之類反面就没有畫兒。所以這些字我又不喜歡認,也不容易記得。

後來是我祖父起頭兒教我念書。我父親(諱衡年)先没教我,大概是因爲忙着去考的緣故,他考中過舉人的。那時代平常總是先念《三字經》、《百家姓》、《千字文》。可是祖父一起頭兒就教我跟我哥哥兩個人念《大學》。我念念念不好就改了念朱子的《小學》,覺着好念多了,后來《小學》没念完又回頭念《大學》了。我到七歲才開始正式上書房,天天早晨上學,晚上才回家。那時候我祖父做冀州的知州,書房在衙門的一個跨院兒裏,所以多半在書房吃午飯。書房好像就只有我跟我哥哥跟一個親戚家的小孩兒仨人兒,因爲那時候我兩個堂房姊姊他們女孩子們都得躲得家裏念書,不能跟男孩子們一塊兒念的。

我們的先生姓陸,字輞軒,是特爲從常州請到北邊來教我們的。他是我大姑婆的長子,照規矩應該稱他大表伯,可是因爲他是我們的先生,所以我們管他叫先生。我祖父費那麼大事從南邊請個先生來,第一是因爲他自己公事太忙,没工夫教我們書了;第二是按"古者易子而教之"的道理,教的學的都認真一點兒;第三是因爲要保存我們的鄉音,非得從家鄉請一位先生來才行。

我們這位先生嚴倒是很嚴,可是我們都喜歡他,因爲他總給我們講書,講字的用法。要知道從前所謂"念書"就是念書,先生不一定講，學生也不一定懂，真是“讀書不求甚解”，可是過了一陣，甚至過了多少年，書裏的意義漸漸的明白了。這種傳統的老法子倒是跟近年來外國所謂耳舌法（audio-lingual approach）相近，先注重聽、念，以後再慢慢的懂。可是我們的先生先講再讓我們念，這是破例的教法。

念書的次序，因爲《大學》在家裏已經念完了，按《四書》的次序該念《中庸》了，但是因爲《中庸》實在是難，所以先念《論語》、《孟子》。我最喜歡《孟子》，其實後來通行的文言也是跟《孟子》最相近。《四書》念完了麼，就是《五經》了。可是我跟着陸先生只念了《詩經》的半部，後半部回到常州以後跟着一位張先生念的。《書經》跟《左傳》是後來我父親教我的。《五經》裏頭麼，就剩了《易經》跟《禮記》没念。其實《大學》跟《中庸》原來就是《禮記》裏的兩章，所以十三經裏没有《大學》、《中庸》就是這個道理。

每天下午四點來鐘放學過後就隨便玩兒，可是晚飯後多半兒還要念詩。詩是我母親教的。母親是當時很有點才的女人，能寫詩、填詞，崑曲也唱的好。我想我後來喜歡弄音樂多半兒是從母親遺傳下來的。吹笛子是我父親教我的，所以成了婦唱夫隨了。晚上念詩我們都覺着比白天念書輕松一點兒，我覺着也好玩兒一點兒。我念的是《唐詩三百首》。我哥哥跟姊姊們另外還念《千家詩》跟别的詩集。可是他們念的詩，我就是没念也漸漸的背得出來了。因爲我們在家里念詩也像白天在書房里似的大家同時哇喇哇喇的你念你的我念我的。有時候我停下來就聽見他們念的東西。我頂記得他們念的吴偉業的《圓圓曲》，我連字都没看見都已經背熟了。還有白居易的《長恨歌》，他們比我們先念，趕我起頭兒念到《長恨歌》的時候都已經聽的半熟了。

我們念了那麽些書始終還没有作文。照老規矩總是很遲才起頭兒作文呐。因爲那時候作文都是作文章,不比後來在小學裏可以説什麽就寫什麽。那時候所謂"開筆"作文是一件大事。我在北邊没到開筆就回常州了。從前開筆那麽遲大概是不但寫東西都得用文言,并且《四書》、《五經》當中除了《孟子》、《左傳》以外不像後來通行的文章,所以總等到念《古文辭類纂》之類的時候才開筆,那就總到了十幾歲的時候了。

可是我們還没學作文已經開始學作詩了,真是没會爬就先學跑了。我哥哥姊姊們倒是真能作詩,我光是跟着他們玩兒玩兒就是了。我們多半兒都作古詩,因爲古詩只須押韻的字平仄對了就行了,律詩還得多半字有一定的平仄,那就難多了。好在我們念書都用常州音,對平仄倒是很容易分。我頂記得晚上練大字用的一首杜牧寫的《赤壁》七絶;那麽四七二十八,每行五個字,第六行還有兩個空兒就題了那年"己亥"兩個字,所以我們總是一頭兒練字一頭兒吟詩,四句完了就念"己亥",把上聲的"己"字念的很高,陽去的"亥"字念的很低。算起來是西歷一八九九,第二年一九〇〇就是庚子,全國出了大變亂,家裏也出了變故,第二年我們就回常州去了。

這一兩年當中,家裏,國裏,事情接接連連的出的真多。先是陸先生過去了,不久我的伯父(諱儀年)在别處任上過去了,最后祖父過去了,我們全家就扶着靈柩回南邊了。在我的語言經驗方面是我第一次聽見外國人長篇的談話。這是在輪船上看他們打紙牌。我就只記得他們説"迷呀迷呀波羅波羅"。可是到今天還不知道那是一句什麼話,是哪一國的話都不知道。到了上海旅館裏住了幾天。我的舅舅(馮聃生)從蘇州來照應我們。他們跟我母親説常州話,對我們小輩就説帶常州音的北邊話。到上海不久我就發現外頭人多數雖然説上海話,可是工人們,拉洋車的,他們都説江北話,就是揚州一類的南官話,因此我對於那種話有一種階級性的聯想。還有一種類似的聯想,就是我們對於北京話雖然不像傅孟真家裏拿它當"老媽子話",可是總覺得那只是日常的隨便説話,常州音就好像高一等似的,因爲我念古書作詩文都是用常州音的。

我們回到了常州青果巷祖上的老房子,一共有三進正院子,一進客廳,一進轎廳,自從曾祖(諱曾向)以下有三房住在裏頭,不過自從祖父過去以後,上兩輩當中只有三叔公三叔婆還在。那時候我還没學會常州話,用人都不懂北邊話,所以管我叫"蠻則",就是"蠻子"的意思。我就跟他們辯,我説只有"南蠻",哪兒有説北邊話的叫"蠻子"的吶?我們家裏上兩輩對我們有的會説一點北邊話,多數只會説常州話,我只用北邊話回答他們。可是跟我們平輩些孩子們對於北邊話連懂都不懂,用人們也不懂,所以就成立了一種人對人的語言方式:就是不久雖然我學會了説常州話,可是跟别房的長輩們雖然他們説常州話,我還是説我的北邊話,只有對平輩跟用人才用我新學會的常州話,如果對長輩們説常州話,好像不恭敬似的。這種人對人的語言方式,一弄慣了以後,是很難改變的。如果要改變的話,非得預先知道難處才改得過來。如果是願意維持那方式的話,當然是很容易的事。前些年跟我們同住的易家樂(Søren Egerod)家,先生是丹麥人,太太美國人。他們的小孩子們一起頭兒父親就跟他説丹麥話，母親跟他們説英文。後來他們回到丹麥還是維持這種人對人的語言方式。所以他們兩個小孩子一小兒就是能説兩種語言①。

我在常州家裏念書，先是一位張先生教我，後來我父親自己教我。有一陣子還找了一位先生教我跟我哥哥的英文。他的發音是純粹的常州音，例如 January，他就教我們念"J-a-n 陣，u 右，a 歐，r-y 立，陣牛而立"②。那幾年我母親多病，父親教的也不很嚴。我就不好好兒念書。到了一九〇四，我還不到足十二歲，忽然父親母親同一年裏先後的過去了。他們别房的大人就商量了把我送到蘇州龐家我大姨母家住了一年，跟着大表哥龐恩長讀了一年書。

蘇州話當然是典型的吴語，後來縣名根本就叫吴縣。這是我學會的第四個方言。龐家原來是震澤人，我姨母是常州話的底子。但是我跟外頭人接觸一多就學會了他們的話了。蘇州話在名義雖然代表吴語標準，但是實際上的地位一年不如一年。一個主要的原因是新式的學校多數在上海，所以近年來説吴語的人都拿上海話當通行的"南邊話"③。比方一個常州人跟一個江陰人要是他們在外頭跑跑的見了面要是不説國語大概就説上海話，仿佛拿滬語當吴語的標準似的，而其實他們要是各人説自己的常州跟

---

① 關於雙重語籍的維持或改變的方法跟幾個要訣，可以參考 Yuen Ren Chao, *Language and Symbolic Systems*，頁 145－148，Cambridge 1968。

② 常州發音是[dzəŋ-ȵiɯ-ʃər-lɪʔ]。又"歐"字常州根本念 *ei*，所以説"a 歐"倒是很準確的。

③ "南邊"這個叫法是我們江浙人狹窄眼光的口氣。有一年我到了廣東對廣東人説，我們南邊人是這麼做法，你們廣東人是那麼做法。他們聽了我的話當然覺得可笑。

江陰話反而很相近的。還有一個原因一般人不學蘇州話是覺得蘇州話的聲音太嬌氣,太嗲(ㄉㄧㄚˇ),特别是ㄠ韻的字,國音[au],上海[ɔː],蘇州就念成[æː],例“好得喇”。這個從[au]變成[æː]的現象并不是蘇州一個地方這樣,連美國東南部所謂“南方音”也有這樣的音變,例如 how,now 念成[hæː,næː]之類。

我在蘇州住了一年又回到常州的家裏。這時候我的伯母從遠處回到常州來照應我們四個小的。(其實大姊已經二十多了。)這是我第一次進新式的所謂“洋學堂”,名字叫溪山小學。先生多數是常州人,就是教英文的沈問梅先生是上海人。我伯母雖然是常州人,但是在福州住過多年,所以我跟她學了一點福州話。這次在常州住了一年,後來除了三年的年假暑假跟偶爾回來看看以外就没有機會説常州話。過了十幾年從外國回來在滬寧鐵路火車上遇見了溪山小學我的國文老師吕誠之先生,他問起我在美國的情形,我多年没説常州話,又得把外國事情用中國話來講,覺得非常别扭。但是不得不這麼,因爲一層他不太懂國語,二層我本來跟他説常州話,要是跟他説國語,覺着不恭敬似的。這個跟上文講的我對家裏長輩説常州話不恭敬剛剛相反,可是都是一樣的心理。

在溪山小學只念了一年就到南京進了江南高等學堂的預科,一進就進了三年(除了年假暑假回常州家裏之外)。學校雖然在南京,但是學生多數都是從江蘇、浙江、安徽各處來的。全校二百七十三個學生只有三個是南京人。一般外路人總笑南京的口音。一層是陰平字念的很低,不過這個跟天津話一樣。但是南京音把ㄚ音念成ㄛ,例如“他回家”念成ㄊㄜ ㄏㄨㄟˊ ㄐㄧㄜ,這是外路人笑南京話的主要的原因。我因爲對於方言有特别興趣,所以不久把南京話居然也學會了。同學南京人雖然少,但是外頭當然容易有機會聽。用入聲,分尖團,丫變ㄛ,當然容易學。有時候根本就是情感上的困難,就是覺着怕人笑。在這三年當中我有一個同住的同學邵繩武是福州人,我跟他交换方言,他教我福州話,我教他常州話,這次我學的福州話比跟我伯母學的全一點。在南京最后一年來了一位名師。因爲他教的是本科,我還在預科,那時又没有旁聽生的制度,所以我就常常在課堂廊檐裏當胡敦復先生的"偷聽生"。

在南京的第二年是一個美國先生教我們的英文,名字叫David John Carver,中文名字叫嘉化。這是我第一個外國先生(他前兩年才過去的)。嘉化先生是 Nashville, Tennessee 人,他説話完全一口的所謂南方口音。例如 haff passt, dzero, li'amp。所以我想這是真正的英文發音了,一直到後來到了美國才知道那是很特别的方音。三年預科没有完全念完,趁游美學務處第二批招考的機會,我就到北京住了一春天預備投考清華的官費。中、英文當然最要緊。中文題目是"不以規矩,不能成方圓"。考的前頭不幾個禮拜我還自修了一陣子拉丁文,當選科之一。用的什麽書忘記了。過了些年要温習拉丁文用 Walter Ripman 的 *Rapid Latin Course*;拉丁雖然是個没有人説的語文,但是這個教科書完全拿它當一個活的語言來教,有回答,有作文,我非常喜歡這種方法;後來我在夏威夷大學教初級中文用文言起頭,也就讓學生開始就在班上説文言,寫回答,跟作短文,結果有的學生都成了漢學家了。

我這話岔的太遠了。再説回頭説一九一〇出洋的事情。我們一班考取的有七十二個人,都一同坐了支那號船到美國。護送這一班學生的是唐孟倫、胡敦復、嚴智崇三位先生。我本來想學電氣工程,到了船上胡先生對我解釋理論科學跟應用科學的關係,結果我想我還是學理論科學罷。可是到了第三年選專科的時候,專修的是數學。

我到了美國在語言上第一個印象就是一般人說話跟嘉化先生的口音很不同。我進了康奈爾大學不久就跟着一般人的聲音改過來了。在大學頭兩年當然得選一門外語,是必修科之一。我選了德文,又自動選了二年級的德文。那時候美國外語教學的習慣是用英文講課文,第二天學生看着外國文口譯成英文。最可笑的是我的二年級的德文先生 Boesche 教授,他雖然是德國來的,可是還是按着一般的習慣用英文上課。一學期念了兩本書 Gottfried Keller 的 *Kleider Machen Leute* 跟誰寫的 *Lebrecht Hühnchen*,可是全學期課堂裏幾乎聽不見一句整句的德國話。我呐,我還照着我的讀書不求甚解的老法子念出聲兒來自修。後來到大考時候——大考當然也是德譯英——居然還得了個"A"。我的法文是從 Scranton, Pennsylvania 的一個國際函授學校學的。我很喜歡他們的教法。他們給你一套蠟筒子的録音跟録音機,跟着課文用的。每一課上完了有作文,有録音問答,你說了寄去,他們不但改你的答文,還能改讀音。近來大概因爲太費人工,所以没有這個函授學校了。在康奈爾這幾年從語言學方面最要緊的一科就是語音學。這是我第一次學國際音標的時候。在那時代語音學還是冷門,一般的語言學更没有成爲學問。這幾年當中我跟胡明復同住,我們没有交换方言,我就學了他的無錫話。

這個我覺得并不太容易,因爲跟常州話太近,反而更得注重微細的分别。

轉到了哈佛的研究院,我在名義上專修的是哲學,但是上了很多的語言的科目。雖然没有語言系,但是已經有語言學入門的一科了。我也選了梵文。博士讀完了又回到康奈爾教了一年的物理。那時候他們正在試驗無綫電,我對於聲學方面特别感覺興趣,所以后來物理大部分荒疏了,就是對於聲學還熟悉一點。

不久我的生活漸漸越來越有意思了。先是清華學校(那時還没成大學)召我回去教物理。没教完一個學期,羅素到北大、師大演講,他們就找我去當翻譯(因爲我的論文題目是《數理邏輯跟方法論》)。我説"越來越有意思了",因爲那一年(一九二〇)就是我初次認得我太太楊步偉的一年,第二年我們就結婚了。我太太雖然是醫生,但是能説好幾種方言。我們結婚過後就定了個日程表,今天説國語,明天説湖北話,後天説上海話等等。最妙的是她雖然進了好幾年的上海中西女塾,可是跟同學們一直用她的帶南京安徽音的南方官話,到這時候才是她第一次給上海話説出聲音來。可見學一種語言簡直可以純用聽覺,聽了潛伏在腦子裏,後來一説就説出來了。這固然未必是學語言的最好的方法,不過現在我發現這個至少是一種可能的方法。

在上海、北京各處講演我當然都用國語。有一次陪着羅素坐長江輪船到長沙去演講,同船有邀請羅素的主人是長沙人。我在路上就跟他學了點湖南話。到了長沙,有一次(民國九年十月二十六日)講完了過後一個學生跑上來問:"趙先生是幾時回省的?"

大概以爲我是湖南人說國語說的不全,不知道我是國語的底子說湖南話說的不全。

差不多這時候我就決定把大部分時間放在語言的研究上了。結了婚不久我們就一同到美國又待了三年。這一次是在哈佛教書,先教哲學,后來教中文,同時上了些語言學的課。接着又轉到歐洲跟着倫敦的語音學領袖 Daniel Jones,還有 Lloyd James。雖然資格較淺,可是我跟他學實際的練習得益最多。到了巴黎在語言方面聽 J. Vendryès 跟 Antoine Meillet 的課,在漢學方面聽 Paul Pelliot(伯希和)跟 Henri Maspero(馬伯樂)的課。上文不是曾經提過,講起小時候到各處學說各種話的經驗較有意思,到後來正式研究語言學就漸漸不如以前那麼好玩兒了。可是跑到歐洲碰到有音位性聲調的語言倒是個經驗。有一次我在瑞典一個火車站買票到 Malmö,我就用平常英德等無聲調語言的語調用半降調說那個地名。說了半天那個賣票的人不懂,后來他恍然大悟,說"哦,你是要到 Mal(51:)mö(35:)",仿佛像國音的去聲加陽平似的。可見理論上知道瑞典語有聲調是一回事,等到聽見他們用才是真知道吶。

民國十四年清華成了大學,同時又開了(國學)研究院,我又被召回到清華了。我教的主要的科目是中國音韻學,附帶的在大學部教音樂欣賞科。從這時候起我就做了十幾年的中國方言調查。第一次調查就是冬天到江蘇、浙江各處做吴語的調查,這一系叫"吴語"不叫"吴越語"是因爲從温州一直到靖江在音韻上都是一個系統[①]。

那幾年我在國語統一的運動上同時也相當的活動。先是參加了國語統一籌備委員會,裏頭一部分的工作是大辭典編纂處,後來出的四册的《國語辭典》,就是從這裏出版的[②]。委員會裏工作最多的最常見面的是汪一庵、錢玄同、黎錦熙、白滌洲、劉半農、林語堂等。我們談談談到《切韻》序裏有"吾輩數人定則定矣"一句,大家就說咱們干麻不組織一個會叫"數人會"來定各種提案再送呈大會跟教育部决定。後來這裏頭工作最要緊的部分,一樣是國音的標準,從民國八年的"因論南北是非古今通塞"的人工式的國音一改改成民國二十一年的完全用北平音的標準;第二樣是擬了一套國語羅馬字拼音法式,在民國十七年由大學院公布作爲國音字母的第二式。

可是我主要的工作還是在音韻學跟方言上。在吴語調查寫完了以後不久就到兩廣去調查粤語。那時中央研究院剛成立,蔡孑民先生當院長,我的康奈爾同學楊杏佛當總干事,傅孟真當歷史語言研究所所長,我就擔任第二組(語言組)主任,到各處去調查方言。這些用表格用録音器作系統化的調查工作是一回事,到各處學説各種話當然又是一回事。我對於兩方面都有興趣,并且學着説一點當地的話,可以使發音人放心説他們本地的話,免得

① 那次調查的報告見趙元任:《現代吴語的研究》,清華學校研究院叢書第四種,xv+地圖+138,北京 1928 年。

② 汪怡、徐一士等編,趙元任、錢玄同校訂:《國語辭典》,第一册書前 48 頁+ 860 頁,第二册 861—2028 頁,第三册 2029—3346 頁,第四册 3347—4485 頁加補遺、補編、索引等共 328 頁,北平 1933 年,長沙 1947 年,臺北 1953 年。

有時誤認爲我是政府派來宣傳統一國語反而想法子對我說國語①。我調查粵語的時候雖然知道潮汕區是閩南語系統,我順便也跑了一趟。可是我到火車站想說潮州話買一張二等票到汕頭,他給了我兩張三等票,我只好用廣州話跟他解釋了。

這幾年調查方言當中打了一個短岔就是民國二十一到二十二年到華盛頓當了一年清華留美學生監督。到各處視查學生的時候順便就拜望些語言學界的人。在勃朗(Brown)大學見着了美國方言調查主任 Hans Kurath 跟 Bernard Bloch,到耶魯大學特爲去拜望 Edward Sapir。他問了我常州話的幾個要點,大約一個鐘頭,把常州的音位系統都差不多弄清楚了,簡直要開始跟我說常州話了。

回國消假,歷史語言研究所在南京北極閣造了新房子,二樓的一半都設了語音實驗室。我的屋子斜對面就是李方桂。我們三個人(連羅常培)合譯高本漢的《中國音韵學研究》②也差不多這個時候。

這幾年當中又繼續作方言調查。最過癮的是調查皖南各處的方言。我太太是安徽石埭縣人,但生長在南京,所以不大會說皖南話。我們一同去,先在歙縣作總站,特別到西鄉學會了說西鄉話,因爲西鄉話是所謂徽州話的典型代表。又找了績溪發音人

---

① 民國九年十月十七日寫逛杭州的(英文)日記有一句說:I got on (to the)杭州 dialect very quickly. ...One very delicious part of my life is that I can feel myself akin to my fellow by talking his dialect. He is often led to think I am from his hometown until I inform him of the contrary.

② Bernhard Karlgren, *Phonologie Chinoise*, 700 pp, Leiden & Stock-holm 1915;高本漢:《中國音韵學研究》,趙元任、羅常培、李方桂翻譯,47+731+地圖,上海,1948年。

記録了績溪話,不過關於績溪方言的報告大部分是好多年後根據胡適之的録音跟楊時逢合寫的[①]。

後來就到江西、湖南、湖北先後不同的時候調查方言。湖北一省調查的最詳細,一共紀録了六十四處的方音跟故事[②]。正在打算到福建去調查,跟當地人都接好了頭了,盧溝橋戰事發生了,我們連家跟研究院都搬到長沙,不久又到了昆明,第二年就又出國到美國。先到夏威夷大學教了一年,上文講的教外國人文言作文、文言會話就是這個時候。接着到耶魯教了兩年。這就是認得語言學家 Leonard Bloomfield 跟 E. H. Sturtevant 的時候。Sapir 跟 Bloch 也先後到了耶魯。那時美國雖然任何學校都還没設立語言學系,但是耶魯的語言學最盛。有一個非正式的語言學俱樂部,每月開會一次聚餐讀論文,附近學校的人也常參加這個會。後來我到了哈佛也常到紐黑文的耶魯語言俱樂部呐。

我在哈佛是去參加那裏中文大辭典編纂處的工作,兼教中文。可是不久珍珠港戰爭爆發,哈佛就開了兩班遠東語言的速成科。我起頭兒教粤語速成科[③]。一夏天才上了兩個月的課,帶着學生到波士頓醉香樓吃飯,他們跟跑堂兒的就聊起來了。有一伙計問我的學生説:"先生,你幾時嚟唐山翻嚟嘅?"他們要開粤語班

① 見趙元任:《績溪嶺北音系》,本刊 34. 1. 27—30(1962),《紀念胡適之院長特刊》;又有較詳的報告,里頭有胡先生吟詩的樂調,見趙元任、楊時逢:《績溪嶺北方言》,本刊 36. 上 11—113(1965)。

② 見趙元任、丁聲樹、楊時逢、吴宗濟、董同龢:《湖北方言調查報告》,本所專刊 vii+總圖+1574+地圖第零至 64 圖+綜合地圖,上海,1948 年。

③ 很少人注意我的《國語入門》是從《粤語入門》翻譯成國語的:Yuen Ren Chao, *Cantonese Primer*, vii+336, 1947, *Mandarin Primer*, viii+336, 1948,都是劍橋哈佛出版部刊行的。

是因爲想到政府也許預備由中國南岸進兵。到了一九四三年政府才大規模的設立陸軍專科訓練班(Army Specialized Training Program:ASTP),我就擔任了中國語言方面的主任。在名義上是每個學生(兵)用十分之六的功夫在語言上,十分之四在别的科目上,不過事實上他們把大部分時間還是用在語言上。前後搭頭一共二百多人,每班教十個月,最后兩個月還附加一點粤語。因爲注重的是説話,所以全用國語羅馬字的教材,只教了少數的最常用的漢字。可是有幾個學生特别加工認字,他們編了一個《大私報》,因爲平常的兵是 private,所以《大公報》變了《大私報》了。這個大概是空前絶後的完全由西洋人編的中文報。

近二十多年在哈佛,在加州大學,在暑假語言學講習所(多半在密希根)各處教書跟自己作研究,當然都是很有意思的工作。當中在一九四五年當了一任美國語言學會的會長,做了一個中國人自然是一件可以特别得意的事情。但是在狹義的語言本身的發展,我這自傳就很少進展了。也没有學會什麽新的外國語文,也没説會什麽新的中國方言。當中有兩個經驗可以值得報告報告。一回是到墨西哥開聯教組織會議。我早晨用我的二五眼的西班牙話叫早餐。過了一會兒,飯廳里用英文打電話來問,先生叫的是什麽東西?又有一次在歐洲開汽車旅行,在瑞士 Brig 城過夜。這是在瑞士的德語區。我因爲第二天要開到 Matterhorn 高山上去,最好送車到車行上上滑油、檢查一下機器等等,所以晚上就拿了一本辭典查了些機件的德文名稱。第二天早晨到了車行誰知道他們一看見我們是外國人,不説他們自己的德國話反而對我説起法國話來了。我説,那不成,我昨兒晚上用的是德文的功,今兒非得用德文才會講汽車的事情呐。

那回開車旅行還遇見一個有意思的經驗。我們連三女來思一家三個人從英國過海再從法國東北經過比利時、荷蘭的長堤，沿着德國的北區一直到丹麥過海到瑞典。路上法國跟比利時人跟我們說法國話；荷蘭人因爲知道很少人會説荷蘭話，跟外國人多半説英文；到了德國他們就跟我們説德國話；在丹麥、瑞典他們又盡量跟外國人説英文。這是他們各國人對我們這些外路人説話的慣例。其實啊，我留心旁聽他們自己當中説話呀，完全另是一回事。在法國的東北就開始説一種日爾曼語系的 Flemish 語；在比利時境内當然是法文跟 Flemish 并存，但是他們自己，特别是北部，都説 Flemish；在德國境内，他們對外國人雖然説通行的高原德文（Hochdeutsch），但是自己説的是窪地德文（Plattdeutsch），所以我們開車從法、荷、比、德近海一帶聽他們説話所得的印象，并不是過一個國境换一種語言，我們的感覺非常像坐着長江輪船從上海到四川一路的口音漸漸的變，并不是一國一國的變的。

最后再舉兩個語言的經驗來作本文的結束。在一九五九年以富爾布賴講座在京都大學講了五個月的學，講的是中國語言的結構。我的日文是不够演講用的，我就全用中國話講，承京都大學的小川環樹教授給我翻譯。可是在最后一次演講我得謝謝給我翻譯的人，總不能請他翻譯謝他自己話煞。所以我只得預備了一篇日語演説，特别向小川環樹先生致謝。這是我生平説的最長的一段日本話。

差不多那時候我在臺大演講了一陣，同時也回到"中央研究院"做點研究，特别注重閩南的方言。上回我在潮州説閩南話不是鬧了個笑話嗎？這一次我要是學會了這種方言我就可以自誇凡是中國主要的方言系中每一系都會說一種了。所以臨動身到日本特别預備了一番用臺灣話的記者談話。可是各報的記者來了，不巧我們一行當中大女兒如蘭赴日的護照簽證的手續没有弄清楚，又忙亂大半個鐘頭，趕手續辦好了就到上飛機的時候了，所以我這全國方言的大考始終没機會考及格過。

但是回頭想想一個語言學者，爲什麽一定要會説各國的話跟各處的方言吶？Edward Sapir 固然會學我的常州話學的很像。可是我的老師 Meillet 他雖然著了講全世界語言的書①，可是他引起各種語言的舉例來不管是希臘、拉丁還是遠東、近東，一出他的口都是純粹的法國口音。Vendryès② 是法國東部口音，向來外國人學法文總是注重前[a]跟后[ɑ]的區别，例如[pat]是爪子，[pɑt]是漿糊，可是他老人家一律念不前不後的[ᴀ]。又如馬伯樂(Henri Maspero)先生是巴黎人，按標準法國國音有四種不同的半鼻音元音，例如 *un bon vin blanc* [œ̃ bɔ̃ vɛ̃ blɑ̃]，可是他跟着一種所謂巴黎土音，他的半鼻音元音只有兩種：[ɛ̃ bɔ̃ vɛ̃ blɔ̃]。可是他們講學理講的還是一樣清清楚楚有條有理的。你要是要聽各種語言的聲音，有的是本地的發音人跟留聲機片或磁帶。所以在一個語言學者的地位并不在乎有本事當一個 Thomas Cook 旅行社的通譯員才以爲榮的。我説了這麽半天也許是想遮掩一下我説不好閩南話的短處吧？

① Antoine Meillet et Marcel Cohen, *Les Langues du Monde*, xiii+1294+26 地圖, Paris 1924 & 1952。

② J. Vendryès, *Le Langage*, xxx+439, Paris 1921.

趙元任先生學術年表

1892 年(清光緒十八年)

11 月 3 日出生於天津,祖籍江蘇常州。父趙衡年,母趙馮氏。祖父趙執詒官至冀州直隸州知州。六世祖趙翼係清代著名詩人與歷史學家。

1898 年(光緒二十四年)

入私塾,學習《四書》,跟先生學會用常州方言誦讀,堅持多年不變。晚上,從母親學作詩,聽崑曲。

1901 年(光緒二十八年)

因祖父去世,隨家人回常州青果巷定居。

1905 年(光緒三十一年)

因父母去世,移居蘇州姨母家,學説蘇州話和用反切説話。

1906 年(光緒三十二年)

回常州,入溪山小學高小接受新式教育。4 月 15 日開始記日記,堅持 76 年之久。

1907 年(光緒三十三年)

3 月,考入南京江南高等學堂預科學習。

1910 年(宣統二年)

1 月由江南高等學堂畢業。7 月參加清華學校第二批庚款赴美留學考試，名列第二。8 月 16 日乘船赴美，9 月入康奈爾大學主修數學，成績名列前茅。

1911 年（宣統三年）

業餘興趣日益廣泛。購買舊鋼琴一部，學習音樂。與同學合購照相器材，練習攝影。8 月學習世界語，次年多次參加世界語會。通過賓州 Scranton 的國際法語函授學校學習法語，收穫很大。

1914 年

6 月獲學士學位。9 月入康奈爾大學研究生院主修哲學，大量閱讀杜威和羅素的哲學著作。8 月 11 日與任鴻雋等人籌建中國科學社，於次年 10 月 15 日成立。同時爲創辦《科學》雜誌投入大量業餘精力。

1915 年

1 月《科學》雜誌在上海創刊。趙元任爲其撰寫《心理學與科學之區别》和《和平進行曲》等。4 月，接到哈佛大學授予的哲學獎學金，9 月 10 日轉到該校研究生院攻讀博士學位。

1916 年

在哈佛大學除主修哲學，輔修心理學和科學史，課餘還選修語言學課及和聲學、對位學等音樂課程。

4 至 6 月與胡適討論對中國語言改革的觀點設想，合寫“The Problem of the Chinese Language”刊於 *Chinese Students' Monthly*，共四篇，其中 I、II、IV 爲趙著，III 爲胡著，首次强調用科學的方法研究中國語言。

1918 年

4 月完成博士論文 *Continuity: A Study of Methodology*。5

月博士畢業後,獲雪爾登旅行獎學金,9月作爲博士後抵芝加哥大學,12月到加州大學柏克萊分校學習。

1919年

上半年在加州大學柏克萊分校學習哲學史、數學史等課程,結識杜威、洛文伯、克瑞博等著名學者。4月在斯坦福大學的美國數學年會上講"Continuous mathematical induction"。6月回康奈爾大學任物理學講師。

1920年

8月17日回到闊别十年的祖國。9月5日到清華大學任物理學教師,17日入選教育部國語統一籌備會,與黎錦熙、汪怡、錢玄同等從事國語運動。10月開始爲英國哲學家羅素訪華演講擔任翻譯。

1921年

6月1日與楊步偉舉行新式婚禮。7月11日結束羅素演講的翻譯工作。8月30日携夫人前往哈佛大學任教。

1月自印通函"First Green Letter",寄送親友。是年,《官話字母譯音法》刊於《科學》6卷1期。

1922年

春,開始在哈佛大學開設中國語言課,工作重點逐漸轉向語言學與語音學研究。

1月譯著《阿麗思漫遊奇境記》由商務印書館出版。

《國語羅馬字的研究》刊於《國語月刊》1卷7期。

1923年

4月自印通函"Second Green Letter",寄送親友。

11 月《國音新詩韵》(附平水韵)由商務印書館出版。

“Ten Objections to Ronmanizing Chinese”刊於 *Chinese Students' Monthly*,18:7。

1924 年

6 月前往歐洲考察進修,拜訪高本漢、Daniel Jones 等各國語言學家,參觀語音實驗室。

1925 年

上半年羈留法國,時而去英國參加倫敦大學的學術活動。自印通函“Third Green Letter”,寄送親友。5 月回國,任清華國學研究院導師,開設方言學、普通語言學和音韻學等課程,正式以中國語言學爲其學術主攻方向。9 月參加劉半農發起組織的“數人會”,討論國語問題。

A Phonograph Course in the Chinese National Language 由商務印書館出版。

1926 年

2 至 6 月先後到燕京大學和北師大做語言學演講,參加“數人會”的國語運動。

《符號學大綱》刊於《科學》11 卷 5、11 期。《北京、蘇州、常州語助詞的研究》刊於《清華學報》3 卷 2 期。

1927 年

10 至 12 月與楊時逢前往江浙等地做吴語方言調查工作,是爲第一次系統從事漢語方言調查工作。

譯文《高本漢的諧聲説》(高本漢著)刊於《國學論叢》1 卷 2 期。《倆仨四呃八阿》刊於《東方雜誌》24 卷 12 期。

1928 年

1 至 3 月與高本漢通信，討論《中國音韻學研究》的翻譯問題。下半年離開清華大學到中研院史語所主持語言組的工作。11 月到廣州，在中山大學講授語音課，12 月赴廣西進行粵語方言調查。

2 至 5 月撰寫《現代吴語的研究》，同年列入“清華學校研究院叢書”第四種，由清華學校研究院出版，1935 年再版，1956 年由科學出版社影印出版，附調查表格。9 月 26 日，《國語羅馬字拼音法式》（與錢玄同、黎錦熙等合制）作爲國音字母第二式由中華民國大學院公布。

上半年《新詩歌集》由商務印書館出版。

1929 年

1 至 2 月在兩廣地區進行粵語方言調查。2 月隨語言組回到北京工作，其間繼續從事國語運動。

譯作《最後五分鐘》（A. A. Milne 著），附“北平語調的研究”，由中華書局出版。

《南京音系》刊於《科學》13 卷 8 期。

1930 年

1 月編寫《廣西瑶歌記音》，刊於《中研院史語所集刊》（以下簡作 BIHP）甲種之一。1 至 4 月編寫《第六代達賴喇嘛倉洋嘉錯情歌》（趙元任記音，于道泉注釋），刊於 BIHP 甲種之五。上半年設計《方音調查表格》，由中研院史語所出版。11 月開始翻譯《中國音韻學研究》，至 1936 年完成。

譯文《上古中國音當中的幾個問題》（高本漢著）刊於 BIHP，1 本 3 分。“A System of Tone Letters”刊於 *Le Maître Phonétique*，

45。“Transcribing Reversed English”刊於 BIHP,2 本 2 分。

1931 年

主持語言組工作,訂購、裝配録音設備。1 至 5 月在親友中調查蘇州和福州方言。

《關於捲舌韵的討論》刊於《國語週刊》13 期。“A Note on ‘let's’”和“‘E’ for Middle e”均刊於 *Le Maître Phonétique*,46。《反切語八種》和“On Using b,d,g(with bars inside) for Unaspirated Voiceless Plosives”刊於 BIHP,2 本 3 分。

1932 年

2 月經史語所批準,赴美接替梅貽琦擔任清華留美學生監督處主任。其間爲史語所訂購語音實驗室儀器。

《註音符號總表》由國語統一籌備委員會發刊。

“A Preliminary Study of English Intonation (with American Variants) and its Chinese Equivalent”刊於 BIHP(蔡元培先生六十五歲慶祝論文集)。

1933 年

7 月參加太平洋關係研究院會議,討論基本英語。8 至 9 月採購語音實驗室的儀器設備。9 月啟程回國。

“Tone and Intonation in Chinese”刊於 BIHP,4 本 3 分。

1934 年

1 月至南京,建設中研院史語所語言組和語音實驗室,做永久計劃。5 月被教育部聘爲音樂教育委員會委員。7 月 8—23 日與羅常培、楊時逢同往安徽做方言調查。

是年,《基本英語留聲片課本》由中華書局出版。

"The Non-uniqueness of Phonemic Solutions of Phonetic Systems"刊於 BIHP,4 本 4 分。"The Idea of a System of Basic Chinese"刊於 *Quarterly Bulletin of Chinese Bibliography*,1:4。

1935 年

5 至 6 月與李方桂、楊時逢前往江西做方言調查。10 至 11 月與楊時逢等前往湖南做方言調查。12 月在南京做湖北鍾祥方言調查。

2 月,《新國語留聲片課本》(甲、乙)由商務印書館出版。10 月,《國語訓練大綱》由南京正中書局出版。是年,《兒童節歌曲集》(陶行知詞)由商務印書館出版。

《方言性變態語音三例》刊於 BIHP,5 本 2 分。《中國方言當中爆發音的種類》刊於 BIHP,5 本 4 分。"Types of Plosives in Chinese"刊於 *Proceedings of the 2nd International Congress of Phonetic Science*。

1936 年

上半年編寫《鍾祥方言記》。4 至 5 月與丁聲樹等前往湖北調查方言。是年,繼續通過演講和廣播從事民衆教育和國語統一運動。

《長沙方音字母》(與黎錦熙通信)、《定縣方音改國音的注意點》刊於《國語週刊》239、243 期。《蘇州方音註音符號與寬式國際音標對照表》、《無錫方音寬式音標草案》刊於《歌謡週刊》2 卷 15、20 期。

"A Critical List of Errata for Bernhard Karlgren's *Études sur la Phonologie Chinoise*"刊於 *Quarterly Bulletin for Chinese*

Bibliography, 3。"A Note on LIA, SA etc."刊於 *Harvard Journal of Asiatic Studies*（下文簡稱 HJAS),1。

1937 年

上半年研究湖北嘉魚方言。8 月隨史語所遷往長沙。

《北平音系的性質》刊於《國語週刊》289 期。

1938 年

1 月舉家由長沙遷往昆明,在昆明繼續主持語言組工作,編寫《湖北方言調查報告》。8 月,應夏威夷大學聘請,携全家赴美任訪問教授。

1939 年

上半年在夏威夷大學任教,編著廣東人學國語的教材 *Mandarin for Contonese*。7 月參加第六屆太平洋科學會議,任中國代表團首席代表,講《中山方言》。9 月前往語言學中心耶魯大學任教。12 月出席美國語言學學會年會。

是年,《鍾祥方言記》由商務印書館出版。

1940 年

每月參加耶魯語言學學會的聚會演講。

9 月,與羅常培、李方桂合譯的《中國音韵學研究》由商務印書館出版。

"A Note on an Early Example of Logographic Theory of Chinese Writing"和"Distinctions within Ancient Chinese"均刊於 HJAS,5:2。

1941 年

7 月前往哈佛大學任訪問教授,在哈佛-燕京學社主持漢英大辭典修訂工作，至 1946 年。

1942 年

"Iambic Rhythm and the Verb-object Construction in Chinese"刊於 *Studies in Linguistics*，2:3。

1943 年

主持哈佛大學陸軍專科訓練班(ASTP)的中國語言教學工作。

"Language and Dialects in China"刊於 *The Geographical Journal*，102。

1945 年

與楊聯陞合作完成《國語字典》編寫工作。11 月，與胡適赴倫敦參加聯合國教科文組織籌備會。12 月，作爲 1945 年度美國語言學會主席做報告。

1946 年

7 月代表教育部與中研院到倫敦參加英國皇家學會慶祝牛頓誕辰 300 周年紀念。10 月獲普林斯頓大學名譽博士學位。11 月作爲中國首席代表，前往法國參加聯合國教科文組織第一次大會。

"The Logical Structure of Chinese Words"刊於 *Language*，22:1。

1947 年

受聘前往加州大學柏克萊分校任訪問教授。10 月到墨西哥城參加聯合國教科文組織會議。

Concise Dictionary of Spoken Chinese(國語字典，與楊聯陞合著)，*Cantonese Primer*(《粵語入門》)和 *Character Text for*

Cantonese Primer 均由哈佛大學出版社出版。

1948 年

被加州大學聘爲 Agassiz 教授,直至 1960 年退休。3 月當選中研院院士。6 月主持聯合國教科文組織暑期講習班。

《中山方言》刊於 BIHP,20A。《湖北方言調查報告》(與丁聲樹、楊時逢、董同龢、吴宗濟合著),由商務印書館出版。*Mandarin Primer*(《國語入門》)和 *Character Text for Mandarin Primer* 由哈佛大學出版社出版。

"The Efficiency of the Chinese Language as a Symbolic System"刊於 *Reflections on our Age*。

1949 年

秋,任加州大學柏克萊東方語言系系主任,學術活動頻繁。

1951 年

上半年從語言學角度撰寫植物名論。

《台山語料序論》刊於 BIHP(傅斯年先生紀念特刊)。《台山語料》刊於 BIHP,23A。

"The Cantian Idiolect, an Analysis of the Chinese Spoken by a 28-month-old Child"刊於 *Semitic and Oriental Studies*,11。

1952 年

3 月到東部參加美國東方學會執委會和科學史年會。下半年研究福州方言。

5 月,《北京口語語法》(李榮譯)由開明書店出版。

1953 年

4 月到普林斯頓大學出席第十屆控制論會議。下半年繼續研究福州方言。

“Popular Chinese Plant Words, A Descriptive Lexicogrammatical Study”刊於 *Language*, 29。

1954 年

6 月獲得谷根函基金會獎資助赴歐洲訪學,在倫敦參加第 23 届國際語言與東方學會議。

“Notes on Speech Archiving”刊於 *International J. of American Linguistics*, 20:2。

1955 年

“Meaning in Language and How it is Acquired”刊於 *Cybernetics: Transactions of the 10th Conference*。

1956 年

“Chinese Terms of Address”刊於 *Language*, 32:1。“Tone, Intonation, Singsong, Chanting, Recitative ,Tonal Composition and Atonal Composition in Chinese”刊於 *For Roman Jakobson*。“Formal and Semantic Discrepancies between Different Levels of Chinese Structure”刊於 BIHP,28 本 1 分。

1959 年

2 至 4 月應邀到臺灣大學做《語言問題》系列演講,次年講義由該校印行。4 至 9 月獲 Fulbright 基金會資助,到日本京都大學講中國語言的結構,並參加學術活動。

“How Chinese Logic Operates”刊於 *Anthropological Linguistics*,1:1。“Ambiguity in Chinese”刊於 *Studia Serica Bernhard Karlgren Dedicata*。“The Morphemic Status of Certain

Chinese Tones" 和"Subsyllabic Imitation Between Two Chinese Dialects"均刊於 *Transactions of the International Congress of Orientalist in Japan*,4。

1960 年

從加州大學退休,延聘三年。當選美國東方學會(AOS)會長。

《説清濁》刊於 BIHP,30 本 2 分。

1961 年

下半年撰寫 *A Grammar of Spoken Chinese*,至 1964 年完成。

《常州吟詩的樂調 17 例》刊於 BIHP 外編,4。"Graphic and Phonetic Aspects of Linguistics and Mathematical Symbols"刊於 *Proceedings of Symposia in Applied Mathematics*,12。"What is Correct Chinese?"刊於 *Journal of the American Oriental Society*,81:3。《語言成分裏意義有無的程度問題》刊於《清華學報》(臺)新 2 卷 2 期。

1962 年

6 月榮獲加州大學法學名譽博士學位。8 月出席第 9 屆國際語言學家會議。11 月開始撰寫 *Language and Symbolic Systems*。

《績溪嶺北音系》刊於 BIHP,34 本 1 分。"Models in Linguistics and Models in General"刊於 *Logic, Methodology and Philosophy of Science: Proceedings of the 1960 International Congress*,5。

1964 年

8 至 12 月繼續撰寫 *Language and Symbolic Systems*，至次年 8 月完成。

"Some Feedback Effects of Communication Technology of Styles of Speech"刊於 *In Honor of Daniel Jones: Papers Contributed on the Occasion of his 80th Birthday*。

1965 年

《績溪嶺北方言》(與楊時逢合著)刊於 BIHP，36。《羅素的抽象原則跟語言教學》刊於臺灣《清華學報》(慶祝李濟先生 70 歲論文集)。

1966 年

2 月獲美國哲學會贊助，從事通字研究工作。8 月 *Language* 期刊將 4 至 6 月卷作爲專刊致獻給趙元任。

1967 年

4 月 3 日，被加州大學授予最高榮譽稱號——教授研究(榮譽)講師(Faculty Research Lecturer)，做專題學術報告"Dimensions of Fidelity in Translation"。8 月赴加拿大多倫多東亞研究系講學。

"Contrastive Aspects of the Wu Dialects"刊於 *Language*，43:1。

1968 年

2 月再次獲得谷根函基金，進行中國通字方案研究，9 月前往歐亞旅行，聽取同行意見。

2 月，*Language and Symbolic Systems* 由劍橋大學出版社出

版。後該書法文本、日文本、西班牙文本分别於1970年、1972年、1975年翻譯出版。8月，*A Grammar of Spoken Chinese* 由加州大學出版社出版。是年，*Readings in Sayable Chinese* 由 San Francisco：Asia Language Publications 出版。

《中文裏音節跟體裁的關係》刊於 BIHP，40。

1969年

2月到康奈爾大學任客座教授，講中國語言結構。3月參加中國演唱文藝研究會成立大會。

《論翻譯中信、達、雅的信的幅度》刊於 BIHP(慶祝李方桂先生65歲論文集)。

"Dimensions of Fidelity in Translation，with Special Reference to Chinese"刊於 HJAS，29。

1970年

6月俄亥俄州立大學授予他名譽博士學位。

《中英文裏反成式的語詞》刊於 BIHP，42本1分。《國語統一中方言對比的各方面》刊於《"中研院"民族學研究所集刊》，29。

"Some Aspects of the Relation Between Theory and Method"刊於 *Method and Theory in Linguistics*。"Interlingual and Interdialectal Borrowings in Chinese"刊於 *Studies in General and Oriental Linguistics*。"The Changchow Dialect"刊於 *Journal of the American Oriental Society*，90：1。

1971年

1月到夏威夷出席太平洋對比語言學會議(PCCLLU)。

《我的語言自傳》刊於 BIHP，43本3分。《漢字通字方案的初步計劃》(張洪年譯)刊於《學海》2 期。

"Some Contrastive Aspects of the Chinese National Language Movement" 刊於 *La Monda Lingvo-Problemo*, 3：7。"Where Chao Went Wrong in Matters of Language"刊於 *Canadian Journal of Linguistics*, 17:2。

1973 年

4 月 16 日至 5 月 28 日回祖國大陸探親訪問,受到周恩來總理接見,與國内同行聯繫增多。

"Chinese as a Symbolic System"刊於 *Papers of the CIC Far Eastern Language Institute*, 4。

1974 年

接受加州大學 Bancroft 圖書館爲編寫《趙元任口述傳記》進行的採訪。

1975 年

1 月自印通函"Forth Green Letter",寄贈親友。8 至 12 月繼續從事通字方案的研究。

Yuen Ren Chao's Autobiography: *First 30 years*, *1892—1921* 由 Spoken Language Services 出版。

"My Field Work on the Chinese Dialects" 刊於 *Computational Analysis of Asian and African Languages*, 2。"Rhythm and Structure in Chinese Word Conceptions"刊於《臺灣大學考古人類學刊》。

1976 年

《趙元任中國社會語言學論文選集》(Anwar S. Dil 編)由斯坦

福大學出版。"My Linguistic Autobiography"等文章收入該書。

"Chinese Tones and English Stress"刊於 *The Dwight Bolinger Festschrift*, Lisse, Holland。"The Phonology and Grammar of 'Skipants' in Chinese"刊於 BIHP 特刊。

1977 年

7 至 10 月進行通字研究。

"The Socio-political Overtones of Chinese Place Names"刊於 *Monumenta Serica*, 33。

1978 年

7 月自印通函"Fifth Green Letter",寄贈親友。

"Further Problems in Chinese-English-Chinese Lexicography"刊於 *Studies of Essays in Commemoration of the Golden Jubilee of Academia Sinica*。

1979 年

6 月《漢語口語語法》(吕叔湘譯)由北京商務印書館出版,爲此版作序。

7 月《中國通字草案》刊於 BIHP,50。《通字方案》成書後 1983 年由商務印書館出版。

1980 年

6 月《語言問題》由北京商務印書館出版,爲新版作序。12 月《中國話的文法》(丁邦新譯)由香港中文大學出版社出版,爲此版作序。

《吴語的對比情況》(倪大伯譯)刊於《國外語言學》5 期。

1981 年

3 月 1 日，夫人楊步偉去世。5 至 6 月回國探親訪問。受到中國政協主席鄧小平接見。北京大學授予趙元任名譽教授稱號。

1982 年

2 月 24 日，在美國麻省劍橋去世，足歲八十九。

《常州話裏兩種變調的方言性》刊於《清華學報》（臺）新 14 卷 1 至 2 期。

（附：趙元任先生是一位博學多才的人文學者，本年表着重反映他的語言學研究和著述概況，其中主要依據趙新那、黄培雲編《趙元任年譜》（商務印書館 2001 年版），參考趙新那編《趙元任生平大事記》、《趙元任語言學論著要目》等文獻資料，由商務印書館編輯部編制而成。）

一部爲現代漢語方言學奠基的經典著作

——重讀趙元任《現代吴語的研究》

許寶華

2008年,趙氏元任先生所著《現代吴語的研究》出版80周年,爲了表達心中對先哲的懷念之情,我曾就這部著作的學術價值,特别是它所體現的學術創新精神寫過一篇拙文,談自己重讀後的一點認識和體會。近悉商務印書館擬再版《現代吴語的研究》,爰將此文稍作修改,忝列書後,以爲推介。

一

八十餘年來,學術界對《現代吴語的研究》一直予以高度評價。《中國大百科全書·語言文字卷》(1988)尊它是"第一部應用現代語言學理論方法調查研究吴方言的著作",《中國語言文字學大詞典》(2007)稱"《現代吴語的研究》是現代漢語方言學真正興起的標誌,是漢語方言學史上重要的里程碑"。

今天,之所以要再版刊行這部爲現代漢語方言學奠基、開創現代漢語方言研究全新局面的經典著作,我個人認爲最重要的目的,是要學習、繼承和弘揚這部著作所蘊含、體現的學術創新精神,在新的時代背景和社會需求的條件之下,開創吴語以至整個漢語方言研究的嶄新局面。

《現代吴語的研究》所藴含、體現的學術創新精神，我以爲至少表現爲下列幾點：

首先，語言理論上體現了結構主義描寫語言學認爲語言是一個體系，研究語言應該從口語入手並系統地加以描寫這一當時區别於傳統語言學（語文學）的先進的語言學理論。

《現代吴語的研究》是一部描寫、分析 33 處現代吴方言的專著，它没有講什麽語言學理論，也未宣稱書中是用什麽語言理論來指導描寫、分析方言事實的，然而這部著作却是充分體現當時先進的現代語言學理論的。

其次，研究方法上開創了走出書齋、實地調查方言的新局面，并且設計、運用了一套結合漢語特點描寫、記録方言口語系統的方法。

具體地説，調查一地方言，一般總是先從調查語音入手，利用以《廣韻》音系爲框架設計的"方言調查字表"作爲調查表格，逐一調查記録方言字音；採用先進的記音工具國際音標、符號和語音儀器，使記録的聲韻調系統寬嚴有度，臻於準確；在記録方言字音的基礎上整理出同音字表，用來進一步記録方言詞彙、語法例句和成篇語料，並進行共時和歷時兩方面的比較研究。這一套調查漢語方言的基本方法爲趙氏首創，並在《現代吴語的研究》一書中得到了成功的運用，在後來的調查實踐中表明它行之有效，也就一直爲漢語方言研究者普遍採用，沿用至今。

再次，首個爲吴語科學定義，開創對現代漢語大方言之一的吴語做全面性研究。

吴語的特點是什麽，"吴儂軟語"到底是什麽樣子的，無人説清楚，古人也説不清楚。是趙元任首先從語言學上爲吴語下了科學定義。他在《現代吴語的研究》第四章“聲韻調總討論”中提出“吴語爲江蘇、浙江當中並、定、羣等母帶音,或不帶音而有帶音氣流的語言”。吴語此一塞音發音方法“三分”的定義科學而簡明。這是趙氏從現代語言觀和語音學理出發,採用科學方法和先進的記音工具調查記録古吴越之地33處方言之後歸納出來的結論。它源於語言事實,經得起實踐檢驗,因而爲語言學界所公認,至今顛撲不破,無可替代。

同時,《現代吴語的研究》也是第一部對吴語做整體性、全面性描寫研究的著作。趙氏根據吴語古塞音聲母今發音方法“三分”這個最大的對内具有一致性、對外具有排他性的共性特點,第一個把古吴越之地33處方言由點到綫到面地聯繫起來,顯示出作爲漢語大方言之一的吴語首次被大體揭示的全貌及其主要語音特徵。在現代漢語方言研究史上,趙氏由此成了對吴語做整體性、全面性研究的第一人,也是漢語各大方言區域性研究中的導乎先路者。

二

《現代吴語的研究》這部現代漢語方言學的開山奠基之作,由於體現了突出的學術創新精神而呈現出與過去我國傳統方言學著作迥然有别的嶄新面貌。比如跟我國傳統方言學中取得很高成就的代表性著作章太炎的《新方言》相比較這一點就很明顯。

章氏是清末一位最負盛名的國學大師,於文字、音韻、訓詁之學造詣精深,但他的語言觀已不同於前賢,當時已受到西方現代語言學思想的影響，認爲語言文字研究應該重視方言俗語，并且第一個提出應將“小學”之名改稱“語言文字之學”。章氏所撰《新方言》已突破“小學之用趣於道古而止”只重視古代文獻不重視方言俗語的局限，運用從現實生活中搜集得來的800餘條方言俗語跟古代典籍中的文字聯繫起來，以古語證今言，以今言通古語，溝通方言俗語與古代漢語的繼承關係，並運用語音演變規律，上探語源，下明流變，從而取得了很高的成就，被學界肯定爲我國傳統方言學的頂峰之作。章氏對此書也自視甚高，曾説“《新方言》之作……自謂懸諸日月不刊之書矣！自子雲以來，未有如余者也”。(《漢字統一會之荒陋》(1907))

然而今天從漢語方言研究學術史的角度看來，《新方言》尚明顯地存在着不足和局限性。比如章氏過分運用通轉之説，難免有牽强附會之處。又如書中《音表》排列了23韻母和21紐目，除説明各種音轉關係外，還對古音做了一些説明，如古無舌上音、輕重脣音不分等，但對章氏當時搜集到的“新方言”的語音的説明書中却都屬於隨文舉例性質，顯得分散、零碎，缺乏對單一方言或片區方言做系統的描寫和闡述，且所用方法和工具都還是傳統的一套，尚未採用國際音標和語音儀器等先進工具。語言觀上，章氏認爲“今之殊語，不違姬漢”，現代方言裏的字詞都可以從漢語以前的古籍尤其是漢代的許慎《説文》裏找出本字來，而没有認識到語言文字發展的複雜性。因之，對待《新方言》這部著作，應該看到它的成就和優長並加以繼承和弘揚，但也不要忽視它的不足和局限，“取其精華，棄其糟粕”，才是正確的治學之道。

如上所述，趙氏《現代吴語的研究》跟章氏《新方言》相比，從理論到方法二者都呈現重大差別。《新方言》是中國傳統語言學向現代語言學轉型、過渡時期產生的一部著作，它明顯帶有傳統方言學向現代方言學轉型過渡的一些特點，它仍然是屬於傳統方言學的一部重要著作。《現代吴語的研究》則第一次大規模地、科學系統地描寫和記録了吴語的語音和詞彙，是中國學者借鑒、吸取西方現代語言學理論、結合漢語實際、運用現代科學方法調查研究漢語方言取得的一項卓越成果，它不僅是現代吴語而且是整個現代漢語方言研究的奠基之作，爲現代漢語方言學的建立鋪墊了堅厚的基石，成了開創現代漢語方言研究全新局面的具有劃時代意義的經典著作。

三

大抵任何一門學問或是做學問總是"前修未密，後出轉精"的，方言學和方言研究也是一項漸進的歷時工程。

《現代吴語的研究》之所以能在20世紀20年代取得極高的學術成就，這由社會變革、學術背景、理論發展和個人天賦學養等多種因素所造成，但如前所述，最重要的是趙氏所具有的突出的學術創新精神。

趙氏學生、前輩學者吴宗濟先生曾經在文章中寫道："説起趙師是哪一學派，曾有人問起我，我還想套那句話：他是没有'學派'的學派，他永遠是自成一派的。……他從不跟尾巴，趕浪頭，而是本着一貫的'拓荒精神'。在八十高齡以後，還在走他自己的道路。"吴老概括地説明趙氏的治學之道，言簡意賅，趙氏一貫本着的“拓荒精神”最爲可貴。《現代吴語的研究》之所以能成爲現代漢語方言學的奠基之作，正是作者秉持“拓荒精神”，開闢學術新境的結果。

80 年過去了，中國社會發生了巨變，我們方言研究者也肩負着新的歷史使命。無論近百年來爲現代漢語方言學做出杰出貢獻的趙氏元任先生等多位學者，還是兩千年間從揚雄到章炳麟等爲我國傳統方言學做出過重要貢獻的學者，都用他們的智慧和辛勞爲漢語方言學的發展積累了十分豐富的文獻資料，鋪墊了非常堅厚的基石。我們將在此基礎上運用不斷發展中的新的理論、方法和工具，弘揚趙氏的“拓荒精神”，開闢新的研究領域，不斷進行學術創新，推動包括現代吴語學在内的漢語方言學的進步、發展和繁榮。

參考文獻：

吴宗濟編：《趙元任語言學論文集》，商務印書館 2002 年版。

胡明揚：《趙元任先生小傳》，載《中國現代學術經典・趙元任卷》，河北教育出版社 1996 年版。

丁邦新：《非漢語語言學之父》，載徐櫻著《方桂與我五十五年》，商務印書館 1994 年版。

蘇金智：《趙元任學術思想評傳》，北京圖書館出版社 1999 年版。

孫　畢：《章太炎〈新方言〉研究》，華東師範大學出版社 2006 年版。